# NEW TESTAMENT FOUNDATIONS FOR CHRISTIAN ETHICS

Willi Marxsen

Translated by
O. C. Dean, Jr.

T&T CLARK
EDINBURGH

Authorised English translation of *"Christliche" und Christliche Ethik im Neuen Testament*
Copyright © Guterslöher Verlagshaus Gerd Mohn, 1989
Published in the United States of America by
Augsburg Fortress Publishers, 426 South Fifth Street, Box 1209,
Minneapolis, MN 55440

This edition published under licence from Augsburg Fortress by

T&T Clark Ltd
59 George Street
Edinburgh EH2 2LQ
Scotland

First Published 1993

ISBN 0 567 29223 1

British Library Cataloguing-in-Publication Data
A catalogue record for this book
is available from the British Library

Typeset by Trinity Typesetting, Edinburgh
Printed and bound in Great Britain by
Redwood Books, Trowbridge Wiltshire

As a sign of his gratitude
for the conferral of the honorary degree
Doctor of Divinity
the author dedicates this book to the
University of Dubuque,
Dubuque, Iowa

# Contents

## Contents

# Preface

The Christian West has not always been Christian.

Hardly anyone will contradict this sentence, although linguistically it contains a contradiction: the same adjective is used with different meanings.

When we speak of the "Christian" West, there is a very broad range of meaning: it includes everything that has been thought, lived, and shaped in a long tradition. This is the sense in which the word is most often used even today. If, however, we ask whether all of that is really Christian, the same word brings a critical evaluation into play. Then we must ask whether what is labeled as "Christian" corresponds to the norm by which it can be designated authentically Christian. It is thus a question of the much-discussed issue of "Christian identity."

Since in our use of language the adjective is ambiguous, and since it is rather seldom that the meaning of the word can be obtained as unambiguously from the context as is the case in the initial sentence above, linguistic discipline is needed. In using the adjective we must make clear what is meant: "Christian" or Christian? If that remains unclear, the genuinely Christian very quickly disappears in the "Christian."

"Christian" politics could then be, say, politics that moves within the framework of rules that have developed in the Western tradition. One can certainly still discuss (and sometimes even dispute) whether in a particular case one follows this or that rule. In both cases we can say that we have remained within the framework of what is "Christian." And what is true for "Christian" politics, is also true for a "Christian" education, a "Christian" marriage, a "Christian" life-style, and much more. But the question always remains, whether what comes out is therefore authentically Christian.

When it is left to the churches—which, it goes without saying, are all "Christian" churches—to bring to bear what is truly Christian, they cannot simply appeal to the fact that they are indeed Christian churches, but rather must name the reference point that is the standard for what is Christian. Likewise, a "Christian" person must show whether and in what way he or she is really a Christian. For we can say without fear of contradiction that not all "Christians" are authentic Christians.

That reference point is generally given as the Bible, and especially the New Testament. Yet the mere naming of this reference point is hardly sufficient. If that were the case, one would presumably have to designate everything "Christian" as Christian, for there is very little called "Christian" that cannot be grounded with reference to the Bible. Hence it is not enough merely and only to give the reference point itself; one must at the same time indicate *how* such a reference is to be made. At this very point, however, there are real difficulties.

We would venture the following thesis: the present discussion among Christians on what is Christian—especially in the field of ethics, which often enough has led to disagreement—has its most fundamental cause in a missing consensus on dealing with the Bible. Then this gives rise to the linguistic problem: a lot of what is put forward as Christian is (only) "Christian." When one speaks of Christian ethics, does one mean "Christian" ethics or Christian ethics? The problem is veiled when we use the same word with distinguishable meanings side by side and indiscriminately.

In the winter semester 1984-85 I dealt with this problem in the lectures given at the seminary in Bethel. In the next two semesters I repeated them in Münster. They are now presented in printed form and offered for discussion.

My concern is not to present an "Ethics of the New Testament." Whether such a thing can even exist in the precise sense of the phrase is not something I want to discuss, especially since the historical information that it provides can and should be taken up by systematic theology.

I begin rather with the uncontestable observation that the authors of the New Testament writings present not only different ethics but also in part ethics that can be brought into agreement only with difficulty. This, however, immediately raises the question: Do they represent a Christian or a "Christian" ethic? We can answer this question, of course, only if we work out a distinguishing criterion.

When that is properly considered, we quickly recognize that the actual problem is a quite old one, even if the authors of the New Testament writings were themselves scarcely aware of this problem and probably could not have become aware of it. When we examine it in historical perspective, however, perhaps it can teach us something for the present.

Thus I would like to address a linguistic confusion that is widespread, of course, but which has to be dealt with not least of all by students. I would like to help and encourage them to find their way in the interdisciplinary realm, especially since they are almost always left there alone. For in this work I undertake the attempt not only to integrate historical exegeses into systematic theology, but at the same time to show that and how systematic issues accompany exegeses. Anyone who wants to move in both disciplines will find this circle unavoidable— and must not seek to avoid it, because in the pastoral office, in the teaching profession, and in the church, one always moves in this circle. Therefore, practice in this area should begin already during one's academic work.

Willi Marxsen
Münster

# Translator's Preface

As the author of the present volume points out in his Foreword, much of the confusion Christians experience regarding theology and ethics is the result of the careless use of language. Words like *Christian, sin,* and even ordinary verbs like *see* can be and are used in more than one sense, and it is often hard to know which sense a particular writer or speaker has in mind. Thus the author seeks to clear up some of that confusion, as well as to provide a fundamentally different way of looking at what it means to be authentically Christian in our world.

Some of the writer's distinctions and language have presented more than the usual challenge for a translator of German biblical and theological works. For example, he makes some of his distinctions visually with quotation marks, such as the difference between Christian and "Christian." For the most part— except in the Foreword—I have written these terms as "nominally Christian" and "authentically, genuinely, or truly Christian" where that distinction is made in the original text.

Similarly, the writer distinguishes between two kinds of seeing: as the world sees and as (authentic) Christians see through the eyes of faith (this is my explanation, not his; he simply writes *sehen* or *"sehen"*). I have written the distinction as "see" and "really *see*" without any quotation marks.

The translation of two German verbs also requires comment. The author frequently uses the verb *wirken* or some related word to describe Jesus's activity and mission. Though a cognate of the English *work,* the German word means much more, especially when used (often in this book) as a verbal noun or participial adjective. It includes such concepts as *be active, be effective, have an effect, create, accomplish,* as well as the idea of *functioning in a particular role or place.* In the present volume the term covers everything Jesus did and was during his time on earth. No English word can convey all these meanings, but as a compromise I have in most cases translated the German terms using *active, activity,* and related words, writing, for example, of the "active Jesus" and "Jesus' activity."

The German verb *prägen* also has no good English equivalent—at least not in the figurative sense often used by German theologians. Its basic meaning is to make an impression in metal (with a die, for example) or to coin (literally and figuratively). Thus it is well suited to use with the Greek *typos* ("example" in Paul), which literally means a die. Except for money and phrases, however, things and people are not *coined* very well in English. Therefore I have chosen the verb *shape* to convey the author's idea. Those who follow Jesus' example are shaped by him, and these shaped people in turn become shapers who shape others with the image of Jesus. (See the section on "The Shaping of the Shaped," pp. 190ff. )

It should perhaps be mentioned that the author frequently adds emphasis to biblical quotations. This has not been noted in the text, however, since there was, of course, no special emphasis in the original New Testament writings.

Finally, I would like to express my gratitude to Horst Gerbig and Volker Gentejohann for their valuable assistance in the translation.

O. C. Dean, Jr.

# Prolegomena

## *Ethics: An Aspect of Theology*

This title is meant as a thesis. With this thesis we intend to dispute the idea that one can isolate ethics in the church and treat it as a topic by itself. Yet ethics is not something added to theology in the sense that it is a consequence of theology. Instead, in our thesis we will maintain that ethics is an integral part of theology. It is an aspect of theology, even though only one of several aspects. And it is essential, for without ethics theology would no longer be theology.

It should be obvious right away that the correctness of this thesis depends on the definition of theology. We will suggest a definition shortly. I would like to begin, however, with a few observations that can be made when we look around today and try to find out how the topic of ethics is treated on the whole in the church. For even though this book deals with ethics (or ethical systems) in the New Testament and hence historical distance must be maintained, ethics cannot be discussed as if it existed in a vacuum. The questions, problems, and disputes originated or have come up in our time. So we must at least mention them here.

## 1. The "Deficit in Ethics"

### a) The Discovery of the Deficit

From the end of World War II until the the end of the sixties the church-going public was mainly concerned about biblical topics. Everywhere interpretations of scripture were always passionately and often even vehemently discussed. This was

1

due in no small measure to Rudolf Bultmann's program of demythologization, which especially created a lot of discension. One side welcomed it and adopted it gladly. They regarded it as liberation because the contents of the faith became intelligible and thus could be discussed with more integrity and intellectual honesty. Frequently it was for this very reason that the other side vigorously rejected the program. Opponents criticized the "modernist" theologians who attempted to destroy the "mystery of faith" by means of reason. The "argument over the Bible"— which was centered chiefly on christological topics—was so fundamental that the Protestant church almost faced a schism.

This concern ceased almost entirely about fifteen years ago or at least disappeared from public discussion in the church. This happened very abruptly and without perceptible transition—we could say overnight. There are various reasons for this, and not all of them have theological or ecclesiastical roots. The rise of the social sciences had an impact on both church and theology. They found they had considerable deficiencies, and now they used all their energy to make up this deficit.

In the process people started to feel that the previous discussion, oriented exclusively toward the Bible, had actually missed the reality of everyday life. Its continuation seemed to offer little promise in view of the new situation. Was there any way it could possibly be helpful in the organization of practical life? After all, the discussion had remained very "academic" or at least seemed so in retrospect. And how did the discussion among experts concern the local congregations? At the 1969 Stuttgart Kirchentag (church congress) the opinion was voiced that the "dispute about Jesus" was really "much ado about nothing." Displayed and carried around on a banner, this slogan hit home and had immediate consequences. Discussions of many topics (not least of all Jesus' resurrection) were simply abandoned without their reaching any conclusions.

Instead, attention enthusiastically shifted to the social sciences, which began to determine almost everything in church and theology. Social and economic issues were discussed; the political decisions of Christians became the subject of intensive consideration; and the responsible treatment of the creation was formulated as a task for the church and the Christians.

Yet these problems could not be solved either, for at the end of such discussions the question could be asked, whether political decisions are not subject to the freedom of one's own conviction. This again raised, at least potentially, the danger of schism—not because of different opinions on Christology but because of unbridgeable differences in political ethics, for example, in the discussion of NATO rearmament.

We do not intend here to answer the question whether we can justly talk about a deficit in ethics at the end of the sixties. Wholesale judgments are always dangerous, and it would be easy to name quite a few things that make this judgment seem questionable at best. There is, however, no doubt that such an impression was widespread. It was most clearly seen in the behavior of students, for many of them were guided by it from the beginning of their studies. They hardly attended exegetical lectures anymore and seminars only to the extent required in their program. Instead they turned to the wide selection of ethics classes, often right in their first semester. Here, they believed, was the deficit that had to be made up. But how can one make up a deficit?

## b) Making up the Deficit

When we speak of a deficit, we mean that something is missing from the whole. Yet before we start to make up this deficit prematurely, we should first take a brief look at the whole. There are two possibilities: we can understand a whole as the sum of its parts or as an organic unity. Our decision in this case will determine our conclusion as to how we can make up the deficit.

In those days no one engaged in such reflections, of course, and it would hardly be fair to make subsequent reproaches for this. In retrospect, however, we can see that things took a wrong turn at this point. For without doubt the growing interest in ethics at that time led to an isolation of ethics. So the decision was made to look at the whole as the sum of its parts, although no one was expressly aware of this. And since it was felt that one part had been neglected, the intention was to emphasize that part in order to make the whole complete again.

This had practical consequences. Again we have to be careful not to make wholesale judgments, yet we could (and still can) see a definite trend. Sermons constantly treated ethical problems, whether the lectionary suggested them or not; religious instruction focused on such problems; and in congregational meetings Bible studies were replaced by discussions of current ethical issues.

It was hard for anyone to see that this was a problem, especially when ministers and teachers remembered their university days. Teaching and research at a university is organized in independent disciplines. The experts are concerned with their respective fields, indeed, often only with small areas within their fields. Yet the future ministers and teachers whom they educate are supposed to be concerned with all of theology in their later professional life. And it is largely left up to them to take the fragments they study concurrently and successively and patch them together into a whole. Rarely do they receive instruction or training in that. So it hardly comes as a surprise that the diagnosed (or only suspected) deficit was made up the way it was: by increasing interest in one (isolated) discipline.

But what if we assume that theology is a whole, in spite of its divisions into disciplines? At least in theory no one will dispute this assumption. As yet, however, it remains an open question where and how we can explain and demonstrate this wholeness. We will first suggest a few definitions in order to give a preliminary basis for this undertaking.

## 2. Definitions

Though we have mentioned theology several times, the word was never defined. Only the context could (perhaps) give an idea of what we meant. Without a context the word is ambiguous and can be used in various senses. Someone speaking of the apostle Paul's theology uses the word differently from someone inquiring about the core of Christian theology. This applies similarly to other combinations or specifications such as scientific theology, catholic theology, Old or New Testament theology, and biblical theology. But if we can still understand the meanings relatively clearly here, despite some distinctions, the so-called genitive theologies pose a different problem altogether: theology of hope, of order, of liberation, etc. In the latter cases we can even ask, why the word *theology* is employed.

Do the people who use it even know exactly what they are referring to? Oddly, theology can even mean "something complicated"—a sermon is supposed to be simple and "not so theological."

If we want to avoid linguistic chaos we have to explain the word each time and more precisely than has been done so far. If we use the word *theology* we have to be ready, willing, and able to answer the question, exactly what do we mean by it. If we are not, then we ourselves are hindering understanding.

There is, however, yet another way. We can attempt (and it will be no more than an attempt) to contribute to clarity by doing our best to use the word in only one sense, thus giving *theology* our own definition. The listener will then know what the speaker means, and the speaker will strive for linguistic discipline. This is the road we will travel here, keeping in mind, of course, the fact that we will not succeed in establishing a standardized use of the word *theology* in the common usage of the language. Yet we must see (and, hopefully, will see) to what extent an effort of this nature can be helpful.

## a) Theology

The first definition we want to give is based on the etymology of the Greek word. We can say: *Theology is talk of God.*

With this definition we have already accomplished something that is by no means obvious in view of the contemporary use of the word: we have expressly included the word *God*. This is important since it provides a certain clarification. Even those who define theology differently and do not use the word *God* in their definition, or use the word in whatever context without defining it, should at least always indicate in what respect the thing referred to by *theology* has to do with God (cf. liberation theology, feminist theology). This should be made so clear that listeners can easily understand it. After all, the word *theology* contains the word *God;* if we cannot see God or even see clearly how the matter concerns him, the word *theology* is misused.

Of course, the introduction of the word *God* into the definition poses another problem: we cannot assume that it is clear what we are referring to with the word *God*. That too we can learn from today's use of the language.

So we frequently hear, for example, the assertion that we all believe in the same God. This is often said perhaps in order to play down the differences between the confessions or sometimes in order to emphasize the community of Jews, Christians, and Muslims. But does this not pretend a consensus that does not really exist? After all, with such a claim we can only express the correctness of a common conviction that we cannot call faith without creating misunderstanding, namely, monotheism. In doing so we presuppose the existence of (only) one God and use the word *God* as a proper name, yet it is the proper name of a "man without qualities," because we forgo the naming of qualities, the description of his work, and the way we can experience him and his work. But are we allowed to suppress all this when we make this assertion? If we are really referring to the same thing, none of this is randomly interchangeable. If we are only mentioning a name when using the word *God,* then this word is literally empty. Then *God* is no more than an empty word-shell waiting to be filled. Not until it is filled, not until the contents are given, does speaking of God become unambiguous. Yet which contents should we name, and how can we justify choosing precisely these contents?

We will defer the answer to this question for the time being and take a look at the (only apparently) inconspicuous word *of* (theology = talk *of* God). We chose this word intentionally, adopting a distinction introduced by Rudolf Bultmann ("Welchen Sinn hat es, von Gott zu reden?" [What sense does it make to talk of God?], in *Glauben und Verstehen* [1925], 1:26). Bultmann distinguishes between talk of God and talk about God and points out that talk about God "does not make any sense at all" because here the subject of the talk (i.e., God) has already been lost. The difference can be explained as follows.

When we talk *about* God, we regard God as an entity that we can study from a distance. Of course, this entity should concern us, but it does not have to. Even if we make correct assertions about it, we can still maintain a neutral position toward it; this would not affect the correctness of our assertions. So in talking about God we can, for example, refer to him as "the Almighty" or "Love" without being affected about it. For we can say this and still hate instead of loving. And how about God's omnipotence? In talking *about* it, we escape it and prove ourselves stronger than God. Using the category of *omnipotence* in talking about God is a problem anyway. We can demonstrate this with a rather absurd example. If the God I am talking *about* is really omnipotent, then he must be able to create a stone that he cannot lift. If he cannot, he is not omnipotent. Yet if he can create such a stone and then cannot lift it, he is not omnipotent either. We could vary this example in many ways.

So we should not refer to an entity we are talking *about* with the word *God*. For if I talk *about* God, right from the start my references miss the entity that I pretend to be talking about.

In contrast to talking about God, talking *of* God is always talking without distance; that is, we are talking of an entity that concerns us unconditionally, that governs us, that pursues us, an entity to which we surrender, with which we get involved, by which we are affected—in short, an entity in which we believe. And we believe in it while we talk of it. So talking of God is only possible in the form of confession, and only in confessing our faith are we really dealing with God.

And this leads to the first refinement of our definition. It is not sufficient to state that talk of God is talk without distance. This assertion remains abstract until we mention the two "entities" between which the distance is removed. Talking is always done by a talker, and this talker has to be expressly named. Thus we have to expand our definition: Theology is *a person's* talk of God. At first glance this expansion seems to state the obvious, but all too often, as we will see later, the obvious is not stated and hence not considered.

Now let us go back to our question: How can the word-shell *God* be filled? A sentence from Luther's explanation of the first commandment in his Large Catechism can help us find the answer: Whatever you set your heart on, that is in truth your god—a really bold statement in view of the widespread careless use of the word *God*!

First, we have to note that in this definition "god" is not the subject but the predicate. Thus the presupposition is not the existence of a god, but that humans always set their hearts on something. This "something" determines their actions and their behavior; it controls them and thus is their god. Here for the first time we can see the connection between theology and ethics.

At the same time, however, questions arise. If what we set our hearts on is our god, then we must admit, if we are honest, that we are constantly changing our gods. Since we consider ourselves monotheists and take this for granted, we resist being revealed as polytheists. So we prefer to distinguish between these gods, speaking in one case of "God" and in other cases of "false gods" or "idols." Yet do we have criteria for such a distinction?

The first step that seems to suggest itself now is to introduce the "God of the Bible." This is what we would like to call God, especially since in most other cases we are referring to very worldly things: money, success, career, health, and sometimes ideals or even other people. We do not deny that these are powers that determine our behavior time and again. Yet in our view they are only idols compared to the "God of the Bible."

As enlightening as this seems at first glance, we still have to ask whether we have not fallen back unintentionally from talking of God to talking about God. We can specify on our own what our idols are. Through our actions and behavior we have demonstrated that we got involved with them, trusted them, and hence believed in them, even if perhaps only temporarily. But can we say the same of the God of the Bible? If we let ourselves be guided by the Bible in filling the word-shell *God,* we find a lot of different contents that are by no means all compatible, since they are often even in tension with each other. But why are we dealing here with God and not with idols? To begin with, these contents are expressions of experiences of *other people*—the authors of the biblical writings—with their God. When, however, these people talk of their God and mention certain contents, *to us* these contents are at first talk *about* God.

It is possible, of course, that in talking of our God we will say things that agree with some of the things the authors of biblical writings have said of their God. Then their God has also become our God. Yet he has not remained our God. Time and again, the things we prefer to call idols have taken the place of this God, whose power we, just like the authors of the biblical writings, had experienced. Thus it is not only a problem to talk superficially of the "God of the Bible"; it even turns out that in our everyday life the God of some authors of biblical writings is only one of a number of gods. Hence the Bible cannot supply us with criteria to distinguish between God and idols.

If we do not want to resort to talking about God, then we can only say of God as much as we know from our own experience. The minute we try to say more of God (in terms of content), we are talking *about* (a) god and no longer talking of God.

Nevertheless, it is not impossible to distinguish between God and idols. This is not accomplished by means of the Bible, but through our own decision. In our everyday life we become involved with many gods and have various experiences in the course of these involvements. If we now consider what these experiences mean to us and what they have given us, what happened to us and what we became through these involvements, we will be able to distinguish between these gods and perhaps finally single out one God. The criteria we accept and apply will vary from person to person, depending on how and where we find meaning in our lives. But the God who promises us meaning, and who in our experience keeps his promise when we get involved with him, will be the one we call "God," and the others we will call "idols." This by no means deprives them of their power. Indeed, time and again we will believe in them and get involved with them. We will set our hearts on them, and when we do, these idols will again become our gods. It is hard to understand, but we always fall for them, although we would really like to stay with the one God, who according to our experience is the only one who deserves to be called "God."

So we cannot distinguish between God and idols by applying a standard from outside ourselves (e.g., from the Bible) and using it to test the contents with which we are presently filling the word-shell *God*. Rather, such a distinction is possible only if we involve ourselves. Theology is not theology without our personal concern. Therefore we must make a second refinement in our definition: *Theology is a person's talk of his or her God.*

We may conclude from this that our talk of our God is possible only in God's immediate presence. But do people talk at all at the moment when God has laid his hand on them?

Hardly, or at best in rare, highly exceptional cases. So our theology, our talk of our God, is always "historical" theology.

Before we go further into this, we should relate the definition we have developed to the thesis put forth in the title of the Prolegomena: Ethics: An Aspect of Theology. If theology is a person's talk of his or her God, then it is always talk based on personal concern. It is talk of an entity to whom this person has surrendered. Therefore this entity governs this person and his or her actions.

Within this complex we can distinguish two aspects and look at each of them separately. We can start with a person's actions and ask about the entity that induced these actions. Or we can start with the entity and ask about the actions induced in the person. Hence there is a correspondence between a person's God and a person's ethics. A change in the definition of one's God will result in a change in one's ethics. If the description of one's ethics changes, one's God will also have to be redefined.

Accordingly, ethics means: *People consider their actions on the basis of and for the sake of the God who governs them.*

This context can be clarified and expressed as a theorem if we utilize the terms *typos* and *mimetes* used by Paul (cf. 1 Thess. 1:6-7). The *typos* is the die, and the *mimetes* is what is shaped by this die and, having been shaped, is itself able to shape. If we apply this image to our definition, we can say that theology is a shaped person's talk of the One by whom that person is shaped. We can now look at the Shaper and describe him on the basis of the shape that he has given and is still giving to a person. Or we can look at the shape and describe what results the Shaper has produced, wants to produce, and can produce in the person.

Basically the sequence does not matter, yet we have to consider one problem here. We can state it in Aristotelian categories. The *proteron physai* (the first thing according to nature) is the Shaper with his shaping action. Thus far it is still true that God is always the subject. We must never forget, however, how this statement came about, namely, by way of a *proteron pros hemas* (a first thing for us). This first thing for us is the shape we have received and on the basis of which *we* define the Shaper. So the act of knowing and the formulation of what is known is always done by a person, more precisely, by a person who experiences himself or herself as shaped. This does not preclude that in this act of knowing (and not until then!) we learn that it is God who makes himself known.

Hence the statement that God is always the subject is always a second sentence. Whenever it is used as a first sentence (most frequently in a statement like, "God has revealed himself here or there"), we are dealing with talk *about* God.

So if we are looking at shaping, we are dealing with ethics. If we look at the Shaper, we are dealing with what may be called dogmatics (or at least what is central to dogmatics). And now we can see that dogmatics and ethics are aspects of theology.

All those who think about themselves and their relationship to their God are in this sense theologians. They think about what immediately concerns them and occupies their minds.

### b) Historical Theology

If theology is people's talk of their God, then we can call them by name and ask how they talked of their God earlier. If we address this question to the Bible, it reads: How did the authors of the writings compiled in the Bible each talk of their God?

We have to stress that this question addresses the authors, not the Bible. At this point our language is often carelessly inaccurate. If we ask, for example, What does the Bible say? we really mean, What do the authors of the biblical writings say? The Bible cannot talk *of* God at all. If we address the Bible directly, all we can learn is what it says *about* God. Yet even apart from that, it is indisputable that all biblical writings (as well as their sources as reconstructed through literary criticism) were written by people. These people cannot be ignored, even though the inaccurate use of language suggests that they can. We overlook the fact that this "personification" of the Bible leads to the unexamined assumption that the Bible has a special quality. When we refer to it as the "word of God," we ignore the fact that there were people who talked of their God because they were affected by him.

If we ask these people from our historical distance how they talked of their God, we realize that they filled the word-shell *God* with very different contents. At first glance these are often not even compatible with each other. If an author talks of his God, for example, as someone who takes pleasure in destroying his enemies (Judg. 5:31), it is hard to identify this God with that of another author who says that God loves all his creatures. Such examples can easily be multiplied. It is impossible, therefore, to take the "God of the Bible" as a point of departure.

Rather, our point of departure has to be the *individual* texts compiled in the Bible, to which we as interpreters have a historical distance. These texts by *authors* in particular situations were written with particular *contents* and particular intentions for particular *listeners* or *readers* in particular situations. The questions "Who? What? For whom?" are constitutive for what we call exegesis here. Thus exegesis is the attempt to repeat in our words what an earlier author tried to say to his contemporary readers with his text. Hence exegesis is always historical exegesis. It is done scientifically, which means that with appropriate methods the exegete tries to get to a better understanding of the old meaning than he could get without using such methods.

In their work exegetes have to forgo any criticism. They must not be influenced by personal judgments of whether the things written earlier by a particular author make sense or not, whether they are logical or not, and under no circumstances whether they are right or not by whatever standards. Every criticism inhibits an understanding of the things the author of the text was trying to say. Therefore a "historical-critical" exegesis is no longer an exegesis. Only after the exegesis has been completed can we (and often we will) criticize the results. And we specify the criteria we apply in our criticism of the author's statements. But this is always the second step, and we must not refer to it with the same word that we use for the first step. Exegesis is only the restating of an old statement in an understandable way and nothing more.

After an exegesis has been completed, and only then, we can also take another step in a different direction. In an exegesis we repeat *everything* that an author tried to tell his readers. If, however, we are interested in certain information, for example, in the talk of God, we can do a *focused exegesis* after we complete our general one. The question then is: How does the author talk of his God in his text and through his text? If this question is to be answered scientifically, we again have to use appropriate methods to get a better grasp on how the ancient author talked of his God.

So the topic of scientific research is not God. This is impossible, because God would then become an object to be viewed and examined from a distance. This would always result in talk about God. The topic of scientific investigation is, rather, theology: a person's talk of his or her God. Whenever, in a so-called scientific theology, we ignore the person talking of his or her God, we are not dealing with theology anymore. For this reason the person should always be expressly mentioned.

Now we must be careful always to stick strictly to our question. We want to find out how that author talks *of* his God and not what statements *about* God occur in his text. This distinction is necessary, if for no other reason, because we have to expect that the author also talked about his God instead of talking of the entity that immediately governs him. And if an author talks about God, we have to ask him where he learned the contents with which he filled the word-shell *God*. They certainly do not come from his own experience.

Of course, it is not always easy to make this distinction, especially considering the historical distance. The main reason is that we concentrate too soon and too exclusively on the occurrence of the word *God,* whereas the author often expresses or indicates the entity that really governs him (i.e., *his* God) by completely different means.

We will encounter this problem several times later on. Yet for its basic significance we should at least illustrate it with two examples, even though we will have to schematize it to a certain extent.

(1) If a (Pharisaic) Jew orients himself toward the law and the law governs his life, then the law is his God. Whenever he talks of the law, he is talking of his God. If we ask this (Pharisaic) Jew why he gives himself to the law and lets himself be shaped by it, he will answer: Because God gave the law. But this statement

that God gave the law (a long time ago)—that is, the predication of God as lawgiver—is a statement *about* God. Its content is a piece of information handed down by tradition but it is not believed in the literal sense. Rather, it expresses a conviction that is held to be true. This can be shown in the following figure.

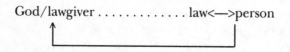

God/lawgiver . . . . . . . . . . . . law<—>person

The person gives himself or herself to the law as his or her god (<—> : theology) and explains this (<—) by talking about God. It is significant that the word *God* does not occur in the theological statement, but we do find it in the statement about God. We will have to explain this later. At this point, however, we can at least see what it means to say that the law is between God and the person.

(2) We find an analogous phenomenon when we talk about creation. The sentence, "In the beginning God created the heavens and the earth," is not a theological statement. Rather, it contains a piece of information that in New Testament times had long since become a conviction beyond any doubt. So the first sentence of the Bible is talk about God, not talk of God. What can we make of that?

Most of time at this point faith is prematurely brought in. Yet this faith merely refers to the information given in this sentence. The person that wrote the sentence is again ignored. Yet we cannot overlook this person, especially since there can be no doubt that someone at some time first wrote this sentence, which has been and is repeated time and again even today. Where did this person get his information?

Bringing the category of revelation into play at this point, which is frequently done, is not very helpful. To begin with, it is anything but clear what revelation is and how we should picture it. Maybe we could think of visions or hearing voices, such as occur later in apocalypses and are claimed by apocalyptics. Yet in this case we have to keep in mind that the faith does not concern the contents of the revelation but these individuals and their claim to have received a revelation. We have to believe them first; then we can believe the contents of the revelation. Hence it is wrong to call the statement that God created the heavens and the earth a statement of faith. Rather, it is a statement that already assumes a faith of a quite different kind. Thus the truth of this statement depends on the answer to the question: Did this person receive a revelation? (And if so, did it come from God?) Of course, this would still be talk about God. And we must also note that in our context there is not even a claim of a revelation. This idea was imported. So the question remains where this person—who was certainly not the same as the author of Gen. 1:1—got the "information" that enabled him to write this sentence. Is there another way to explain this?

There is a hint in the older creation story, which unfortunately comes second in the Bible (Gen. 2:4bff.). It starts with a human being. That he is a man is of minor importance; this simply corresponds to the "natural order" that was taken for granted at that time. It is important, though, that the story starts with an individual human being. He finds himself in a garden that provides him with food and shelter. And now this human being understands himself as created by (a) God. With this he expresses the idea that he cannot credit himself with his own existence but is a creature of his creator. And this is indeed a statement of faith, that is, a theological assertion. This human being talks of the entity on which he is simply dependent from the very beginning: "God created me."

It is a statement of faith, because this human being chooses between various ways of understanding himself. After all, he could have seen himself as a product of chance or as a toy in the hands of, and at the mercy of, capricious powers. Yet he chooses the confession, "I am a creature, and God has created me." This theological assertion cannot have been derived and therefore cannot be refuted either. In his faith this human being (the creature) is certain about the things he believes (having been created by his creator). And yet he will find again and again that other people do not share his faith.

Now this believer experiences an expansion of his horizon and adapts his faith to this expansion. If he sees himself as a creature of his creator he can do no other than to see his fellow human beings as creatures of his creator too. Then he looks beyond the ends of the garden and sees countries, rivers, unknown people, and later also earlier people, his ancestors, nature, etc. From his faith it follows that everything comes from the hand of *his* creator. And finally the time will probably come when he can say, "The God who created me created the whole world."

One thing is clear: the statement of faith (i.e., the theological assertion) reads: God created me. But the statement that in the beginning God created the heavens and the earth is not a statement of faith but a consequence of this assertion. This is no problem until we reverse the order. Then a sentence that is only possible as a last sentence is made a first sentence. But if we start with it, we start with talk about God. We inadvertently take the consequence of a statement of faith as information. Then we can hardly avoid getting into trouble when we talk with natural scientists, especially since we are also using the language carelessly. Instead of saying "creation *story*," we speak of a "creation *report*."

So the task we have is to reconstruct assertions of God from statements about God, because this is where they originated. Therefore we must understand them and can use them only in this context.

In the context of ecology, for instance, if we finally develop a widespread interest in treating nature more carefully, the contribution of the church cannot simply be the replacement of the word *nature* with the word *creation*. It is easy to see that this is not sufficient, for the word choice does not make a difference in the concrete measures to be taken. In this case the church turns out to be just hopping on the bandwagon.

Only if we believe ourselves to be creatures of a creator can we speak theologically of creation. Especially today we cannot tacitly presuppose this point but have to state it expressly; otherwise the wild idea could arise all too easily that we can speak (theologically!) of creation first and that on this basis we as individuals can and should believe ourselves to be a creatures. It was not for nothing that Luther began the explanation of the first article in his Small Catechism (entitled "On creation") with the words, "I believe that God created *me,*" and only after that continues, "along with all creatures." Here Luther converted talk about God back into talk of God.

As we will see later, the same must to be done in many other cases of talk about God that we find directly in scriptures of the New Testament or in connection with them. Sentences like "God became man," "God raised Jesus from the dead," "Jesus sits at the right hand of God," and even "Jesus will return at the end of the days" contain information, but they are not statements of faith. We have to say of these sentences too that they were spoken for the first time by particular people at particular points in time. Ever since, however, it is almost always just the contents that have been repeated. And so in order to understand these sentences and use them theologically, we must ask the first persons who uttered them why they formulated the sentences exactly the way they did. We have to ask them about their theology, their talk of their God. If we can explain the origin of these sentences on this basis, then those who talk of their God in the same way with the same contents may (perhaps) be able to repeat these sentences as a consequence of their faith—or possibly use different formulations instead.

After the exegesis is complete, we can ask the authors of the writings about their respective theologies. Since this specific questioning still occurs in the context of historical exegesis, we arrive at the result of historical theology by working out how the authors of the individual scriptures talked of their God to their readers in their time. As far as we can reconstruct earlier versions or sources by means of literary criticism, we must in turn ask their authors how they talked *of* their God and not what they said *about* God. On all literary levels we must be careful to let theology remain theology and not inadvertently present talk about God as theology.

If we limit ourselves to the New Testament, our task is to trace a history of theologies. This history started before the composition of the earliest New Testament writing, Paul's First Letter to the Thessalonians—that is, before A.D. 50. For this time we depend on reconstructions. Then this history covers the period of the New Testament from A.D. 50 to about 130; after that it continues into our immediate past.

We have to be extremely careful to do nothing more than trace this history. There is no place for criticism yet. As we continue our work, however, we cannot forgo criticism of the respective theologies. And for this criticism we need a criterion to go by. This criterion cannot be chosen at random; it must be developed and substantiated.

## 3. The Criterion of a Christian Discussion of God

### a) The Necessity of a Criterion

Criticism of the theologies of the New Testament authors would be unnecessary if all of them (including the authors of the reconstructible sources) talked respectively of their God in the same way and with the same contents. If that were the case, we could indeed say that the talk is always of the same God, and we could speak of the God of the New Testament (though this would be an ambiguous abbreviation), who would then be the Christian God. Yet this could only be a result of our work; we could never presuppose it and use it as a point of departure.

Yet even a first brief glance at the different theologies makes us doubt that we can achieve this result. We can show this with a classic example. If Paul talks of his God as one who accepts him on the basis of faith alone, apart from works of the law (Rom. 3:28), and the author of the Letter of James talks of his God as one who does not accept him on the basis of faith alone but also demands works (James 2:24), then it is hard to say that both writers are talking of the same God. Is the word-shell *God* not filled quite differently? Such examples can be multiplied (as we will see later) if we compare how Mark talks of his God and how Matthew and Luke talk of theirs, how John talks of his God and how the Johannine writers talk of theirs. Time and again we find differences that resist harmonization. At first it may sound bold, but it will prove correct that the authors of the New Testament scriptures not only talk differently of their God, but also fill the word-shell *God* with different contents. Some complement each other and thus present no serious problem. But some contradict each other. Then it is inevitable that we go from a distinction to a separation, for now it is necessary to ask which author talks "correctly" of God. This question can only be answered by means of criticism.

We have to make sure, however, that with our criticism we do not change our presentation of these theologies. Historical theology has to remain historical theology. Nonetheless, it has to be judged, and judgment is not possible without evaluation. So we have to find a criterion by which to evaluate. And this can only be successful if we decide beforehand which kind of evaluation we want to make.

### b) *The Efficacy of a Criterion*

When we compare different people's talk of God we usually ask, who talks of the "true God." We have to be careful, though, not to ask this question in the form of talk about God. But if we ask it in a strictly theological way, we realize at once that when Paul talks of his God, he talks of the God who is the true God *for him*. It is this God who governs him. Paul let himself be shaped by him by getting involved with him. In and through involvement with this God (in faith) Paul *lives* the truth of his God. He vouches for the truth of this God with his own existence.

The same is also true for the author of the Letter of James; it is true for Mark as well as for Matthew and Luke; it is true for John as well as for the Johannine writers. They each get involved with their God, and each vouches for the truth of his God with his own existence.

Thus it is quite impossible to answer the question of the "true God" objectively, especially since it would always yield talk *about* God. Only people who talk *of* their God can answer it. And they will talk only of the God that is true *for them*. Their confessions of their God are not open to discussion and therefore can be neither supported nor discredited by any criterion.

This tension between the unavailability and the binding nature of truth still exists today. If people today talk of their God, they are speaking of the Shaper who has shaped *each one of them*. By their confessions of this Shaper they stand for the truth of their God as people who have let themselves be shaped by the Shaper (and would like to be shaped again and again).

At the same time they have repeatedly learned through experience that many people around them have themselves been shaped by a totally different God and now vouch for the truth of that other God. So there is no criterion by which to settle the question of truth, neither then nor today. And such a criterion would have to be imported from outside anyway.

It is an entirely different story if people talk of their (for them!) true God and claim, "My God is the *Christian* God." This happens very often nowadays. Using this adjective they claim to make the unavailable truth binding. But can this be done?

We can assume that Paul and the author of James, that Mark and Matthew and Luke, that John and the Johannine writers were convinced that the God of whom they speak is the "Christian" God, and that they would have said so, if this term had existed then. Yet the question is whether this conviction is true. If they talk of different gods, not all of them could be talking of the "Christian" God. They may have had the best of intentions, but that does not mean they succeeded. So they have to allow us to examine the situation.

It is likewise true that if people talk of their God today and in doing so take for granted that they are talking of the true God (otherwise they would not get involved with him), and if they then claim that their God is the Christian God, then they must substantiate this assertion (but only the assertion, not their faith, that is, the fact that they got involved with the—for them—true God). For if this substantiation fails and their assertion is wrong that their talk of God is Christian talk of God, then this does not concern their faith itself or the "quality" of that faith, but only the classification of that faith, that is, the label.

So we have to remember that neither the granting nor the denying of the term *Christian* can decide the question of truth. *Christian* is merely an adjective that aids description. The two must be kept strictly apart, especially since they are often confused in current interpretation and use, and this can easily have serious consequences. Since *Christian* is then immediately understood as a statement of quality, judgment as *non-Christian* is perceived as a deficiency. And we naturally do not want to admit that our talk of our own God (which really is talk of the true God!) is not talk of the Christian God. Are we no longer allowed to assume that we are Christians? And if talk of God by the author of a New Testament writing is labeled non-Christian talk of God, this is viewed as a qualitative devaluation of this author and his writing. But is this text not part of the New Testament? We can only avoid such disqualification if we strictly adhere to our principle that the word *Christian* is to be used only for description and nothing else.

With the help of such a description we can now distinguish critically between the different theologies. What we want to check is the assertion that a certain theology is a Christian theology. For this check we need a criterion. This will indeed be imported from outside and be applied both to the individual theologies of the authors of the New Testament scriptures and to a modern person's talk of his or her God. All of these theologies are contrasted with *one* theology, specifically the one that forms the standard for deciding whether the other theologies can be *designated* Christian or not.

With this we have stated our task: Is it possible to describe and define *the* theology to which the adjective *Christian* can be applied in a methodically controllable way? And is it possible to substantiate why this is possible for this theology but not for another one?

In solving this problem we will answer the question of ethics not only provisionally, but also definitively.

### c) Christian Ethics: An Aspect of Christian Theology

If ethics is an aspect of theology, as we have tried to demonstrate, then it follows that Christian ethics is an aspect of Christian theology. We know this from the definitions. Those who speak of the Christian God talk *of* this God only if they get involved with this God in their lives. They are living their God and thereby proving the truth of this God.

This also means that if the word *Christian* does not express superior quality but simply makes a classification, then we must not think that Christian ethics is "better" than other ethical systems. It is merely another system. When we develop Christian ethics and describe other ethical systems in the following chapters, it will not be in terms of superior or inferior value.

For this reason also, no one today can be forced to live by the standards of Christian ethics. But we can very well expect other people to look at their ethic and find out which god determines it. If it is the Christian God, they can claim that their ethic is a Christian ethic. If it is not the Christian God, they should in all honesty no longer refer to their ethic as "Christian," but this does not make their ethic inferior. Since and if their God, of whom they speak, really is the true God to them, then they will obviously stick to their ethic. For it is, after all, the better ethic *for them.*

# I. The Approaches

If after the discussion in the prolegomena we now attempt to define Christian theology and—directly connected with it—Christian ethics, we may assume general agreement that we must get our orientation from the beginning. It is disputed, however, where this beginning lies. Thus we have to address the related problems at least briefly.

If we put the New Testament scriptures in chronological order, we find a series of theologies that at times developed simultaneously. Between A.D. 50 and 130 authors talked of their God through their texts to other people. They did not start over again each time but in their talk referred to talk of God by predecessors. Hence they understood themselves as people living in a tradition. But where did this tradition begin?

Occasionally these authors use statements of or about God that they found in the scriptures that were later compiled in the Old Testament. Yet they do not consider this the beginning of their talk of God, at least not the immediate beginning. Rather, the interpretation of things taken from these old writings has been somewhat modified in the meantime. The kind of modification can be classified differently, that is, as a destruction, but also as a surpassing, of previous talk of God. And the place where this modification happened is called Jesus Christ.

Thus these authors see in Jesus Christ the real beginning, at least the beginning of what we can call Christian. For all the authors of New Testament scriptures appeal to and relate to Jesus Christ and know themselves obligated to this beginning. In whatever tradition they may stand and formulate their talk of God, they are convinced of their faithfulness to this beginning.

23

Of course, that poses a problem for us. This beginning is unavailable to us in written form, for we have no texts from the time before A.D. 50. Hence none of the theologies we find in the New Testament scriptures (not even the one Paul formulates in his letters) can serve in its present form as a model for the definition of Christian theology, for they do not form the real beginning. If we want to go back to that beginning, we must depend on reconstructions.

That such reconstructions are not always easy to achieve is obvious. Occasionally we even have to work with hypotheses, and thus the results (sometimes) remain disputed. It seems easier then, to stick with the texts we have, take our bearings from them, and rely on Paul's letters, since they just happen to be the oldest documents that still exist. Referring to these letters is almost an automatic practice.

Yet if the real beginning was before A.D. 50—a fact that cannot be honestly disputed—we have to admit that the seemingly simpler solution is an inadequate and therefore bad solution. We cannot escape a task known to be necessary merely because we would run into problems carrying it out. We must take it on, but we will have to be careful to proceed with our reconstructions most circumspectly. The steps in our work have to be verifiable.

One more problem should be mentioned, especially since its solution is obviously far more difficult. As of now there is no consensus on whether the beginning of Christianity is to be seen in the life and work of the earthly Jesus, or whether the real beginning came at Easter. For the time being the word *Easter* must remain an empty word-shell. Only later will we be able to give it some content.

This alternative of whether things began with Jesus or only with Easter cannot be resolved simply through reconstructions because of a peculiar circumstance. We find the chronologically earlier events only in relatively late documents, whereas earlier documents hardly ever mention the earlier events. The Gospels, written in A.D. 70 and later, are the earliest texts that tell us something about the life and work of Jesus. Paul, on the other hand, mentions next to nothing on this topic in his letters, which were written about A.D. 50 to 56. So if we base our reconstructions on Paul's letters, we will only be able to go back to Easter (and before that to the death of Jesus). Yet if we base it on the Gospels, we can go back to Jesus' life and work. And if we assume a rectilinear devolopment (work of Jesus, death of Jesus, Easter, primitive church, Paul, Gospels), we get the impression from the literary documents that have come down to us that during the time following Easter, no one was interested in Jesus' life and work. In that period Easter seems to have been considered the beginning. Only later did people become interested (again?) in Jesus' life and work. In this way Jesus' life and work *became* the beginning, but only long after Easter. This is odd, to say the least, and requires explanation.

It seems obvious to understand *beginning* in a temporal sense and reconstruct it from the Gospels, while skipping over Paul's letters, so to speak. In this case we would have to say that Christianity started with the life and work of Jesus.

There are, however, objections to this procedure. There is no doubt that the Evangelists(!) knew about the end of Jesus' life and about Easter. So one may assume that in their presentations of Jesus' past this knowledge guided them (at least in part) and influenced those presentations. From this the conclusion has been drawn that the primitive church(!) always saw and presented the earthly Jesus from the perspective of Easter. In other words, from the very beginning faith in the resurrected One determined the presentation of the earthly One. If this is true, then there really are good reasons for understanding Easter as the actual beginning of Christianity. As a further argument it is also possible to point to the oldest literary documents, Paul's letters, which seemed to support this theory.

We can, of course, ask whether it is allowable to take what is accepted as truth by the Evangelists and apply it to the earlier(!) primitive church. I think it can be shown that such an inference is superficial. Yet this requires a more thorough discussion. For the time being we will leave open the question of where we must see the beginning of Christianity, in Jesus' life and work or not until Easter. We should, however, point out some consequences of the different answers, especially since they open up other questions that have to be answered.

If, on the one hand, we take Easter as the beginning of Christianity, we must answer the question, What significance do Jesus' life and work have for the Christian faith? Was the earthly Jesus only a kind of forerunner of the resurrected One? It is often told that Jesus led the people around him to faith, but never to faith in his person. (This came later in the Gospel of John.) So what kind of faith did Jesus lead the people to? Faith in God? Certainly. But what kind of God? It cannot have been Christian faith, if this faith did not exist before Easter.

If, on the other hand, we see the beginning in the life and work of the earthly Jesus, things only seem simpler. Now we have to answer the question, What significance does Easter have for the Christian faith? Is it a resumption (however conceived or originating) of something that already existed before? Then Easter would have no other content than the revival of the old faith, because afterward the content of the faith was the same as before. But this contradicts the widespread opinion that the resurrection of Jesus (along with his cross) was the central event that determined everything. If this is really true, the time before Easter seems again to be deficient. But is it possible to see the beginning of Christianity in the life and work of the earthly Jesus without his subsequent exaltation?

This can be put in two short formulas. If we take Easter as the beginning, we have to explain the pre-Easter Jesus. If we see the beginning in the pre-Easter Jesus, we have to explain Easter.

We have to mention a third possibility according to which the alternative is resolved by either sweeping aside the problem of Easter or ignoring it. The father of this idea was Hermann Samuel Reimarus, whom we will soon discuss in detail. Since Reimarus thought that Easter was a deception of the disciples, he understood the development of Christology as a consequence of this deception. Hence he was only interested in the historical Jesus, whom he tried to reconstruct. He said the church should orient itself only toward the historical Jesus; by its invention of Christology it had gone astray.

This abandoning of Christology promoted by Reimarus has lasting effects even today, and most remarkably in the area of Christian ethics. Here we can very often see a great reserve vis-à-vis any Christology, the question being whether it turns Jesus into something entirely different from what he really was and wanted to be. So Christology is eliminated by ignoring it. Looking for ethical instructions in the church means asking what Jesus said about a problem. He is perceived as the uncorrupted beginning and thus the norm. If one wants to know what is Christian, one looks to the "historical Jesus." A consideration of Easter can be, and is, omitted. Hence, in this view, we can do without Christology. Reimarus has indeed remained modern!

How shall we proceed in view of this seemingly rather obscure situation? Again, we should remember that through our definitions of Christian talk of God and of Christian ethics an *evaluation* cannot be reached—nor are we allowed even to attempt one. Since there is no agreement on the true beginning, we will not make a decision on that beforehand; instead we will give two descriptions, one based on the assumption that the beginning was Jesus' life and work, the other one based on the assumption that it was Easter.

This gives the direction in which we will go in the following pages. Since with the Gospels we can go back into an earlier time than with Paul's letters, we will start with them. Our questions are, What can we find out, through reconstruction, about where and how Christian talk by people of their God began? and What can we say in this context about these people's ethics? Then we will have to approach Paul's letters with the same questions. In this way we will look at two possible beginnings.

# A. Ethics Oriented toward Jesus

This title has been chosen intentionally because the traditional formulation, "The Ethics of Jesus," is too imprecise. I am convinced that there is no way to establish the ethics of Jesus. This has to do with the "quest for the historical Jesus," which we will go into shortly. Moreover, in defining Christian ethics we must not and indeed cannot disregard Christology. The two are directly dependent on each other. Through the insight that the quest for the historical Jesus has failed to produce results, we can even say that we are directly confronted with Christology, even before Easter. Hence Christology turns out to be not only indispensable—this could be a postulate—but unavoidable if we proceed in a methodically deliberate manner.

## 1. The Basic Problem: Christian Ethics, an Aspect of Christology

This title is a modification of the title of the prolegomena. For a Christian, Christology is the specific form of theology. In talking of Jesus as the one who shapes them, Christians are talking of *their* God.

> With this we state at the same time that the understanding of the first article of Luther's catechism is only possible on the basis of the second article. If we want to proceed from the first to the second article, we almost always slip into talking about God.

Yet what does it mean when a person talks of (and not about!) Jesus?

### a) The Quest for the Historical Jesus

In discussions and hence in the literature two terms are often used synonymously: *earthly Jesus* and *historical Jesus.* We should make a distinction, however, since this can easily produce misunderstandings.

The *earthly Jesus,* in contrast to the resurrected Jesus, refers to the Jesus who worked on earth from his birth to his death. In this context it makes no difference whether or not what is told about him is historically accurate. Not so in the case of the *historical Jesus.* Here we are dealing with a presentation of the Jesus working on earth *apart from any human interpretation.* The question is, How did Jesus understand himself? and not, How did other people understand him? When we look at his activities we are only concerned about the historical facts, and when we look at his preaching we are only concerned about his *ipsissima verba,* his very own words. We should use the term *historical Jesus* only in this exact sense. Otherwise we should speak of the earthly Jesus.

This terminological distinction is not an arbitrary one; rather, it is required by the concern of Hermann Samuel Reimarus (1694-1768), with which the quest of the historical Jesus began.

Between 1774 and 1778, in Wolfenbüttel, Gotthold Ephraim Lessing edited parts of Reimarus's work as anonymous fragments without naming their author. One was entitled, "On the Purpose of Jesus and His Disciples."

According to Reimarus we have to keep the two strictly apart. The "purpose of Jesus" was to be the *political* messiah of his people and liberate them from Roman dominion. On his way to Jerusalem he expected an uprising of the people there, which did not happen. So Jesus failed to achieve his purpose. On the cross he admitted his defeat with the words, "My God, my God, why have you forsaken me?"

His disciples, who had hoped to become officials in the messiah's empire, had come to enjoy traveling around and did not want to go back to their original work. So they started to pursue their own "purpose": they intended to lead comfortable lives as preachers.

To achieve this purpose they invented "Easter." They stole the body of Jesus and claimed—though not until fifty days later—that he had risen. Based on this "Easter" they wrote their version of history, falsifying the picture of the *historical* Jesus. If he had intended to be the messiah of his people, understanding himself as an earthly, human figure, the disciples now created the image of the *earthly* Jesus, presenting him as the Son of man and thus giving him the features of a heavenly divine being who while he was alive had already announced his imminent return. And this return was to be expected shortly.

Since in the Gospels we are always dealing with the earthly Jesus—that is, with a picture of Jesus painted over with the colors of Easter—our task, according to Reimarus, is to scrape off this second layer. Only when we do that will the historical Jesus become visible again under the image of the earthly one. And that historical Jesus is what Reimarus was looking for.

It is true, of course, that Reimarus was motivated by a profound hatred of the church. He proved critically that in its appeal to Jesus the church was not appealing to the *historical* Jesus but to an *image* of Jesus that originated through deception, as he believed he could demonstrate. So the church was a product of this deception, even into the present time. With this theory Reimarus inevitably met resistance, but this does not discredit his methodological insights.

On the contrary, these insights seem, at least initially, to make sense. If the church appeals to Jesus, it really cannot appeal to its own created *image* of Jesus. And so, after some hesitation, the question of the historical Jesus was attacked, since it seemed not only reasonable but also plainly necessary. Interest was focused on it for almost a century and a half, until after World War I and in part even today. Most of the books on Jesus published in the last three decades or so give evidence of this. But at the same time they show that reaching a consensus on the figure of the historical Jesus has been impossible.

Perhaps this problem is unsolvable. That would have to be demonstrated and substantiated. As long as this has not happened, the question remains—unless we can show that the question of the historical Jesus was itself improperly asked. Naturally, a wrong question cannot yield right answers. And indeed it has turned out in the meantime that the question was asked in the wrong way.

The long history of the quest for the historical Jesus cannot be presented here, but I would like to mention at least two insights that were gained.

First, if we look for the historical Jesus and base our research on the Gospels, we find many traits and themes that are, or seem to be, incompatible. Thus we need *selecting criteria* in order to decide what is authentic (historical fact) and what is not. Where do we find them? Albert Schweitzer stated in his history of the life-of-Jesus research (*The Quest for the Historical Jesus,* first published in 1906 under the title *Von Reimarus bis Wrede* [From Reimarus to Wrede]) that each generation had formed its own image of Jesus. From the multitude of divergent traits, themes, and sayings it had picked those that suited its own interests and concerns and held them to be historical. So researchers had decided on the criteria themselves, as Reimarus had done before. Of course, this is not the way to find the historical Jesus, but is it possible to do research at all apart from one's own interests? If not, then the historical Jesus must remain hidden in the obscurity of the past. So Albert Schweitzer's book was dubbed the "funeral hymn of the life-of-Jesus research." But is that true? Most of the more recent life-of-Jesus books ignore Schweitzer's observations—which was the only way they could be written. Also, they almost always ignore a second insight.

If we look for the historical Jesus, we cannot immediately turn to the Gospels. We must, instead, be familiar with and take into account the *problem of the sources.* In the course of more than a century, German Protestant researchers in particular did an excellent job of clarifying this. They developed a set of instruments with whose help one could at least hope to get results that were methodologically better substantiated than those achievable by Reimarus.

The Gospel of John had to be ignored in the quest for the historical Jesus. The relationship of the synoptic Gospels to each other could be explained with the theory of the two sources. Literary criticism helped to reconstruct small units and led to the theory that the Jesus tradition began with individual bits of tradition. It was obviously a very long road from these beginnings through the collection and compilation of individual traditions into early sources and finally to the Gospel of Mark, which then (together with the sayings source) was used by the Evangelists Matthew and Luke.

As early as 1847 Adolf (von) Harnack proposed in his inaugural dissertation the thesis, "Vita Jesu scribi nequit," that is, the life of Jesus cannot be written. And indeed the entirely different arrangements of the individual traditions showed that it is impossible to write a biography of Jesus. The question of the historical Jesus could only be directed to individual traditions and answered separately in each particular case.

Yet again criteria were needed to decide what is historically authentic and what is not. No agreement could be reached on how to find these criteria or which criteria to use. The problem seemed unsolvable indeed.

With the birth of form criticism after World War I it began to dawn on people that the question of the historical Jesus was asked the wrong way. Yet this happened very slowly, for at first form criticism was considered an obstruction that made it difficult to find the historical Jesus too fast and too directly. And this turned out to be the case.

It is problematic, of course, to speak of form criticism in general, since individual approaches are sometimes considerably different. Yet if this is the main concern of a critique of form criticism, it misses the crucial point: All approaches share the knowledge that the authors of the individual traditions were themselves not interested in historical facts. So if we examine the historical authenticity of things related in these texts, we are investigating them with an interest that we ourselves bring to the texts, but it is foreign to the texts themselves. Hence we cannot expect an immediate answer. In addition, we are denying ourselves an understanding of the texts by asking the wrong question.

We can illustrate this point through a comparison with dramas that deal with historical events. If, for example, we examine Heinrich von Kleist's *Battle of Arminius* for the actual history of that battle, we will get no useful data and at the same time deny ourselves an understanding of what Kleist was trying to say with his work.

Most of the time the insight gained was expressed in the terminology that had been used in the quest for the historical Jesus, and this hindered recognition of the real problem. Previously, distinctions had been made between "historically authentic" traditions and those that were merely "church formations." Now it was said that all the texts that could be reconstructed by means of literary criticism were church formations. With these texts the primitive church did not want to *report on Jesus* but—as it was summed up—to *proclaim Jesus*. Different "life situations" (Sitze im Leben) in the primitive church were postulated, such as worship, apologia, paraenesis, and exhortation of the Paraclete. The life situation specified the purpose a text was supposed to serve, and the purpose determined the literary form in which the history of Jesus was recounted. So we were dealing not with historical reports but with what was called *kerygma*.

So form criticism had surprise and disillusionment in store for those who were interested in the historical Jesus. Ever since Reimarus they had tried to reach behind the primitive church to the historical Jesus. Now, after over a century of hard work, they had to realize that they were dealing with the primitive church even in the earliest Jesus traditions. Had they gone in a circle? Was there any way at all to find the historical Jesus?

Some were ready to abandon the quest for the historical Jesus altogether. Here we must mention Rudolf Bultmann and later on his school. Bultmann saw no point in pursuing the quest and asserted that if we tried to verify the kerygma in regard to the historical Jesus, we would give rise to the suspicion that we want to secure the historical basis of our faith. But a faith that needs securing is no longer faith—to say nothing of the fact that the results of historical investigations keep changing and thus are always uncertain. Hence the only possible model for faith is the kerygma of the primitive church. Since it was postulated that the primitive church had come into being through Easter, that became the real beginning, and this gave rise to the "scientific dogma" that all presentations of the earthly Jesus are determined by faith in the resurrected One.

Others (above all Joachim Jeremias) continued the quest for the historical Jesus, because they believed that only the word of the historical Jesus could give the proclamation of the church authority. Yet if this was true, they had to ask whether the proclamation of the primitive church, which obviously had no interest in history, happened without authority. In addition, the search for criteria of authenticity now had to start anew, as did the dispute over which criteria were appropriate and which were not.

Even some parts of the Bultmann school again raised the question of the historical Jesus, now dubbed the "new" quest for the historical Jesus. The kerygma, it was claimed, had to get at least some "orientation from the historical Jesus" or else it would lose the foundation on which it claimed to be built (Gerhard Ebeling). And it was said that the kerygma owed its *existence* to Easter, but not its *content,* which came from before Easter (Ernst Käsemann). So they had to keep looking for the historical Jesus and solve the problems that had originated through the insights of form criticism. It seemed impossible to abandon the quest. It was too deeply ingrained in everyone's consciousness, especially since also in the life of the church it was almost never given up. The problems posed by scientific research were often simply ignored.

And it was indeed not possible simply to outlaw the question of the historical Jesus. But those who wanted to answer it now had to argue in two directions. It was not sufficient to show why something was inauthentic, as had mostly happened before; one also had to show why something could be called historically authentic. For now it had to be assumed that *all* reconstructable texts had *originated* in the primitive church. So two things were possible: they could be authentic or inauthentic. It was always the primitive church that was talking, and not Jesus. Yet were there criteria by which the two could be distinguished?

In my opinion, none will be found, because there cannot be any. In order to understand this we must first ask whether the term *primitive church* was not introduced prematurely to designate the group to whom we owe all our Jesus traditions. The term is dangerous, because it immediately suggests a date: in Luke's conception (as well as in the still influential conception of Reimarus!) the primitive church did not exist until Easter (or Pentecost). Whether this is historically accurate must still be tested. First of all, however, judging by the results of form criticism, we must ask whether such implicit dating, given with the term *primitive church,* can be defended at all?

Form criticism postulated "life situations" that did not exist until these later times. Yet not only are some of these situations questionable, but the fixation of our interest on them also keeps us from seeing what form criticism really accomplished and can hardly be proved wrong, namely, that all the Jesus traditions were formed by *people.* When this happened can only be determined from case to case. But however far back we go, there were always people who talked of Jesus. It is simply unimaginable that such talk began only with Easter and thus only in the post-Easter primitive church. There is no reasonable objection to the assumption that there was already talk of Jesus during the time of his activity. Hence the beginning of the Jesus traditions must lie in that period, whatever changes and embellishments were added later. Jesus himself did not leave us even one line. It was always other people who talked of him from the very beginning of the traditions. What kind of people were they?

There were various people and groups who could talk of Jesus: followers, opponents, and neutral observers. Our traditions show that they come only from the first group. Tales by opponents (who certainly existed) and neutral observers (who most likely also existed) do not appear in the synoptic tradition. That means, however, that the entire reconstructible Jesus tradition was "biased" from the beginning. (This is only a description, not a negative judgement.) But something that is biased cannot claim to be a historical report. On the other hand, if people wanted to render a historical account based on their commitment, they could never achieve their intended purpose, that is, to tell others of their commitment or to lead them into a similar commitment. The presentation was necessarily biased, and thus an inquiry into the bare facts of history is indeed futile. Even if we still decide to look for these facts because we want—for whatever reasons—to find the historical Jesus, we would not succeed, as two considerations will show.

First, we must consider that (the historical) Jesus without doubt said and did much more than tradition recalls. And those to whom we owe the oldest traditions experienced more with Jesus and heard more from him than they later told. So what we now have is only a relatively small selection. This raises the question, By what criteria did these persons make their selection? The answer is obvious and almost sounds trivial. The people who told of Jesus told only what *they* considered worth telling, because *they* considered it important or crucial. But they did not tell what they took for granted, because it was not so important to them.

This raises a further question: Would the historical Jesus have selected the same things the authors of the texts selected? Or would his selection have been different because in his opinion a different evaluation of importance had to be made? There is no answer to this question, since there is no method by which we can find an answer. So the very selection of the things told makes it impossible to bypass the people and get back to the historical Jesus.

Even more important is the second consideration. The persons who talked of Jesus always talked *as they understood things*. There is no other possible way to tell something.

This again raises the question, Did the historical Jesus understand his actions and his preaching in the same way that these people presented it later? And, what is more, did the historical Jesus understand himself the way these people said he understood himself? There is no answer to this question either, since there is no method by which we could find an answer.

The consequence of this is inevitable: *The historical Jesus cannot be found*. From the traditions we only learn how the authors of the texts understood Jesus' actions, his words, and hence Jesus himself. There is no way to bypass these people.

For this reason we should abandon the old way of asking the question and formulate more precisely a new question (as already occasionally proposed). *The quest for the historical Jesus* has to be replaced by *the historical quest for Jesus*.

If we are looking for the historical Jesus, the statement of our goal (the historical Jesus) already determines the nature of this goal, namely, Jesus before any interpretation by people. But if we try to examine Jesus historically, we only state the direction of our investigation. How far we get in this direction remains open.

If we investigate Jesus historically, we never get any farther than the *people* who talk of Jesus, and we find Jesus only together with these persons. According to prior definition, this is not the historical Jesus.

Naturally, the failure of the life-of-Jesus studies may be disappointing to those who still believe that the historical Jesus is crucial and want to argue with his self-understanding (which frequently happens in dogmatics). Actually, however, this failure contains an opportunity: we finally have another chance to do theology. In seeking the historical Jesus we inevitably end up with "talk about." But in investigating Jesus historically we have to deal with the people, because we cannot bypass them. And now we can question them regarding *their* God. But their God is Jesus (in the first place, at least). We will elaborate on this later.

We cannot talk about the "ethics of Jesus" anymore either. This manner of speaking suggests that we are referring to the historical Jesus and that it is essential to reconstruct the authentic (historically genuine) Jesus material. And since this is unavailable, we have to speak of *ethics oriented toward Jesus*. The real issue is the ethic developed by people in their orientation toward Jesus.

Often Jesus and Paul are contrasted and compared with each other. The difference is frequently stated as follows: Paul looks back on what Jesus expected as imminent, that is, the coming of the kingdom of God.

Yet this is an error. We can really compare only the *people* who talk of Jesus with *Paul,* who also talks of Jesus, though quite differently. Hence we have to clarify whether the people who met Jesus differ from Paul, in that expectation has become fulfillment. We will see that this is not the case. A precise use of the language can keep us from approaching a problem improperly and then arriving at the wrong solution. Thus it is a fundamental rule that we should no longer say, "Jesus said," but instead, "according to _____ Jesus said." In this way we will avoid errors and misunderstandings.

From all this it follows that the quest for the historical Jesus has to be replaced by the historical quest for Jesus, that is, the quest for the witnesses who, being impressed by Jesus, developed ethics as an aspect of their Christology.

## b) The Beginning of Christology

*(1) Structure: the proclaimed agent.* The beginning of Christology is usually seen as the point where (as Rudolf Bultmann puts it) the proclaimer becomes the one proclaimed. For that is what Christology is all about: Jesus is the *object* of faith, and Christology says who he is—and in what way—as the object of faith.

*Christology* is an unfortunate term, because *Christ* is already a majestic christological title. When we call Jesus *Christ,* we have just one of many possible forms of Christology. The term *Christology,* however, presupposes that *Christ* is understood already as a proper name. Thus we would be more precise to speak of *Jesusology,* because it is of *Jesus* that we make various statements. We can do this in the form of titles; Jesus is the Christ, the Son of God, the Savior, the Redeemer, etc. Or we can look at the *work* Jesus has accomplished: he died for us, reconciled us with God, etc. In summary we can say that it is always an *image of Jesus* expressing some sort of qualification of him. The traditional term *Christology* should be understood in this sense.

Hence Christology starts at the point where Jesus becomes the content of proclamation, the object of faith. According to traditional understanding this happened *at* Easter and *through* Easter. Thus the beginning of Christology is always placed at Easter, as Reimarus had already done.

The presentation of the resulting course of history seems to make sense at first glance: while Jesus was active on earth he did the proclaiming, and only later was he proclaimed. Yet has this really been the case only *since* Easter? And (we must ask this question separately) did it happen *through* Easter?

If we seek Jesus historically, this view is no longer so obvious. There can be no doubt that Jesus preached. Yet we can no longer find this proclamation itself because we always keep coming upon people who in their stories present Jesus the way they understood him. Thus these persons are drawing images of Jesus. To the extent that Jesus is evaluated in these images directly or indirectly, we are dealing at least implicitly with Christologies. Hence the ultimate answers attainable in a historical quest for Jesus are Christologies.

The people drawing these Jesus images are communicating them to other people. It is obvious why they are doing this: they want to tell others what this Jesus means to the storytellers themselves, so that he will have the same meaning for others; they want to stimulate an interest in Jesus. In other words, they are proclaiming their Jesus images. Thus in our historical quest for Jesus it is always the proclaimed Jesus that we find. He can be found only as an object of faith.

Yet we must now take a closer than usual look at the contents of these proclaimed Jesus images. They do not by any means only portray a proclaimer. We also find narrative passages in addition to his words. Here Jesus is proclaimed as one who heals, discusses, responds to particular situations in a particular way, etc. If we ask who is (historically) behind these traditions, it is not enough to answer, they presuppose a *proclaimer.*

The fixation on this point is a legacy of the quest for the historical Jesus. Here was the primary focus in the search for Jesus' proclamation. This proclamation of Jesus was then compiled into a doctrine of Jesus, and a part of this doctrine was Jesus' ethics.

We can avoid this problem only if we do not one-sidedly assume a proclaimer, who became the content of proclamation, but instead speak of the *active* Jesus who is presupposed by all traditions. Jesus' proclamation was merely a part of his work.

In summing up the oldest traditions, we would have to say: *An agent is proclaimed.* This is the basic structure of every Christology.

In the picturing of Jesus in the Jesus images different accents could be placed. The activity could be described, the agent could be described, or both could happen at the same time.

If we ask here about the sequence, there is an obvious assumption that will be confirmed later when this sketch is filled in with details. Christology began with people understanding and presenting Jesus' work as a qualified activity. This is something we could call an *implicit Christology*. It is implicit, because it is first the *human being* Jesus to whom a qualified work is attributed. Even here we can already call it Christology, because this work—however differently designated—was always attributed exclusively to *Jesus*. An explicit Christology came about later in describing the agent on the basis of his activity.

The overcoming of the one-sidedness by talking of the agent instead of the proclaimer allows us at least a glimpse of an important problem for ethics. We can only mention it briefly here but will elaborate on it later.

Attempts to present the "ethics of Jesus" use his words almost exclusively. The result is the claim that Jesus proclaimed a new ethic. Does this not inevitably lead to an understanding of ethics as "law" and make Jesus appear as a "new Moses"? The imperatives lack an indicative.

Omitting the narrative parts results in ignoring the relationship between speeches and narrative. The Jesus who acts, however, is proclaimed in the Jesus images as someone who lives his own proclamation. People experienced Jesus' proclamation on the one hand and his actions and way of life on the other as interpreting each other. We could say: By Jesus' actions toward people they experienced the indicative that enabled them to act the way they were invited to by the proclamation.

This discussion at least calls into question the widespread opinion that Christology originated at Easter and through Easter. And we must make a strict distinction between these two. "At Easter" only gives a date. With "through Easter" we are talking about events that occurred on that date and made it possible now (and only now!) for Christology to develop. In order to show this we must fill the word-shell *Easter,* and later we will do that. For the time being we will restrict the meaning of *Easter* to the giving of a date: some time after the crucifixion of Jesus. This restriction is possible, because for now we can get along without filling this word-shell.

The question of the beginning of Christology is the question of when Jesus became the object or content of the proclamation. We should now see the answer clearly: Jesus became the object of proclamation the moment people started to speak *of* him. Even if we cannot reconstruct traditions that arose at the time of Jesus' activity because an exact dating still remains uncertain, we can take for granted that there already were such traditions in Jesus' lifetime. People told people of Jesus: the historical truth of Mark's later statement that "his fame began to spread throughout the surrounding region of Galilee" (Mark 1:28) should not be doubted. Such narratives form the core of the synoptic tradition, which from its very beginning was christological.

We can certainly ask—and discuss—whether (the contents of) Easter caused changes, revisions, or even a reevaluation of the Jesus images. But the images themselves, and hence Christology, originated before the date of Easter for the very reason that Jesus was the content of proclamation from the beginning. This raises the question of who spread these earliest traditions.

*(2) Place: the Galilean churches.* In the quest for the historical Jesus a distinction was usually made between *historically authentic*

*material* and *formation by the church*. Based on this distinction form criticism established that all traditions were formed by the primitive church in particular life situations. Since it was taken for granted that the primitive church did not exist until Easter (or Pentecost), the already mentioned "scientific dogma" developed that all narratives of the earthly Jesus presuppose belief in the resurrected One. Thus Reimarus's conception was still maintained—at least in principle. The bearers of these traditions were believed to be the group that Jesus had gathered and who had traveled with him through Galilee and finally to Jerusalem. When these people started to talk of Jesus after his death, they could no longer simply tell the past as they had experienced it; it was always at least partly determined by the "Easter experiences" that they had had (or invented, according to Reimarus) in the meantime.

So a unilinear development is assumed, roughly corresponding to the conception that Luke had (though not before the eighties or nineties) about the course of history.

activity in Galilee

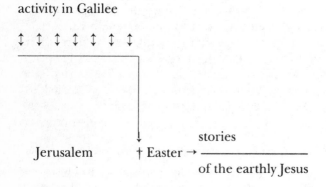

We run into problems with this construction, however, when we try to use it to explain the literary findings.

First, it is at the very least amazing that the synoptic tradition started out as individual stories, for after Easter *the disciples* could see the finished work of Jesus as a whole. Would it not have been much more logical to write a coherent sketch of his activity that could later be expanded? Remarkably enough,

Luke is the first one to think of this. He quotes as a condition for the election of the twelfth apostle that he know the way Jesus traveled, "beginning from the baptism of John until the day when he was taken up from us" (Acts 1:21-22), from having traveled this way himself with Jesus. Yet the history of the texts went in the opposite direction. Not until much later were the individual texts combined into a coherent history.

Thus it was Luke's idea that the twelve were the bearers of the Jesus tradition, which makes sense in the context of the Evangelist's conception. Yet it is not very likely that this was the case. Jesus' companions could hardly have discussed and preserved their individual experiences *while* they traveled with him, in order then to tell them as individual tales after Easter. Rather, the literary findings suggest a bigger and more varied group of bearers.

The disciples were indispensable for the "scientific dogma," of course. Only they had the "Easter experiences," so only they could tell stories of the earthly Jesus out of their faith in the resurrected One. Did they do this in Jerusalem? If so, how do we explain our literary findings? Or did they go to Galilee so that there they could tell of the earthly Jesus out of their faith in the resurrected One? How are we to picture this?

On closer examination, the "scientific dogma" turns out to be mere postulate anyway. Where in the reconstructed texts of the synoptic tradition can we really find an "Easter influence"? Certainly in some late traditions, but the bulk of the synoptic tradition talks of Jesus in the same way that people could and did talk of him during his lifetime. And long after the date of Easter people still talked like that—even in the sayings source, which, in unanimous scholarly opinion, contains no passion or Easter kerygma.

Very often we assume that texts that were written after Easter have to be determined by Easter in their contents. But this assumption turns out to be a prejudice if it cannot be verified by the texts.

For whether or not the authors of texts knew something about Easter cannot be decreed ahead of time. We can only learn from their texts what they knew. Any conjectures about what else they might have known or must have known, based on the dating of the text, remain pure speculations.

A look at the texts, however, also shows that even if the

authors should have known about Easter, it did not influence the the their writings in the earliest synoptic texts, in the first compilations, and even in the sayings source. So why did they make no perceptible use of their knowledge?

The problems we face here were created by taking Luke's conception of the course of events as historically correct. Then this context was used in an attempt to explain the results of literary criticism and form criticism. Methodologically, however, this is a more than questionable enterprise.

Our point of departure cannot be a historical construction, to which our literary findings are adapted; we must begin rather with the findings themselves. If they are the basis of our attempted reconstruction of the course of events, we avoid such problems. But then, of course, another problem arises. We will have to abandon many familiar ideas that we have considered so certain that they have achieved the status of "dogma."

The bearers of the earliest traditions at the time of Jesus' activity and also of the later synoptic traditions (roughly until the sayings source) cannot have been the primitive church in Jerusalem; they must have been churches in Galilee. And if we try to picture of Jesus' activity (based on our literary findings), then this is indeed the most obvious assumption. We can illustrate this with the figure below.

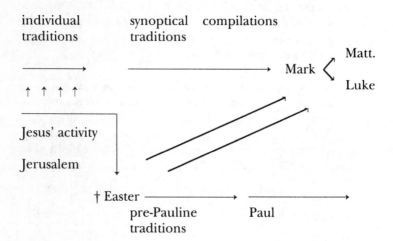

Traveling through Galilee, Jesus is active in many different places. Some people join him and follow him. Most people stay behind—even those who are impressed by him in various ways through his activity. But those start telling of him, of his words and deeds, of events and encounters. In the context of our traditional understanding of the primitive church, of course, it is problematic to speak of Galilean "churches." Nor can we draw an accurate picture of these "Jesus groups." We can only say that they must have been bearers of quite diverse Jesus traditions and that through them the news of Jesus was spread. And this happened in his absence: Jesus' journey to Jerusalem did not stop the process; people kept on telling of him.

And they told of him *in the same way* they told of him when he was active. There is no perceptible "break." We do not know whether the people in Galilee learned about Jesus' journey to Jerusalem or, more important, about the events in Jerusalem. We should not be too quick to assume either modern means of communication or an early consolidation of these "Jesus groups" into an organization that would have facilitated the flow of information. We have to be faithful to our literary evidence. For a long time after the *date* of Easter the synoptic tradition records no knowledge of Jesus' death or of the *contents* of Easter. This happened much later and then only sporadically.

Therefore we must deal with a fully independent Galilean line of tradition. It begins with individual traditions at the time of Jesus' activity, runs through the history of the material in the synoptic tradition, and finally leads through the early compilations to the writing of the Gospel of Mark.

The Jerusalem events produced a second, entirely different line of tradition, which can be reconstructed from several pre-Pauline traditions. Literarily it surfaces in Paul's letters, which later started a tradition of their own. Characteristic of this tradition is the fact that it sees the completed work of Jesus as a whole, and on this it bases its proclamation. The contents of the proclamation can be aspects of this whole: in the beginning, primarily the interpretation of Jesus' death, which was a puzzle that simply required an explanation, and later also the interpretation of his coming (cf. Gal. 4:4). But the contents could as well be statements on the *person* of Jesus: the one resurrected by God, or on his *work:* Jesus is the one with whom faith came (cf. Gal. 3:25) or the one in whom God reconciled the world to himself (cf. 2 Cor. 5:19), and so forth.

If we assume this simultaneity of two lines of tradition running independently for a relatively long time (which we can conclude from literary evidence), we can explain some peculiarities that otherwise pose problems.

*(a) The distribution of the material.* It is often asked why Paul is almost completely silent about the life of the earthly Jesus. This is hard to explain if we postulate the twelve as carriers of the Jesus tradition and assume that Paul met Peter three years after his conversion. In the Jerusalem line of tradition, however, the Jesus stories were not passed on, because it had different interests from the beginning. Conversely, in the Galilean line of tradition we find, with few exceptions, none of the creedal formulas that already existed rather early.

*(b) The statement of faith.* There is a saying going back to Bultmann that corresponds to the one already quoted (the proclaimer became the proclaimed): The one who called to faith became (through Easter) the one *in* whom people had faith. After what we have said so far, we may have to be more cautious. One may indeed be able to assume that the *historical Jesus* (who is intended here) did call to *faith* (and not to faith in his person). Yet in the Jesus traditions he is *proclaimed* as one who calls to faith. Thus Jesus was the "object" of faith from the beginning, and not just after Easter. But this is stated differently in the two lines of tradition, and with remarkable consistency. In the Galilean branch (the date of) Easter does not mark a break. In the history of the synoptic tradition, including the synoptic Gospels, Jesus is always proclaimed as the one who calls to faith and never (as in the Gospel of John) to faith in himself. (The two exceptions, Matt. 18:6; 27:42, are very late modifications of Mark 9:42; 15:32.) Faith *in* Jesus (Christ), *in* the *kyrios,* etc., is found only in the Jerusalem line, and there from the very beginning. There Easter influence can really be seen. Easter had no influence on the line from the Jesus traditions to the synoptic

material. What the Jerusalem line means by *Easter* is expressed here with the title *Son of Man,* as we will see. This title is not found in the Jerusalem line.

*(c) The interpretation of Jesus' death.* In the Jerusalem line we find from the beginning the interpreation of Jesus' death as a vicarious suffering or an expiatory sacrifice, usually expressed with words such as, "He died (was crucified, given, etc.) *for us.*" So the *death* of Jesus is understood as an event in which God acted for the salvation of humanity. This interpretation of his death, which later became almost exclusively dominant, does not exist in the Galilean line. The two exceptions (Mark 10:45; 14:24) can easily be explained as singular imports from the Jerusalem line. They remain alien elements in the Galilean line. In the bulk of the individual traditions of the synoptic corpus Jesus' death is not even mentioned. Nor is his work interpreted in such a way that Jesus *wanted* his death in order to achieve salvation for humankind through it (or, judged by the assertions of the Jerusalem line, *exclusively* through it). Rather, the activity of the earthly Jesus has a meaning in itself. In this work Jesus *risks* persecutions, prosecutions, and possibly death (cf. Mark 3:6). Later on, after his death had become a fact, and news of it had reached Galilee, it was possible to say of Jesus' *way* that despite apparent defeat it had been a way with and under God (e.g., Mark 8:31) or to compare his death to the fate of the prophets (e.g., Luke 13:34-35). So there was no soteriological understanding of his death.

This outline of the literary findings shows that there were two independent lines of tradition that for a long time did not influence each other. Whether the carriers of these two traditions were aware of each other, knew each other, and were in touch with each other is an idle question, since it cannot be answered. Yet it is striking—even assuming a closer contact—that both preserved their independence. For each line remained faithful to its own language and its own concepts. Mutual influences reveal themselves only relatively late, and then only hesitantly.

Since the Jerusalem line later prevailed, chiefly through Paul's influence, it was hard for most scholars to see the independence of the Galilean churches. If "the" primitive church was the topic, one took for granted that it did not exist until after Jesus' death and owed its existence to the "Easter events." Accordingly, it is postulated that synoptic tradition material, which originated "in the primitive church," was based on Easter; in exegesis the soteriological understanding of Jesus' death is superimposed on the so-called announcements of the passion (Mark 8:31). And if followers of Jesus in Galilee are even mentioned, they are not called a church but a "Jesus sect" (W. Schmithals). Since Reimarus the view that what is "actually" Christian came to exist after and through Easter has predominated. Thus whatever has not been influenced by Easter must not be called Christian. This certainly applies to the "historical Jesus." And it also applies to the Galilean followers of Jesus who are still oriented (only) toward the earthly Jesus and have not yet integrated the Easter kerygma into their tradition. We will see that this widespread opinion cannot be defended in its present form.

*(3) Christology and Ethics.* Since the Galilean churches preserved no reports *about* the historical Jesus but instead Jesus images that always presented him as the proclaimed One, their tradition was christological from the beginning. We have neither early traditions of Jesus' opponents nor neutral presentations. Rather, the traditions come from people who became involved with Jesus, were shaped by him, and talked *of* him under the influence and in the context of that shaping. This happens in very different ways and in the beginning always fragmentarily. Since Jesus always traveled around the country rather than staying in one place, his work could also be experienced only fragmentarily. There was no way that something like a "school" could quickly form and make it possible at an early time to sum up his activity and present it systematically. Thus the conditions here were entirely different from the Jerusalem tradition. So in regard to the Galilean tradition we have to ask whether we can find and present christologically a common line—expressed or implied in the various individual statements—that shows us the

experienced work of Jesus as a logical whole. In the following paragraphs we will attempt to answer this question.

Only in this context can we also clarify the relationship of Christology to ethics. We can already give a hint in advance by introducing a term that is not exactly usual but reveals the problem. The work of Jesus consisted in *turning people inside out.* Then these people turned inside out talked of him and emphasized different things.

On the one hand, people could speak of the "inside-out turner." In this way the things that constitute Christology came into play. It could be done by means of titles (and *inside-out turner* would be such a title), yet this is comparatively rare. More often Jesus is talked of as someone acting with authority (e.g., driving out demons with the finger of God). On the other hand, emphasis could be put on the very act of turning inside out. And here we are dealing with ethics.

If we are now interested only in the inside-out turner, Christology easily loses its character as theological statement: we are no longer talking *of* Jesus but *about* Jesus. Conversely, if we are only interested in the act of turning inside out, which regrettably often happens in ethical discussions, we overlook the fact that it is people turned inside out who are talking of the inside-out turner. Yet these people who are turned inside out present Jesus as someone who let himself be turned inside out by the one whom he calls his God. So Jesus was experienced as someone who—as one turned inside out by his God—announced his God to the people around him and offered his God to them by the way he himself lived. Both the announcing and the offering, the proclamation and the activity of Jesus, belong inseparably together, even if in many traditions we find only one of the two.

We can see clearly here how Christology directs our attention toward theology. The experience of people that Jesus announced his God to them and offered him through his life-style could in the Greek-speaking area produce the sentence: God became human. Yet we have to pay close attention to how this sentence came about, for otherwise we are in danger of misusing it. In the Hebrew-Aramaic language area it would have been impossible, because it would have had to read: Yahweh became human. No Jew could have said that, and later on Christians did not say *that* either.

The reason is obvious. The meaning of the name Yahweh was defined. In regard to ethics, it was defined as the lawgiver. Yet people did not experience Jesus as one who presented the lawgiver to them, but *his* God as the Father. Jesus' turning inside out was thus understood as his redefining Yahweh. And this "redefined Yahweh" is who Jesus offered the people around him. Jesus did not thereby *become* Yahweh or a redefined Yahweh; rather, Yahweh remained Yahweh. Jesus, however, was experienced as a theologian in the exact sense of the word: a person who, turned inside out by his Father, talked of his Father and offered people his Father through his way of life.

A problem arises because of the fact that in the Greek-speaking world (as well as for us!) the word *god* is not clearly defined, but is a word-shell. Whoever can fill this shell with "Father" (and this person alone!) can say that in Jesus' activity *God* was at work. Then as well as now, only people who experience *their* God in the work of Jesus are able to fill the word-shell with "Father." In other words, only people who are turned inside out by Jesus can say that in the inside-out turner Jesus they have met the One who turned Jesus inside out, namely, the God *of Jesus*.

Only by reversing this situation could one produce the sentence, "God became human." And the sentence makes sense only if the word-shell *god* has been filled *beforehand,* as in Gen. 1:1 (cf. pp. 14-15 above). The sentence is misused if we take it as it is as the point of departure for our argumentation.

It is now clear that we can never ignore the people who are talking. These people turned inside out are people *to* whom something has happened through the work of Jesus. And what happened to them is nothing less than what is supposed to happen *through* them. Thus Christian ethics is an aspect of Christology.

## 2. Different Images of Jesus, Different Ethics

Christology, as I have attempted to show, is an image of Jesus drawn by people. So if it is true that Christian ethics is an aspect of Christology, we have to look at the Jesus image drawn by people in order to formulate the ethics that *these people* would consider Christian ethics.

There is general agreement, however, that we find various Christologies in the New Testament and also in the pre-New Testament period. People drew various images of Jesus, and this raises some questions.

If people drew different Jesus images, did they also have different ethics? This would be the obvious conclusion. If this is the case, we must ask how these ethics relate to each other. They could complement each other. A later ethic could be seen as a development of an earlier one. We would have to demonstrate this, though, for it cannot be assumed. Rather, we must grant the possibility that these ethics may disagree or even be mutually exclusive; we cannot disallow that from the beginning. The exegeses could show that people who draw different Jesus images also have different ethics. This poses a systematic problem. The fact that each person draws an image of *Jesus* implies that each ethic, being an aspect of a Jesus image, claims to be a *Christian* ethic. This claim is subject to examination (the *claim,* not the people's conviction of having drawn the right conclusions from their Jesus images). And this examination requires a criterion.

After our previous discussion it should be clear that we can develop a standard for Christian ethics only in connection with that Jesus image which people formed during or after their encounter with the acting Jesus. Yet such a Jesus image is precisely what we cannot find directly anywhere in the New Testament. We have to reconstruct it.

This is the task to which we now turn. We must work in a circular fashion. Our points of departure are the Jesus images in the texts. If they agreed, our inquiry would be unnecessary. But since this is not the case, we must go back from these Jesus images to the image that originated as closely as possible to the actual work of Jesus. If this reconstruction is successful, we must then go from there in the opposite direction, tracing the development that resulted in the scriptural images of Jesus.

In the context of this tracing we can and must ask the question whether the later Jesus images, and hence the later ethics, were faithful to this beginning or deviated from it. When they were faithful, we can also call the later ethics Christian ethics, but not when they went astray.

Achieving this task would really require a full development of the history of the synoptic tradition. This would have to be done both analytically (from the synoptic Gospels back to the beginning) and constructively (from the beginning to the synoptic Gospels). That cannot be done in this book. So we must proceed by example and restrict ourselves to a few further references. The examples are selected so as to allow us to see as easily as possible the relationship between Jesus image and ethic.

## a) Images of Jesus in the Texts

In the New Testament we find four detailed images of Jesus. Each of the Evangelists presents one of his own and says in it how *he* sees Jesus and what Jesus means *to him*.

The fact that we omit John in this context needs no further explanation. Later we will have to discuss the Gospel of John separately. In the synoptic Gospels I presuppose the two-source theory. Matthew and Luke use Mark's image of Jesus as their model but accentuate it differently. This explains the similarity of the three images, as well as their differences.

We will limit ourselves here to a comparison of Mark and Matthew, concentrating for the time being on only one point that is—or could be—ethically relevant.

Mark draws his image of Jesus as the presentation of a path from the start of Jesus' activity in public through Peter's confession near Caesarea Philippi to the days in Jerusalem. It is characteristic of this path that it is not a continuous progression. In the first or Galilean period the continuity is repeatedly interrupted by what we call (following William Wrede) the messianic secret. Whenever the glory of Jesus is recognized, orders to keep silent prevent its ongoing recognition. Who (the person) Jesus is must be experienced ever anew. This corresponds to the reaction of the disciples. In Jesus' presence they experience extraordinary things but seem at once to forget them. Later they show incomprehension in similar situations. They do not see that what was once possible through Jesus could be possible again. And then when they really recognize Jesus as God's Son at the confession of Peter, they are told that Jesus' way is leading him into suffering. So each time the glory of Jesus shines for only a moment; the rest of the time it remains invisible. The suffering, however, is visible.

How can we describe the ethical aspect implied in this Christology? The readers of Mark's Gospel are invited to join Jesus on the path he takes with his disciples. They are supposed to become disciples too. Yet the one who calls them is not immediately the Son of God but a person. Only when they get involved with this person do they realize that they are dealing with someone who transcends human nature in the direction of God. This knowledge does not remain a "possession" of the disciples, however; it has to be gained ever anew. Hence Jesus had to begin his activity ever anew, and the disciples had to venture to follow him ever anew. The old world around them, in which these persons-turned-disciples find themselves and in which they are really living, hinders their perseverance as disciples. The life of a disciple can be lived only in a way that makes suffering visible. The follower is with Jesus on the road to the cross.

We can also put it another way. Those who have once become Christian soon fall back into being human. They have to wait to become Christian again, and even if they become Christian again, they cannot maintain their status. So according to Mark it is not possible to say that someone *is* a Christian. Only being human is permanent. This is because Jesus cannot be permanently known as the Son of God.

According to Mark people live in the old world. They cling to this old world and live by its laws. The lack of faith is normal for them. From time to time, however, they succeed in stepping out of this old world. In such a *kairos* they recognize the Son of God in the person Jesus. Then they *become* Christians and as Christians face suffering. Yet soon they fall back into a lack of faith and have to wait to be called into faith again.

Matthew has a different view. Christologically we can see that already in the fact that Jesus's journey does not commence with his appearance in public but with the infancy narrative placed before it. In contrast to the Gospel of Mark, the person Jesus of Nazareth does not have to be *qualified* again and again by his disciples as the Son of God. In Matthew the repeated qualifications are replaced by statements on Jesus' *quality*. This is done with the help of Jesus' genealogy (Jesus *is* the son of Abraham), scriptural quotations (in Jesus' life, prophecies *did* come true from the beginning), and the motif of true birth from a virgin. Thus Jesus is portrayed as someone with a *character indelibilis* (indelible character) right from his birth.

Matthew's anthropology corresponds to this Christology. The alternative is no longer faith or no faith, but faith or little faith. Even those of little faith are still people of faith; they did not fall away from faith: they only fell back into a state of little faith. Now they are urged to leave their little faith and regain their (full) faith. They can accomplish this if they do *everything* that Jesus told them to do during his life on earth.

In Mark people are invited to *become* Christians and, when they fall back into their human nature, to become Christians *again and again*. In Matthew, on the other hand, we can say that people *have become* Christians (through their baptism). As a consequence, we have to distinguish between good and not so good Christians now, and the not so good ones have to strive to become good Christians again.

This comparison, which we have only briefly sketched here, already shows how different Jesus images result in different ethics and, conversely, how different ethics are based on different images of Jesus. What can we do with these findings, which thus far are only exegetical?

The fact that both images of Jesus, and accordingly both ethics, are found in the New Testament can easily obscure the problem that must be dealt with. We can appeal to both of them, and therefore we can call both Christian. But are *both* of them really Christian?

More clearly than from the Jesus images themselves, we can see from their ethical aspects that the harmonization of the two is impossible; fundamentally they are mutually exclusive.

Therefore we cannot avoid making judgments. Yet this is possible only with the help of definitions. And here we run into problems when we look at our present time. Can we define who in our day may be called a Christian?

Our imprecise use of the language gets in our way, as numerous examples can demonstrate.

If we start with average churchgoers, we can call all of them Christians. We distinguish them, for example, from Muslims (as in Lebanon they distinguish between Christian militia and Shiites). Yet not every member belongs to the core group of those who are active in a church. According to Matthew's conception we could distinguish between (merely) "nominal Christians" and those "who earnestly want to be Christians." According to Mark's conception, however, nominal church members could (almost) never—and even members of the active core group not always—be called Christians.

Without a precise definition the word *Christian* is almost useless. But do we realize that for such a definition it is not sufficient to use certain adjectives? We can succeed only if we look at the particular image of Jesus, that is, at the Christology.

Corresponding to this is the fact that the understanding of baptism is not at all the same among Christians. The use of the same ritual everywhere does not mean anything until we explicate the content of this ritual. (Thus it is meaningless in the ecumenical dialog to be content to assert that the use of the same ritual as a sign of unity.) Does baptism give the baptized a new nature as an indelible character, or do we have to see baptism as an offer which, having really been made, is an irrevocable offer? This has serious consequences for the development of a Christian ethic.

What is the status of baptized persons? Have they become Christians who now strive to be as good Christians as possible? Or have they received an offer giving them the chance again and again to become Christians anew?

Of course, we can try to construct a system harmonizing the alternatives. To get a definition we would then proceed as follows. We begin with the word *Christian* and try to fill it with content. We take elements of Mark's conception and elements of Matthew's and claim that being a Christian requires both. Yet in our hurry we miss two points. First, in the New Testament the two conceptions are given *separately,* and each of them is complete in itself. Second, the two conceptions were developed *one after the other.* This forces us to ask whether this was a logical development or a development in the wrong direction. Not until we have answered this question can we decide whether a systematic harmonization is possible at all.

So for the definition we cannot start with the word; first, we have to look at the phenomenon and describe it, and then we can give it a name. If we go by Mark's conception and apply to it the adjective *Christian,* this word is "used up." But then we have to examine whether Matthew's conception is faithful to the concepts we defined before as "Christian."

If it is true that the definition of *Christian* has to be based on the beginning, we might be inclined to see this beginning in Mark's conception. As long as we stay with the images of Jesus in the texts, we can assume that Mark's is closer to the beginning than Matthew's. We have to be careful, however, because Mark's conception is a late one, at least relatively speaking. It is roughly from the year A.D. 70. Hence we have to ask whether it was faithful to the beginning. Yet this question can only be answered if we reconstruct earlier Jesus images on the basis of the ones in the texts.

### b) *Images of Jesus Reconstructed through Literary Criticism*

If the hypothesis put forth above (p. 45) that the history of the synoptic tradition began during Jesus' lifetime is true, we can assume that only partial traditions could arise at that time. Different people in different places in Galilee told what they had heard, experienced, and learned in their encounter with the active Jesus. So what is important now is to reach these oldest images of Jesus. We will briefly summarize the problems arising in this context.

(1) Even in their present form the synoptic Gospels still show that their authors used available partial traditions in the

composition of their respective Jesus images. This is true even for Matthew and Luke, who used the work of Mark (i.e., a lengthy, coherent text). Yet in our reconstructions of the partial traditions we have to proceed with more caution than is exercised in most cases. It is a fatal mistake simply to use the scissors, because when the Evangelists edited the material, they did not just combine it additively without making changes; they created transitions, often rewriting the beginnings and endings of the originals. Frequently they even changed an original itself in order to place their special accents.

And if we use the scissors, as is common practice in creating lectionaries, we do not really get texts but only fragments of texts, that is, fragments of the present Gospels. Yet since lectionary readings are not texts, they cannot be analyzed exegetically as such, but only in the whole context of their respective Gospels. Through literary criticism, however, we try to establish *texts,* and that means units that existed earlier independently. Only such texts can be analyzed because only here can we ask what the (original) authors wanted to tell their readers and listeners with the text they composed. Hence the process of literary criticism has to undo changes the Evangelists made in the original texts.

(2) After the literary criticism is completed, the result is a number of individual traditions that were used as sources by the Evangelists in this or similar form. If we look at all these traditions, the impression is confusing. The reconstructed images of Jesus show considerable differences, not only in regard to form and genre, but also and above all in regard to content. Differences in form and genre can be explained by the different authors of the individual traditions. But different content prompts the question whether it is possible at all to restore a passably consistent Jesus image from images so divergent. This is only possible if we can find a way to bring order.

(3) After the literary criticism we already have a criterion that permits at least a preliminary arrangement, namely, the age

of the traditions. Parts of Matthew and Luke that have parallels in the Gospel of Mark turn out to be pericopes that give a revised version of Mark's text. Hence the original independent unity can only be reconstructed from Mark. Here the literary findings help us determine the age. In this context our attention is immediately drawn to the history of the synoptic tradition.

It is harder, however, if the literary findings give no such help. Then we must find other criteria for determining age, perhaps investigating where the traditions originated. If, for example, a tradition shows that it originated in the Greek-Hellenistic area, it cannot be old—at least not in its present form. Hence we have to disregard it in our search for the beginning. In this way we can make a negative selection with reasonable accuracy. On the other hand, material originating in the Jewish area cannot be considered old for this reason alone, even if we can translate it back into Aramaic. All the material comes to us in Greek, and it may have been translated early or late. Opinions on this often differ, and the dividing line between older and younger remains in flux.

We must be satisfied with the assertion that literary criticism and the subsequent evaluation of individual traditions bring results of very limited usefulness. At best we can say that a certain corpus of very likely older Jesus images can be sorted out, but if we look at the contents of this corpus, we still see various incompatible images of Jesus. It is apparently impossible to find *the* Jesus image in this way.

There is also, however, an entirely different question. How is it conceivable that in his activity Jesus made such completely different impressions on the people who tell of him? Some saw in him a person who sovereignly transgressed the law of God by healing on a sabbath; others saw a person who plainly radicalized the law by demanding even more than was required by the commandments of the law ("you shall not kill" vs. "be angry"; "you shall not commit aldultery" vs. "look lustfully"). Some could see in him a person who gave himself to the oppressed and to sinners (to the lost sheep of Israel exclusively); others, a person who not only did not renounce the scribes but even let himself invited by them. We could easily augment such examples. And for this very reason we get the impression that we can appeal to Jesus for various and often contradictory things. The impressions he made on people were obviously not consistent. Hence the reconstructed Jesus images are not suited to a direct appeal to Jesus. But there is another way.

### 3. "The" Image of Jesus: Christian Ethics

We are proceeding from the hypothesis that in his activity Jesus pursued a consistent goal.

Even though this hypothesis has a high probability, we have to see that it is only a hypothesis, since there is no method by which we can reach the historical Jesus (cf. p. 37 above). We can find out neither how Jesus understood himself nor what he wanted to accomplish with his activity. All we have is the statements of people.

### a) Methodology

We always have to start with the immediate eyewitnesses, whether or not we can reconstruct their narrations exactly. Each of them experienced only a part of Jesus' activity, and always in concrete situations. They experienced how he acted provocatively. Sometimes they heard helpful or encouraging words from him, and at other times harsh rebukes. People heard Jesus reveal the situation of certain people before God in parables, they heard him tell stories to demonstrate correct behavior, and so forth. Many different people passed all this on, sometimes mentioning where they heard it, who was involved, and what the situation was, but often without such information. What was concrete in the beginning assumed the character of general statements.

If we take into account this origin and this early way of passing on these individual stories, we can see that the result was a wealth of divergent individual statements. Thus at first there was no way for a consistent image of Jesus to come about.

How then could this diverging material be kept together? An attempt was made to find a "center." One way to do this was to use the material selectively; similar or related things could be compiled into early collections to show a typical trait of the Jesus image. But it could also be done by writing summaries and in this way expressly stating such a center.

Here we have a circle. The point of departure was the various individual traditions, which had become available in the meantime. Even if their contents were incompatible, they always had a common point of reference: Jesus of Nazareth. This provided the name for the center but, nevertheless, only the name. The problem now was to fill this name with content that was as unambiguous as possible. Even though this definition of the name, and along with it the naming of the center, was not done until later, the people who did it assumed that from this center the obviously divergent individual traditions not only could be understood but in their opinion also had to be understood. We could say that the center was now the new text. The older individual traditions were considered interpretive elaborations of this text.

This circle is due to the situation and unavoidable. We can demonstrate this with an simple example. If I want to draw a single portrait of my father, I depend on the many individual images I have from various encounters with my father. At first glance, and especially to an outsider, these images may seem entirely divergent. If one looks at them in isolation, they may even be contradictory in some details. Yet I can later draw *the* portrait of my father. Even if it was formed only later because it could only be formed later, I will still be convinced that *the* portrait of my father factually precedes every individual image. Judged by this portrait the contradictions only seem to be contradictory.

We can also put it this way: When people tried to derive *the* image of Jesus from the Jesus images, they expressed what *they* wanted to define as "Christian."

In the two following sections we will fill this with content, and for this purpose we will refer to Mark 1:14-15 and Matt. 11:2-6. Yet we should consider ahead of time what such definitions can accomplish. They were not made at the beginning, at least in regard to their formulation, but they are supposed to be valid for the beginning. They are always assertions made by people at a later time. What did these people express with them? And what could these people (only) express with them?

First, we may assume that if several persons (summarizing older traditions) each drew a Jesus image that they claimed to be *the* image of Jesus, then they were expressing their individual faith. This was the Jesus they wanted to surrender to, and the surrender to this particular Jesus is what they defined as Christian faith—even if this term itself was still unknown.

In our comparison of Mark's image of Jesus with the one in Matthew we saw not only that there could be different definitions but that there actually were different definitions. And the same thing could have happened earlier too. Hence it should be obvious that it is impossible to state quasi-objectively what has to be (systematically) considered Christian. We can never bypass the people who drew their image of Jesus.

So if today we (now systematically) define what we want to consider "Christian," we can only do that by consensus. And then the obvious approach is to assign the term *Christian* to the oldest achievable formulation of a center. At least there seems to be no other criterion we could bring into play and substantiate. It should be an agreeable assumption that the definition of *Christian* cannot be made arbitrarily but has to be founded on the beginning.

Yet that means that this definition has to be found in history. Historical findings, however, are always uncertain and subject to verification. This can result in a lack of consensus on the definition of *Christian*. One could get rather uncomfortable with this idea. Should it really be up to the historians to decide what can be called Christian and what cannot?

Yet this uneasiness would only be justified if by using the term *Christian* we wanted to do more than give a description, that is to say, if we wanted imply a moral judgment (cf. pp. 21-22 above). But this is not the case, and therefore it must not be done.

Mark's image of Jesus was the true Jesus image *for him*. The same is true for Matthew, who drew his own (entirely different) image of Jesus. Each one expressed with his own Jesus image his faith, of which he was certain. They relied on their respective Jesus images, and these images determined their ethics.

So the dispute is not about the worth of the Jesus images for those who were guided by them in their everyday lives. The dispute only concerns the labels.

If we call the oldest Jesus image we find in history *Christian,* this term is "used up." We cannot assign the same designation to other Jesus images that deviate from this one. But this does not say anything about the worth that these Jesus images have for those who rely on them and in doing so stand firm in their faith.

Now we will look at two early images of Jesus, which each author regarded as "the" image of Jesus. In my view they belong to the oldest images of Jesus, therefore we will define the term *Christian* in connection with them. As mentioned before, we should keep in mind that we are making a historical evaluation that is open to later correction. Whoever considers a different Jesus image older will define the term *Christian* differently.

We can mention two points to support our evaluation. First, we find the two Jesus images in different lines of the tradition, the Gospel of Mark and the sayings source. If we succeed in showing a common feature in them, this is evidence that this Jesus image was already widespread at an early time and hence probably rests upon a consensus. Second, the circle is important again in this context. If the individual traditions, or at least the majority of them, can be understood as interpretive elaborations of these Jesus images, then this gives further evidence that the early summaries can be considered accurate.

### b) Mark 1:14-15

We will give this summary a more detailed treatment, for in this context we must look at a few questions that will further our discussion.

Experts dispute whether Mark used older themes or even texts that he had at hand in his composition especially of 1:15 (and if so, what these sources said). Yet there is agreement that with this statement (1:14-15) the Evangelist intended to give a summary of Jesus' activity—and we must add—the way *he* sees it. He places this (subsequently written) summary at the beginning of Jesus' public activity. So for Mark these verses have a programmatic character. For him they form "the" Jesus image.

For easier understanding, I offer the following translation, which indicates the structure and gives some paraphrases; some Greek words, however, have to be left in Greek for now:

> After John was handed over, Jesus came into Galilee,
> *proclaiming the gospel of God* ("and saying" replaces a colon):
> > *the kairos has become full*
> > *and*
> > *the basileia of God has drawn near;*
> *(therefore) turn around* ("and believe in the gospel" =) *by trustingly relying on this gospel.*

In this sentence there is a circular movement. The starting point is that Jesus proclaims the gospel of God. Then the content of this gospel is quoted in two lines. This is followed by the call to turn around. The call to turn around is presented as an invitation to rely trustingly on the gospel (of God), which Jesus, coming to Galilee, has proclaimed.

I have rendered the verb *believe* as "trustingly rely on." This brings the ethical aspect into our view right at the beginning: if we rely on this gospel, we let ourselves be governed by it in the life we are living.

It is very important now that we not leave the term *gospel* as a variable. In the language of the church (and even of the New Testament) it is used in different senses. Today we very often do not even know what a person speaking of the gospel means by the word. At best we can figure it out from the context. In Mark 1:15, however, we are lucky: the term is defined (and this is the only place in the New Testament where such an express definition of *gospel* appears).

According to Mark (!) the content of the gospel is the announcement of a time. Yet more precisely we must first say that we have two announcements of time that seem to be contradictory, at least at first glance. In the first line we see a perfect tense: a period of time *has been* completed, because the *kairos* has come. In the second line, however, the perfect seems to be taken back again. For that which has come near is imminent, but for this very reason it is not here yet. Often this contradiction is characterized with the terms *already* and *not yet*. By relating these two terms to each other we try to express the idea that something that seems to be contractictory has to be kept together anyway.

In order to understand this we have to explain the concepts used here. This brings us to another problem. If we assume that Jesus was active in a Jewish environment, then people had to employ familiar concepts in order to describe his activity. Only in this way were they able to communicate intelligibly to others what they had experienced. At the same time, however, Jesus' activity was understood as something that—to put it quite neutrally for now—differed in some way from things that had been familiar. This too had to be expressed understandably.

Thus to understand the summary it is not enough just to look at the text written by Mark. Right from the beginning we must observe that with this text the existing and hence familiar concept was modified. If we want to see this modification, we must first sketch the background before which and based on which the modification was made.

*(1) Contemporary background.* It is often said that the Old Testament forms the background before which we must see Jesus' activity. Yet this is very imprecise and can easily lead us astray. If we refer to the Old Testament in this context, we must always add: in the way it was understood in the time of Jesus.

In both of the summary's time announcements we find concepts that do not come directly from the Old Testament but from so-called late Jewish apocalypticism.

Apocalypticism was a religious movement that gradually developed starting around the end of the third and beginning of the second century B.C. in Palestinian Judaism as a continuation of prophecy and thus at the same time as its successor. The movement got its name, though not until much later, from the literature that originated in it, the so-called *apocalypses* (i.e., revelations). In these apocalypses the still hidden course of things to come is revealed in order to inform believers of what will happen in the near future.

The concept of history in apocalypticism is dualistic. Two aeons are confronted, the present one and the one to come. The present aeon is an evil time and will remain thus to the end. Nothing good can be expected from it. But when God comes (in "his day"), he will bring a new world in a new time, which will have eternal (i.e., unlimited by time) duration. The thoroughly pessimistic character of apocalypticism is overcome by an optimistic view of the future: the glory in the kingdom of God. So hope is concentrated on the turn of the aeon, which in some apocalypses is announced as imminent. Yet this hope is not simply and only a looking forward, but also always involves anxious expectation, and this is where ethics comes in.

At the turn of the aeon the dead are raised and have to appear together with the living before the judgment seat of God.

In this context the figure of the Son of man is sometimes important. A transcendent heavenly being, he already exists now, yet is still hidden. The turn of the aeon will bring his Parousia. He will become visible and (the concepts vary somewhat) either will himself sit in judgment in the name of God or will act in court as the prosecuting attorney or the attorney for the defense.

The books will be opened, and then it will be determined whether the conditions for admission to the kingdom have been fulfilled.

So human beings have to be concerned about creating the circumstances necessary for their admission to the kingdom later on. They can do this by holding to the law and fulfilling its commandments.

Whoever wants to keep the law has to know it first. This obvious presupposition brings a special problem to our attention, namely, the privileged status of Israel. In the time of Jesus people were convinced that God (through Moses) gave his law exclusively to Israel, and thus only Israel is in a position to be admitted to the kingdom through keeping the law. Hence Israel had every reason to "delight" in the law (cf. Ps. 1:2). Yet this delight by no means removed the seriousness that follows from the obligation to strive to keep the law. In the time of Jesus people even did more than required; they wanted to be quite strict. So the task of the scribes was to "interpret" the old law. They casuistically elaborated the individual precepts and thereby regulated the lives of Jews down to the last detail.

Even though many of these regulations seem strange, we should not overlook the concern behind them. People tried to take very seriously the God who had given the law. His will, so far as it could somehow be perceived, was to be followed with painstaking exactitude.

The Pharisees in particular excelled at this. We should not be deceived by the distorted image (Pharisee = hypocrite) created by Matthew (cf. Matt. 23), which has affected even our time. Indeed, we have to consider the Pharisees as models of moral behavior for their time. The Pharisee Paul is a case in point.

The fulfillment of the law required considerable effort from each individual Jew and in two respects. First, they had to gain a detailed knowledge of the many individual commandments. This was hardly possible for the lower classes. Hence the Pharisees spoke scornfully of them as "country folk." Second, they had to exert considerable effort to do what was required in each individual case. For they were obligated to do *everything* and to do it *always*.

Since God was a just God, he would administer justice at the judgment. And because of God's justice it was held (at least in principle) that anyone who had violated even a single commandment had committed a sin. Here sin was understood as an individual act against a commandment. Even this was an act of disrespect toward God. Therefore the sinner would not pass judgment and would be condemned to eternal death.

Of course, the people also knew about God's grace and his forgiveness of sins. Yet this grace did not mean that *all* sins would be forgiven at the judgment. Rather, grace consisted in God's being able to limit his justice. If the instances of fulfilling the law outnumbered those of transgressing it, God could disregard the transgressions (sins)—but only then. So God's grace was real, but it had to be earned.

Hence the Jews of Jesus' time lived in anxious expectation on their way to the turn of the aeon, because it would then be decided whether they would reach their goal: admission into the kingdom of God. This high goal was worth every effort.

And if the apocalyptics (as happened every so often) then announced the end of the aeon as imminent, expecting the imminent parousia of either God or the son of man, this was additional motivation to make a special effort in keeping the law, for the time that people had left was now very short.

The activity of John the Baptist must also be seen in this context, despite some peculiarities characteristic of his manner. Many details remain obscure, because the portrait of the Baptist has been painted over with Christian colors. Hence opinions differ somewhat even among experts. When, however, tradition gives the Baptist's proclamation as, "Repent, for the kingdom of heaven has come near" (Matt. 3:2), this means: since the turn of the aeon and judgment are imminent, it is important now for everyone to try even harder to keep the law.

The imminence of the end of this aeon could be expressed with the metaphor of a measuring cup that is filled with time (with hours and days). If it is full, then "the time is fulfilled" (as is often translated), and hence the aeon would have reached its end. Then God (or the son of man) would come and (after the resurrection of the dead and judgment) would bring in his kingdom with the new eternal aeon. In this kingdom (according to the popular metaphor) all who had survived judgment would sit at table with God for the "meal of the end time."

*Theologically,* this means that the law was the god of the Jews. For they *directly* confronted only the law. That was what they set their hearts on, as Luther put it; the law "shaped" them. At that time one could almost identify God with the law and say that

God was present in his law.

> We must recognize the "theological shift" that has occurred here. The wording of the law was the same in the time of Jesus as in the time of ancient Israel—if we disregard the scribes' "interpretations." Yet the law had a different function, since the relationship between God and law was seen differently. In ancient Israel the law was understood as an offer by God. If people accepted this offer, they could make their lives "more worth living" and make coexistence more successful. But now the law was understood as a duty the people had to perform, no matter what. And thus God was no longer seen as the one who helpfully wanted to stand beside the people with his offer, but as the lawgiver who obligated the people to abide by the law. So what the people dealt with directly was the law.

> Yet even if God was present in the law, the people were really alone with the law. Because the real, visible coming of God was yet to be. Nonetheless, the people were neither helpless nor hopeless; after all, they had the law and knew what they were supposed to do. The Jews (and *only* they, since only they had the law) had the big opportunity to make great efforts and thus to meet the admission requirements that God had set for his kingdom.

*(2) Modifications in the summary.* With regard to ethics apocalyptic thought was characterized by the idea that people still have time to do something about their future destiny. This was believed to be true despite the reigning expectation of the imminent end. In this case, the time left to humanity may be short, but people still have a chance to fill this time and, in view of their goal, to fill it with intensive activity. By contrast, the gospel says there is no time left. This deprives people of the chance to do something about their future. Yet they are not given this message as a threat but as gospel. People must learn to see that they have no need at all for such a chance.

This is expressed by the *two* lines of the *one* announcement of time. In them the connection is with apocalyptic thought, insofar as it is adopted. Yet at the same time it is wiped out. This very sequence is significant.

If we read each line in isolation, we could well understand it apocalyptically. We would probably have to start with the second line, "The *basileia* of God has come near." This would announce the expectation of the imminent coming. Now the first line could follow: "The *kairos* is fulfilled." This uses the metaphor of the measuring cup. Hence the statement would read, "Now is the turn of the aeon."

Yet the sequence is really reversed, resulting in a statement that seems at first glance to be illogical and then even nonsensical. For what kind of sense can it make to talk first of the turn of the aeon as having *already happened* and then of God's *basileia* as only *near*? In the latter case the turn of the aeon is still to come. But does it make any sense at all, in terms of apocalyptic thought, to talk of the turn of the aeon as having already happened? For all we can see and experience, the old aeon's clock is still running. Thus we cannot state accurately (which means, apocalyptically) that the turn of the aeon is now here.

And indeed it is not stated this way. The apocalyptic conception is negated when the term *kairos* is used here instead of the term *chronos* that we might expect.

> The difference between the two terms, both usually rendered in English as *time,* is that *chronos* refers to time as a line, that is, passing time, whereas *kairos* refers to a point in time as a (positively or negatively) filled instant that has no duration. So when Paul talks in Gal. 4:4 of the fullness of the *chronos* (!), he is saying (in the context of his train of thought in his letter to the Galatians) that God made a caesura by sending his Son; the time passing before then had come to an end. In this case (in contrast to the summary) the apocalyptic conception is directly adopted.

The question now is: What can it mean that on the one hand the still existing old aeon is said to have "become full," although its time (*chronos*) is still passing, while on the other hand this same continuing old aeon, referred to as *kairos,* is claimed to have ended? We can understand this if we see that this text does not try so to speak objectively to give a date—as the turn of the aeon is a date—but to address *people.* We first have to take a look at people and their ethical possibilities. As long as they live in the old aeon, their options are to try to take care of their future themselves. Now it is true that for the time being people are still living in the old aeon, and the turn of the aeon is a date in the future. The things that people (in the context of apocalyptic thought) had to and wanted to take care of in this old aeon will come to an end. In that respect it is really possible that the old aeon has ended *for them,* even if around them it still continues. For in the middle of this visibly continuing old time, *kairos* is announced to the people as a new possibility *for them.*

The second line explicates the contents of this possibility: the *basileia* of God is imminent. It is not here yet, but it is now about to come. Compared to apocalyptic thought, one crucial thing has changed. If the old aeon has ended *for the people,* they have no time left to do something to earn their admission to the *basileia.* Since they cannot do that anymore (for "lack of time"), and since the *basileia* is going to break in anyway, they no longer even have to do it. The *basileia* will come *as a gift.* So the announcement of time is an offer to the people. It is up to them whether the *basileia* reaches its goal, that is, whether it comes as a gift.

This makes it immediately clear that God is now defined differently. So far God has been the one who *required* of the people the fulfillment of conditions without which he would not admit them to his *basileia* and to communion with himself at his table. And since God had bound himself to his conditions, it was not even possible for him to act differently. Now, however, God is the one who wants to give his *basileia,* and with it communion with himself, *for free.* So what we have here is nothing less than the offer of a "change of Gods" (cf. pp. 8-9 above).

The next question is: When and how does the *basileia* (and with it the giving God) reach the people? For the presence of the *basileia* is not what is asserted, only its nearness—but that as an immediate offer. This question is answered by the imperative following the announcement of time: "Turn around!"

This imperative urges the people to *re-act* to the offer of the giving God. They *can* accept it now, and this acceptance consists in their turning around.

> Linguistically it might be helpful to make a distinction in translating the Greek word *metanoein*. If we are talking about something that people *must* do, we should say "repent"; the exhortation "repent!" is made because the judgment is imminent. Yet if we are talking about an offer made to the people, which they *can* accept, "turn around" is the more appropriate expression.

Those who let themselves to be turned around because of the offer no longer travel the road they were on previously in the old aeon, as ordered by the demanding God. On this road they had tried to reach God (eventually). They had the law behind them and God always ahead, remaining for the time being at a distance.

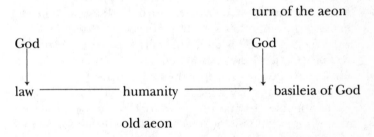

turn of the aeon

God            God

law ———————— humanity ————————→ basileia of God

old aeon

If people turn away from this road, they no longer have the demanding God ahead of them; now they have the giving God behind them.

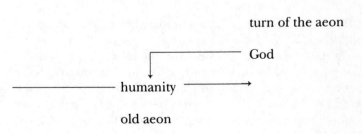

turn of the aeon

God

——————————— humanity ————————→

old aeon

Since this God offers his communion "even now," people can even now, through their lives, be on the road together with him. The *basileia* of God can be present for them even now in the middle of the old aeon.

Here too it is helpful for better understanding to differentiate in translating. If *basileia* refers to the state after the turn of the aeon, we should translate it "kingdom of God." If, however, we are thinking of the presence of the *basileia,* then "lordship of God" is the better expression.

Both translations are already inherent as possibilities in Hebrew-Aramaic usage, which we have to see behind the term *basileia* of God. In the context of apocalyptic thinking, first of all, the *basileia* of God could be connected with the conception of the state after the turn of the aeon (thus "kingdom of God"). In the Judaism of that time, however, it was also possible to say that people "take the *basileia* of God upon themselves." Of course, the translation "kingdom" would not make any sense here, but "lordship" would. These people want to have God as their Lord. Yet they have God as their Lord in that they strictly—more strictly than usual— abide by the law. This could be called "acceptance of the *basileia* of God," because it was believed then that the people who would one day come into the kingdom would live by the law there. For the law is the law of the kingdom.

The people who take the *basileia* of God upon themselves are now already doing the same things that the people in the kingdom will one day do. In this aeon, of course, they are doing it, because it is demanded of them and because it is their own decision. After the turn of the aeon people will do it because they live in the kingdom.

If we also distinguish in the summary between lordship and kingdom, we could say, the kingdom of God will enter as the lordship of God. This way we avoid the misconception that a change in the old aeon is intended. The world around us is the old world and will remain the old world until the turn of the aeon. The *basileia* of God will never be present as the kingdom; also it would be entirely wrong to assume that the intended meaning is that the old aeon will slowly develop step by step into the kingdom of God. If the people turn around, however, that which is expected as the content of the kingdom will come to them in the form of the lordship of God and will happen through them. Now the people will live the lordship of God, and they will live it for other people.

If we want to give this content, we can begin as follows. What is expected at God's table after the turn of the aeon is *a world that is whole*. God is offering this "whole world" to people even now, and they receive it *when they live it*. This yields contents we can state negatively and positively. In a whole world there is no anger, no covetous look, and swearing is unnecessary, for whoever sits at God's table will naturally always speak the truth. These tablemates will live in peace. They will live for each other what they have received from God.

Where the lordship of God happens, people dare to live this perfection. It is daring because it happens in the middle of the still ongoing old aeon. This is why living the lordship of God will not and cannot last. For all we know the old aeon remains the old aeon and retains its power, even over people. For them this means that now they can live in imminent expectation ("has come near"). Yet in contrast to apocalypticism, in *this* imminent expectation they do not look at a date that is imminent but still leaves them some time. There is no time left. And this is why in each moment in which people move further along the line of time, they are living in a new imminent expectation. Their concept becomes an attitude.

This explains the circular movement expressed in the summary. Jesus is portrayed as one who offers the gospel as an announcement of time. This gives people an opportunity to turn around. And if they turn around, they start to rely on the gospel and at the same time are invited to rely ever anew on the gospel that Jesus has offered and continues offer.

*(3) Jesus image and Christian ethics according to Mark.* In the summary that Mark places before Jesus' activity, he gives *his* image of Jesus. On the one hand he lets us know how *he* understood the individual traditions he had before him and,

on the other, how *in his opinion* we are to understand the individual stories he compiled in his Gospel.

This has consequences, first of all, for exegesis. If we want to analyze a pericope from the Gospel of Mark, we must proceed on the basis of the summary. We need not decide here whether an individual story reconstructed by means of literary criticism (i.e., a pre-Markan one) is to be analyzed as such or differently. All that matters in the exegesis of the pericope is Mark's intention, not that of the author of an earlier individual tradition. According to Mark, all that follows the summary has to be understood as explication of the programmatic statement in 1:14-15. It does not have to contain the complete statement of the summary—often it offers only one aspect—but it must be clear that it is an aspect *of the summary.*

Thus the two kinds of exegesis are to be kept distinct. Indeed, we must allow for the possibility that some of the authors of the individual traditions would not have agreed with the content of Mark's summary. They would have understood Jesus and his activity differently from Mark. The question would then be whether it is possible to write a different summary. Since, as we said, the content of the individual traditions diverges, the writing of a summary is indispensable. Otherwise we have contradictory Jesus images side by side and thus leave the reference to Jesus arbitrary, as the history of the life-of-Jesus studies demonstrated in the quest for the historical Jesus. Yet we have no earlier summary by another author that might serve as an alternative to the one by Mark.

Nonetheless, we must be exact: with his Jesus image *Mark* shows how *he* would define *Christian.* So if we look at his Gospel from the viewpoint of his summary, we should observe two things: Jesus is presented not only as someone who announces the gospel as the offer of his (i.e., the giving) God but also as someone who relies on this offer himself and is living the gospel. We can summarize the two in the following definition: Christianity deals with eschatological existence; more precisely: wherever eschatological existence happens, we can call it *Christian.*

The term *eschatological* is to be taken literally. The plural *ta eschata* means "the last things," that is, the things that have to do with the turn of the aeon and whatever follows it. In apocalyptic thought this always means future things. Eschatological existence, however, always happens in the present. Thus people who are living eschatologically are anticipating the future.

What this means can be illustrated by the following diagram:

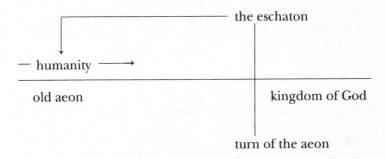

Thus *gospel* means that the people are offered eschatological existence even now. And the one who offers this to the people is doing so as one who exists eschatologically himself. In other words, Mark understood Jesus as someone who lived his God for the people around him. In traditional terminology we can say that he lived the indicative for them. If the people rely on this indicative, they turn around and start living eschatologically themselves. In turning around people start to believe the very gospel that Jesus brought and lived. Hence the Jesus who acts is God's gospel for them. So those who rely on Jesus (= believe in him) are themselves now living the God of Jesus and are living him for other people.

Yet our diagram still needs modification. Since eschatological existence takes place in the old aeon, it will not last. This does not mean that the kingdom of God is coming in, but that the lordship of God is happening through the people. It does not happen once and for all. God's lordship must happen again and again, and it is meant to happen again and again. Here too we have a close relationship between Christology and ethics.

If we proceed from Mark's summary, literary findings gain christological and thus theological significance: the individual Jesus images and their being joined into one Jesus image.

The origin of the Jesus tradition suggests that it started in the literary form of partial traditions. Again and again, Jesus was active in different places at different times, always in new ways and always with different details. So at first (in terms of literature) only partial traditions could develop. With his summary Mark interprets individual events as follows: *Each* individual event was the breaking in of the kingdom of God into the old aeon in the form of the lordship of God. The individual Jesus images are understood as *kairoi* that happened now and then along the line of the *chronos*.

Traditions came only from these individual *kairoi,* but there is no reflection on what happened between the *kairoi.* For Christology such reflection is not unimportant, even though it is only possible from the standpoint of later development. This brings a point to our attention that people were not aware of in earlier times. Hence it can be surprising or even provocative when we state it: between the *kairoi* there was a lot of "everyday." What happened through Jesus in those times was quite "normal" human activity—which means for Christology that we do not assume a special quality for Jesus. If this were the case, he would have had to be continuously active in a qualified way. Hence the fact that the Jesus tradition started out as individual traditions is the literary expression of the fact that God's lordship always happens as *kairos,* which does not last.

Yet by compiling many Jesus images Mark runs the risk of having one *kairos* immediately follow another. So he takes steps to prevent this. On the one hand, he adds chronological and geographical data that connect the individual traditions but at the same time keep them apart by creating spaces between them. On the other hand, and above all, he uses the so-called messianic secret (cf. p. 52 above). With this the Evangelist achieves in his Jesus image a presentation of Jesus as someone who always had to begin anew with his activity.

The consequences for ethics are that people can (and should!) enter into eschatological existence ever anew and always afresh. To this extent they live *constantly* in near expectation. They are always expecting to live the lordship of God.

This results in the following modified diagram:

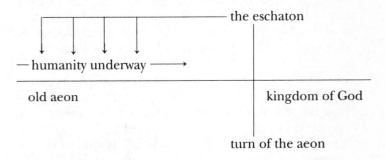

Hence, according to Mark, Christians are people who had once (or several times) experienced and lived eschatological existence and thereby *became Christians,* yet (despite these experiences) are now waiting *as human beings* to experience eschatological existence again, that is, to *become Christians* again.

### c) Matthew 11:2-6

In addition to Matt. 11:2-6, John the Baptist's query to Jesus can be found in Luke 7:18-23. Both Evangelists adopted a bit of tradition from the sayings source. Comparison of the two pericopes shows that Luke's version is longer; the additions are apparently Luke's. Thus the shorter text given by Matthew is more faithful to that of the sayings source. Yet even Matthew seems to have made one change in the original.

When John hears in prison about "what *the Christ* is doing," it is unnecessary to ask who Jesus is. He is *the Christ.* This question, however, is not necessary when we read about the activity *of Jesus*. Since *Christ* was understood even at a very early time as a proper name rather than as a christological title, we may assume that *Christ* has replaced an original *Jesus* here.

So the original may have read (approximately) as follows:

When John heard in prison about the deeds of Jesus, he had his disciples ask him: Are you the one who is to come, or are we to wait for another? And Jesus answered and said to them: Go and proclaim to John what you hear and see: the blind see and the lame walk, lepers become clean and the deaf hear, the dead rise and the gospel is preached to the poor. And blessed is anyone who takes no *skandalon* (i.e., offense) at me.

It is at once clear that here we have a summary. Its author sums up stories about deeds of Jesus after the fact and presents them as the reason for the Baptist's inquiry. Because of Jesus' extraordinary deeds, John wants to know who Jesus *is*. He could be "the one who is to come." This very general expression refers to a figure who is expected to come immediately before the turn of the aeon, in order to introduce the end time. But since John is not sure, he wants from Jesus an express confirmation of his "quality." Nonetheless, he does not get an answer to this question. Instead, Jesus refers to the work that is accomplished through him. Yet this was the reason for the question. So apparently everything is left open.

The gist of Jesus' answer can only be understood if we realize that it does not simply give a report. Rather, it uses formulas from prophetic tradition (cf. Isa. 29:18-19; 35:5-6; 61:1), whose contents were adopted by apocalypticism. All the things quoted were expected for the end time.

In Jewish apocalyptic thought the future was pictured very "massively": the raised dead would exist in their old bodies again, except for the flaws and infirmities that plagued them during their lives in the old aeon.

So by using these formulas the author of the summary tries

to interpret the deeds of Jesus; they are anticipations of eschatological events. If we express this in the terminology we discussed and used in the context of the exegesis of Mark's summary (cf. p. 72 above), we can say that in Jesus' activity the kingdom of God has already repeatedly entered this old aeon as the lordship of God. So we get the same figure as in the summary of Mark.

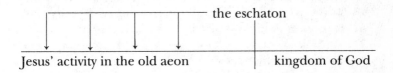

We also encounter other peculiarities again. The old aeon does not change. It remains the old aeon. Not every sick person is cured. But from time to time, here and there, and always by the activity of Jesus, an inbreaking of the eschaton occurs.

Also, by the fact that the activity of Jesus is presented by means of available tradition, it is clearly impossible to see the true nature of this activity directly. The occurrence of God's lordship is indeed always a *visible* event. What cannot be seen, however, is whether such an event is an occurrence of the lordship *of God*. This, after all, is the reason for the Baptist's inquiry. Apparently the visible events were ambiguous.

Thus it is understandable that the Baptist would like to know for sure. He just asks in the wrong way, or with the wrong question, if he wants to find out who Jesus *is*. This will only provide him with information about Jesus' nature. He wants a direct christological statement on the *person* of Jesus, in order to use it as a basis for his evaluation of Jesus' deeds. At this point he is corrected. Only people who understand Jesus' *deeds* "correctly" can understand and confess Jesus' nature. Then and only then can they evaluate Jesus properly.

For this reason it is true that those are blessed "who take no offense at *me*." The offense consists in the "detour" around Jesus. The answer requires John (and every reader of the summary as well) to decide *by himself* where every activity that he experiences comes from. There is no advance certainty (based on a pregiven Christology). We all have to take the risk of making our own decisions, and we have to do this again and again.

What the author of the summary intended to tell his audience will become clearer if we consider where and when he wrote it. This happened at a time when people were looking back on the then completed activity of Jesus, and it happened in a "Galilean" church (cf. p. 45 above). This church is asked by outsiders: "Who are you?" And it asks itself the same question.

The question is understandable because at that time there was a Baptist movement beside the Christian movement and in competion with it. Each of them claimed to be the eschatological church, one of them based on Jesus, the other on the Baptist.

Yet is it enough for the Jesus church to make its claim by simply referring to Jesus? The question "Who are you?" can only be answered after the question "Who is Jesus?" has been answered. And this is why the author of the summary has the Baptist ask this very question. Jesus' answer thereby becomes transparent for the current problem of the church.

This answer explains to the Jesus church why a reference to Jesus is not enough, even if a christological title is claimed for him. *That* cannot legitimate its claim to be an eschatological church. It can be legitimated and made acceptable only by pointing to what happens in the church and through the church.

What happens in and through the church is indeed life that is lived visibly, but it is not unambiguous, not even if it is exemplary, just as Jesus' activity was not unambiguous either. Yet Jesus' activity was meant to be a proclamation. Repeatedly in his activity the breaking in of God's lordship occurred. Likewise the *activity* of the church should now be a proclamation. But the church has to see that this activity can be misjudged and become offensive, even if it is done perfectly and thus attracts attention. If, however, this activity is understood as proclamation, it *can* happen that some people (first of all, some of the Baptist group) who "hear and see" will experience in the activity of the church the inbreaking of *God's* whole world. Then they will know that this is not the church working through its own efforts and accomplishments but *God* working through the church. Then and only then, will people "know the tree by its fruits" and see in the Jesus church the eschatological church—and in Jesus they will see the one who initiated the living of the end time, the one "who is to come."

> In traditional terminology: the "ethics" practiced by the church draws our attention to "ecclesiology," and from there to "Christology."

The church must not yield to the temptation to reverse this sequence. Activity in public must not commence with a claim made by referring to Jesus. This claim competes with other claims. Nor is the church allowed to substantiate or secure its claim by pairing its christological statements with ecclesiological statements and then basing its argumentation on the latter. The church can argue with outsiders only with its activity.

And this is how it really proves to be the church of Jesus. Because—and this is what the author of the summary tells his readers—whoever appeals to Jesus appeals to the *active* Jesus.

### d) Summary: The Son of Man

The figures on pages 77 and 79 show that the summaries, which were both written in retrospect, are based on the same Jesus image. Since they occur in different contexts of tradition (the Gospel of Mark and the sayings source), we can assume that they originated in different places. Thus it is easy to understand why the authors used different material in their texts. This does not, however, affect the common basic structure.

If we proceed from this basic structure we find different means of expression. To name a few examples, we can state that Jesus was understood as a theologian. More precisely, this means that Jesus was understood as someone who talked *of* his God (cf. p. 50 above). Shaped by his God, he shaped the people around him by living his God for them. If we stay closer to the concepts used, we can state (without saying something new) that Jesus was understood as someone who again and again lived the kingdom of God as the lordship of God. This means that he was understood as someone who even now, in the middle of the old (evil, unredeemed, sin-dominated) world, dared to live the healed and whole world expected in the future. We can sum up this anticipation of the future by saying that Jesus was understood as someone who existed eschatologically.

We get the same results if we look at the Son-of-man sayings in the synoptic tradition and the synoptic Gospels. For we can also call *Son of man* a "summary" even though the term is not common in this context. For this title is also used to draw *one* Jesus image in retrospect.

Of course, the problems connected with the Son of man are the subject of dispute among the experts. Yet, as we will briefly demonstrate, we can understand the starting point of the development and, in connection with it, the origin and elaboration of this Jesus image.

> The *concept* of a coming son of man originated in apocalypticism (cf. p. 65 above) as a further development of motifs in Dan. 7. We have to distinguish the son of man from the expected messiah, who was not a typical figure of apocalypticism. Rather, the messiah was a *human being* to whom "political" expectations were attached. At some time in the future (some thought sooner, some later) someone would turn out to be the messiah and would unite the scattered people of Israel and lead them to Zion, where the kingdom of David would then come into being once again. It was quite possible that this person was already alive. It would then become apparent that he is the messiah. The son of man, on the other hand, was not a human but a *transcendent figure.* He did exist already, but was still transcendentally hidden. Not until the turn of the aeon would the son of man come out of hiding, appear visibly and recognizably to all people in his parousia, and then play a role in the judgment.

The question is, How was this traditional concept first connected with Jesus and then directly applied to him? We can follow the order of events if we begin by arranging our findings.

Apart from four exceptions we find the term *Son of man* only in the Gospels and then only on the lips of Jesus. And here it is striking that Jesus always talks of the Son of man in the third person, as if he were talking of someone else.

Thus if the findings leave undecided at first whether *Son of man* refers to Jesus himself or to someone else, there can be no doubt on another point: when the *Evangelists* have Jesus talk of the Son of man, *they* think that he is referring to himself. The question now, however, is whether this was already the case in the synoptic tradition.

With the help of literary criticism we can reconstruct three groups of Son-of-man sayings. The motifs occurring in them are always separated. There is no overlapping.

*(1) Talk of the suffering, dying, and rising Son of man.* This group occurs in Matthew and Luke only in places that go back to a Markan original (Mark 8:31; 9:31; 10:33-34). Most likely they were written by the Evangelist Mark and thus form the youngest group. It is certain that these Son-of-man sayings refer to Jesus himself. The traditional concept did not include a suffering, dying, and rising Son of man. Even though Jesus talks in the third person (and thus the form of the older Son-of-man sayings is retained), it is clear that they were elaborated by using motifs from the Passion.

Since this group accentuates a trait indispensable for Christian ethics, we will have to come back it later (cf. pp. 134ff. below.)

*(2) Talk of the presently active Son of man.* This group can be found on all levels of tradition, even though only sporadically, and is differentiated within itself. The Son of man has authority on earth to forgive sins (Mark 2:10); he is lord (even) of the sabbath (Mark 2:28); he has nowhere to lay his head (Matt. 8:20); he came eating and drinking, and the people say he is a glutton and a drunkard, a friend of tax collectors and sinners (Matt. 11:19; Luke 7:34).

In this group motifs of *Jesus' activity* are connected with the Son of man. The traditional concept, however, did not include activity of the Son of man in the old aeon before the turn of the aeon. So there is no doubt that these Son-of-man sayings also refer to Jesus, who in the meantime became identified with the Son of man.

*(3) Talk of the coming Son of man.* Only in this group are apocalyptic concepts directly adopted. As suddenly as lightning strikes, the Son of man will be here. Therefore we must be ready for his hour, or else we will not pass the judgment (cf., e.g., Mark 13:26; 14:62; Matt. 24:27, 37, 39, 44; Luke 12:40; 17:24, 26). If we had only this group, we would never suspect that Jesus was talking of himself and announcing his own coming (again). Rather, according to this group he would be announcing the coming of the Son of man (quite in accord with apocalypticism), who would have to be distinguished from Jesus.

If we find that the Evangelists later identify Jesus with the Son of man when they use this group, then we have to assume that by then the parousia of the Son of man has been replaced by the Parousia of Jesus.

If we want to understand the development of the Parousia concept (the replacement of the Son of man with Jesus) in the history of the synoptic traditions, we can find help in several Son-of-man sayings (like those in the third group) that speak of the coming Son of man, but expressly distinguish between Jesus and the Son of man.

"And I tell you, everyone who acknowledges *me* before others, the *Son of Man* also will acknowledge before the angels of God; but whoever denies me before others will be denied before the angels of God" (Luke 12:8-9).

"Those who are ashamed of *me* and of *my* words in this adulterous and sinful generation, of him the *Son of Man* will also be ashamed, when he comes in the glory of his Father with the holy angels" (Mark 8:38).

These sayings, demonstrable in Mark and the sayings source, probably go back to a common basic formula. Even if we cannot reconstruct it exactly, this formula is still recognizable.

An obvious consideration shows that these words must be relatively old. It is hardly likely that sayings that expressly distinguish between Jesus and the Son of man were formed after the two were identified. And these are the sayings that help us understand the subsequent development.

The point of departure is Jesus' activity, which in the meantime is regarded in retrospect. The question—now and then—is, what does this activity mean for people and what is their position on it? They can rely on it, or they can avoid it. Though this is a decision they must make in the old aeon, this same decision will one day be confirmed by the Son of man in the judgment at the turn of the aeon. So the expected judgment is already past now. Those who rely on Jesus do not need to be afraid of the future anymore.

On this basis it is easy to understand how the term *Son of man* came to be applied to Jesus. He was seen as someone who by his activity offered an anticipation of the judgment of the Son of man. Thus, first of all, his activity could be interpreted as the activity of the Son of man, and then if his activity was the activity of the Son of man, then Jesus could be classified as the Son of man.

Thus, first the sayings of the presently active Son of man were formed, and later (presumably through Mark) those of the suffering, dying, and rising Son of man. It is noteworthy that *Son of man* never became an actual title; Jesus is never addressed this way. Through the use of the third person, the emphasis was placed on the function.

So the Galilean churches look back from the qualifying activity of Jesus to the Son of man, who is present as the one who is active. But these churches live in an environment in which people under the influence of apocalypticism are waiting for the coming of the Son of man, and they themselves have not given up the concept of the Parousia. Now, however, they can modify the content of this concept, for they already know the one who is to come. Hence, unlike those around them, they no longer simply await the coming of the Son of man; they now expect the coming of the Son of man *Jesus*. And since he has been there already, they are involved with him even in the present. The Son of man Jesus is directing them today.

> At this point an obvious parallel should at least be mentioned. By means of the concept of the Son of man, the Galilean church could express the presence of the one who had shown them the way in which they were now traveling. Yet in content this is no different from what was expressed by the concept of the resurrection of Jesus in another line of tradition (in which Paul lived).
>
> The idea that "he is (still) coming even today" could be expressed with totally different (always pregiven) concepts, because people had learned that "what Jesus stood for is still going on."

If the Son of man Jesus is still guiding people today, this means that these people exist eschatologically. We find the same connection that occurred in the two summaries: Jesus' activity was understood as anticipation of the future.

This is precisely what is characteristic of "the" Jesus image, into which the diverging Jesus images of the individual traditions were merged at an early time. And since this Jesus image does not occur first in Mark (i.e., around A.D. 70) but was already in the sayings source and, moreover, in all layers of the synoptic tradition, where it is expressed with the concept of the Son of man, we can give the following definition. The *Christian* Christology is that Christology in which eschatological existence is experienced and lived. *Christian ethics* is the actualization of this risky activity.

## 4. The "Development" of the Jesus Image

When we now speak of "development," we are looking at dogmatics—and at the same time at the still ongoing tension between the exegetes and the dogmaticians. The individual pieces of the synoptic tradition did not *originate* as development of this (one) Jesus image. Rather, this (one) Jesus image was subsequently reconstructed from the Jesus images already present. Thus development means that the (individual and diverse) Jesus images that originated earlier are to be *understood* on the basis of the subsequently reconstructed (one) Jesus image. But is this possible? And how is it possible?

We will first use Mark again for clarification, because the problem is most evident there. If it is true that with his initial summary Mark indicates how *he* understands Jesus' work, then all events told later are to be interpreted on the basis of this summary. If we want to analyze a pericope (in the exact sense of this word!) from the Gospel of Mark, we cannot restrict our exegesis to this pericope alone. Rather, we have to ask how *Mark* wanted this pericope to to be understood. In order to know this we have to proceed from Mark 1:14-15. For Mark the individual pericopes are developments of his Jesus image.

Very often it is possible to reconstruct from these pericopes pieces of the *pre-Markan* tradition. If we want to analyze these pieces, it is not a matter of how Mark understood them later but of how in each case the *authors of these individual pieces* understood Jesus' work. The two views, that of Mark and that of the author of an individual tradition, may coincide, but they do not have to—not even if it is an almost identical event that is related. Whether they coincide has to be established; it cannot be presupposed.

So an exegete always has to conduct two exegeses, that of the pre-Markan piece of tradition and that of the pericope. If (as presumably happens in most cases) we begin with the exegesis of the original tradition (which, however, must always be reconstructed first), we cannot directly carry over our results to the exegesis of the pericope. The latter *must* be based instead on Mark's Jesus image. This means, however, that Mark's Christology is the "canon" for interpreting the individual pericopes(!) of Mark's Gospel. This brings a dogmatic element into our view—first, of course, in a historical perspective.

For both of the exegeses we are conducting are historical exegeses. We are always concerned with what the respective authors (Mark and the author of the individual tradition) wanted to tell their contemporary readers. The difference is that in our exegesis of the pre-Markan tradition we are dealing only with that piece of tradition. Of course, it may contain a Jesus image (and insofar "dogmatics"). But this is determined exclusively from that piece of tradition itself. Our exegesis of the pericope, on the other hand, must not be restricted to this pericope alone; we have to proceed from the Christology (and thus from the "dogmatics") of Mark. So Mark's dogmatics (which may not even be recognizable in the pericope itself) determines how the pericope is to be understood. To that extent we can speak of a "dogmatically guided" exegesis, which nonetheless remains a historical exegesis, since we are trying to establish what intentions Mark had at the time.

The same is true for the Gospels of Matthew and Luke and for the material these Evangelists used. If we want to analyze a pericope from one of these Gospels, we first have to establish the Jesus image of that Evangelist (and thus his "dogmatics"), which can be seen most clearly if we observe the editing work of that Evangelist and draw conclusions from it. We can establish two Jesus images that are significantly different from that of Mark (as we will see below—cf. pp. 231ff.) but do not agree with each other either. Hence it is true here also that the exegeses of pericopes(!) of the Gospels of Matthew and Luke have to be "dogmatically guided" by the respective Jesus image. And again we have to keep them strictly separated from the exegeses of originals that were used by these Evangelists. Here too we have to avoid the common mistake of entering the results of the exegeses of the pre-Matthean and pre-Lukan traditions directly into the exegeses of the pericopes from the two Gospels.

If exegetes realize that they must make not only two exegeses but even two different kinds of exegesis, they will contribute to settling the troublesome tension between exegetes and specialists in dogmatics or ethics. They will see that despite apparently identical material, the results are different and sometimes contradictory. They can neither determine nor even want to determine which of these results are used in dogmatics. For as exegetes they have no criteria for deciding which results should be called "Christian." Since they have no criteria, it cannot be their task to make this decision.

We can illustrate this problem with Luther's preface to the Letter of James. Luther analyzes the letter historically, of course, and then states the result of his exegesis: The author of the Letter of James wanted to admonish people who relied on faith without works for their justification before God. But he did this in a way that made the doing of works a precondition for justification before God. Luther lets this result stand as the result of historical exegesis. Yet he is not thinking of using it immediately in his preaching, for the result of a correct(!) exegesis is first subject to criticism of its content by what Luther calls a "touchstone," which he finds in Paul. Only this touchstone can decide whether the result of the exegesis may be called a Christian statement.

If exegetes (as exegetes) tried to decide what can be called Christian and what cannot, they would risk their independence. The knowledge that we always have to apply a touchstone to the results of an exegesis provides exegetes with the independence necessary for their work. Thus they cannot (again: as exegetes!) interfere with the work of the dogmaticians and ethicists. And the dogmaticians and ethicists will never be in the situation of being disturbed by exegetes.

First of all, dogmaticians have to take into account the exegeses. And when they see (as the exegetes can show them) that there are two different exegeses, one based exclusively on a piece of tradition and one "dogmatically guided," they can see where they have to begin their work.

For the dogmaticians and ethicists are basically in the same situation as Mark, as Matthew and Luke. Therefore they are now asked about *their* Jesus image. But they are not allowed simply to use it (most of the time implicitly); they have to make it explicit and describe it. And they must state why, in their opinion, it is *the* image of Jesus. What reasons can they give?

One possibility (and most of the time this will be the point of departure) would be to appeal to the dogmaticians' own tradition. But can this alone substantiate the Christian character of this particular Jesus image? They would have to explicate their presuppositions, and these assumptions themselves require substantiation. Eventually they will be led to the path described in the last section.

Now the dogmaticians must decide if they agree with the definition proposed there or if they want to label another Jesus image "Christian." In the latter case they again face the necessity of stating their reasons. This substantiation is not possible through historical exegesis, for such exegesis can substantiate not only Mark's Jesus image but also those of Matthew and Luke or, for that matter, almost any other Jesus image, even if they are mutually exclusive. Historical exegesis is overtaxed when we try to use it in dogmatic substantiations.

For this reason discussions in dogmatics cannot call on historical exegesis for substantiation. It is not possible for Christian ethics (or a Christian sermon) to appeal to a correct exegesis. As Luther already pointed out (see above), such an appeal is not enough. In practice this is almost never observed. Disagreements among exegetes always concern what the *author* of a text considers Christian but not what can be called genuinely Christian. In the latter case the issue can be settled only by forming a consensus. So when we look at the origin of all reconstructed Jesus images, we cannot interpret them as developments of this one Jesus image.

Individual Jesus images were first accounts of impressions that *individual* people wrote after *individual* encounters with the active Jesus. This happened at different times, in different places, in different situations, and under different conditions. Inevitably, only a narrow and very limited aspect of a comprehensive Jesus image could be seen. This image took time to come into being at all, and it was formed as many aspects were combined into one image. Our examples were the summary of Mark, the Baptist's inquiry, and the Son-of-man sayings.

So our task must now be to develop under dogmatic guidance the aspects of eschatological existence that are discernible in the individual pieces of tradition. For there (and *only* there) is where we are dealing with Christian ethics.

*a) Individual Aspects of Eschatological Existence*

Eschatological existence must be understood in the context of contemporary Jewish or Jewish apocalyptic thought. Today we would say by analogy that *Christian* existence must be understood in the context of *secular* existence. Thus statements on eschatological existence and on Christian existence always have a polemical character, for each presupposes the possibility of another form of existence with which it does not want to be associated. Hence we must grasp the nature of this polemic. What does it refer to? What is its approach? Whom or what does it concern? And then this polemical character must be retained as a part of new statements. Otherwise polemical statements will soon turn unnoticed into positive statements, which will then be repeated as such. In this way the original cause will be lost.

> We can illustrate this problem, in a somewhat simplified way, with a slogan from the Reformation. *Sola scriptura* (scripture alone) was then used to polemize against "scripture *and* tradition." Today we hardly remember that this was a polemic. *Scripture alone* has become a positive statement; we consult the scriptures when we want to present the life and teachings of the church. Both must be "in accordance with the scriptures," for church life is based on scripture. *It* is the required point of orientation. The earlier (polemical) concern has faded. If we felt bound by this *concern* (and not just by the *formulation* of the concern), we would have to see that an appeal to the New Testament scripture is an appeal to tradition. The Reformers did not see this and probably could not have seen it. Thus the Reformers' concern has been compromised, because the old wording was adopted, but the polemical statement was used as a positive statement.

Thus we must take care to understand the nature of the polemic as exactly as possible.

*(1) Luke 6:5 (D).* We will start with an old segment of tradition that we find in codex D in the place of Luke 6:5.

On the same day he saw a man doing work on the sabbath. He said to him, "Man, if you know what you are doing, you are blessed. But if you do not know, you are cursed and a transgressor of the law."

The context is clear. The norm for the peoples' deeds is the law, for God has given the law and demands its strict observance. Whoever asks for God's will is referred to the law. This goes for individuals as well as for the community. Thus the law is also something we could call a civil code of law. Regulations on the prohibition of work on the sabbath were especially strict and exact. Here there were occasionally disputes concerning the question, What kind of work can still be done on a sabbath under certain circumstances? A much discussed example was whether a child who had fallen into a well on the sabbath could be rescued on that sabbath. The stricter school of scribes considered even this prohibited; other scribes held that it was allowed. So we could raise the question whether Jesus is depicted here as someone who advocated a more liberal practice in observing the law, or who even placed himself beyond the sabbath regulations completely.

Yet such considerations misunderstand the story. The issue is not what work may be done under what conditions. For the work this man is doing is not specified. Nor is it, by any means, a matter of doing away with the sabbath regulations altogether, for there is still the possibility that this man working on the sabbath will be condemned. Hence the crucial point is not the sabbath regulations as such. In this regard there are no directions as to what to do.

Rather, it is characteristic that for the same concrete activity happening in the presence of all two judgements are possible: the man is "blessed" or "cursed." In our terminology this means that we cannot see from the activity itself whether eschatological existence occurs here or not. The decisive factor is the doers and, more precisely, whether *they* know what they are doing or not.

It is immediately clear that this knowing or not knowing cannot be superficially related to the activity; this man knows, of course, that it is sabbath, that he is working, and what he is doing. But does he know what *he* is doing by doing it? Hence the knowing or not knowing must concern the entire context in which the work is done and in that context, first of all, the man himself and *his* God. Does this man know about God or does he not?

If he does not know about God, he has only the law, and that is what he must hold to. That is also what the community in which he lives must hold to. It orders its life according to the law. If they both also see God behind the law (and this is what they do, of course), then this God is characterized by the law. It is a God who has set up requirements to be followed exactly. His will is to be fulfilled. Since his will is directed toward human deeds, people fulfill his will when they hold exactly to the law— and only then. Judgment will take place in like manner. Concretely occurring deeds will be measured by the law. If people's deeds deviate from the law, they are transgressors of the law, whom the community will rightly judge. At the same time, they will receive the curse of God because of their deeds.

This piece of tradition polemizes precisely against the assumption that we can judge people directly by what they do in the presence of everyone. It does so by steering our attention away from the doing to the doer. The latter is decisive. For if the people "know"—that is, if they know what they are doing by their doing—they can be blessed, even though what they are doing on the sabbath is the very thing that is condemned by the law. Thus if we see the knowing in its entire context, it can only refer to God. For if the God of these people is not the law but the Father, then they are "knowers." They are people who know about Jesus and who *therefore* know what they are doing by their doing. For a deed that is done together with the God of Jesus is eschatological existence.

We could now raise an objection and ask whether this is true of any kind of activity. And since this is disputable, we could then look for examples of the kind of work this person could have been caught doing. After all, the whole context includes not only the doer and the deed but also the purpose of the deed. For this we have examples in the synoptic tradition also, for example, healings on the sabbath.

Yet this is exactly what is not seen in our story. And it is not supposed to be seen, because we would again run the risk of concentrating on the activity and thus fall into casuistry. For we would superficially judge the doer by this particular deed.

This segment of tradition begins with the following briefly stated situation: a man does something that necessarily offends everyone who sees it. This obvious fact is by no means questioned fundamentally, as the second answer shows. Yet it can be questioned, if the God of Jesus is taken into account and it involves doing his will. So the intention of the text is as follows: if we watch a stranger's actions, we can soon determine whether these actions conform to the law (or to the rules observed in that particular society), but we cannot determine whether these actions constitute doing the will of God.

This is exactly what cannot be determined, because eschatological existence is never evident as *eschatological* existence. Likewise we can say that whether Christian actions are really Christian is hidden from all onlookers. For the decision on this depends exclusively with the doers. They are the immediate addressees of God's will—not the things they do. And since no one can look into the doer's heart, a theological judgment is not only impossible but also forbidden. This knowledge can only lead to tolerance.

Of course, this does not apply to the doers. For they are still questioned—particularly about their God and thus for the motivation behind their actions.

Lately it has again become very fashionable to speak of "anonymous Christians." This refers to people who do not consider themselves Christians but who act in ways we would expect from Christians. Here we can only give a warning, for we are making inferences from the purely visible deed to the people performing it. In addition, of course, we can ask about the intent of such judgments. Are we not claiming people for Christianity who put absolutely no stock in it themselves?

The segment of tradition about the man working on the sabbath looks backward from activity that has already happened. What if we go the other way? What if the activity has yet to be done and we ask, *What* are we to do?

*(2) Luke 10:29-37.* We will illustrate the problem first with the parable of the good Samaritan, which has widely been considered a paradigm of Christian conduct even today. In answer to the question, What characterizes Christians? we hear that they practice love of neighbor, just as the good Samaritan did. But does that get at the real point of this bit of tradition?

The reconstruction of the (pre-Lukan) beginning of this text is not possible with final certainty, because v. 29 was composed by Luke himself. With the words "wanting to justify himself" the Evangelist wrote a transition from Jesus' preceding discussion with the lawyer. The lawyer's question, "Who is my neighbor?" presupposes, however, that he has at least been urged to love his neighbor. This admonition was possibly preceded by the question, "What must I do to inherit eternal life?" For this question is not found in the teaching of Mark 12:28-31, which Luke used as a model for vv. 25-28. Luke could have taken it from the beginning of the parable and placed it in v. 25.

So the original beginning of the traditional story must have read roughly as follows. [A lawyer asks, What must I do to fulfill the will of God? He is given the] admonition: love your neighbor as yourself.

By asking, Who is my neighbor? the lawyer slips into casuistry, for he would like to distinguish between those whom he is supposed to love and those to whom God's commandment does not apply unconditionally. We should not be too quick to criticize at this point, for basically this question not only makes sense but is also justified (and was discussed in contemporary Judaism, as Matt. 5:43 demonstrates; cf. p. 99 below). No one can love everyone if loving means more than merely a benevolent attitude, that is, if it means concrete action. People who want to love have to make distinctions, or else they will become overburdened. The question, Who is my neighbor? is asked in order to make love practicable.

Yet Jesus refuses to answer this particular question. Instead, he answers with the example of the man who has fallen among robbers. The priest and the Levite pass him by, and only the Samaritan gives the the maltreated man the necessary help. That it was, of all people, one of those Samaritans—despised by the Jews—who served here as a model, must have been offensive and shocking to the Jewish hearers of the story. But this is not the real point at all.

This comes in Jesus' subsequent question, "Which of these three, do you think, was a neighbor to the man who fell into the hands of the robbers?" The lawyer accepts the question and gives the right answer: "The one who showed him mercy." The story then ends with Jesus' admonition: "Go and do likewise."

This command is completely misunderstood if we take it as an encouragement to do in similar situations what the Samaritan did. This would lead us into casuistry again. If we meet poor, weak, sick, suppressed, or victims of robbers, we have to show love for our neighbors. Basically, this is not wrong. But it would mean acting and behaving in a *human* way. It still does not touch upon the particular issue here (and in *Christianity*), for it does not observe that the direction of the question has been reversed. *Who* is my neighbor? has been replaced with To whom can *I* be a neighbor? *The Samaritan* was the neighbor. The admonition to go and do likewise does not urge us to love our neighbor but to be neighbors ourselves and act as people who are neighbors.

This reversal of direction makes the lawyer's question, Who is my neighbor? irrelevant. If he is a neighbor himself, then he is a neighbor to anyone he meets. Before the deeds are discussed, we must ask of the doers, Are they neighbors? If this is the case, they can no longer select the person to whom they want to be a neighbor. Nor do they have to: they have that person right in front of them.

It might be helpful in our reflections on Christian ethics if we could practice using the language more precisely. In the term *love of neighbor, neighbor* can be subject or object. In common usage it is the object. So we are talking about love directed *toward* the neighbor, and the one practicing this love is not specified. We only mention a deed and the one affected by it. Thus the commandment can be formulated as, "Love your neighbor." This commandment can be given to anyone, and anyone can try to obey it. We may be successful in trying and, depending on our efforts, may expand the circle of our neighbors or those whom we want to regard as neighbors. If we accomplish a lot, we earn a lot praise. Yet can we as doers be characterized by our deeds? And can a person's deeds, which are a matter of that person's *own* decisions, be called eschatological existence?

Hence this kind of love of neighbor (love toward the neighbor) should not be called authentically "Christian," even though there is no doubt that it entered our culture in the context of the Christian tradition. Rather, what is specifically and characteristically Christian is that it is *a neighbor* who is loving. Also we can no longer talk here about a *commandment* to love, since anyone who is a neighbor *exists* as a neighbor, which means that this person loves. It is obvious that here love of neighbor is also happening in the traditional sense. But it no longer has to be commanded.

To put it concisely, Christians are given the commandment to love their neighbors. And real Christians are loving neighbors.

Yet this poses other questions. For example, are there not also Jesus traditions in which he not only exhorts love of neighbor but even love of the enemy? And most of all, how can a person become a neighbor? We will examine these questions in order.

*(3) Matthew 5:43-44.* The sixth antithesis (by Matthew's count) states: "You have heard that it was said, 'You shall love your neighbor and hate your enemy.' But I say to you, Love your enemies . . ." (Matt. 5:43-44).

The history of the tradition of these antitheses is not always clear and cannot be presented here. But since we forgo on principle the reconstruction of "authentic" sayings of Jesus, it plays a less important role than it is often given. Here we only presuppose that the third antithesis (Matt. 5:31-32) was written by Matthew.

The structure of the antitheses is always the same. An initial thesis states what was said "to those of ancient times." The following antithesis is introduced by "but I say to you." The first impression is always that the old demands are increased, sometimes to the extreme. Hence we often read about the rigorism of Jesus' demands and find the following interpretations. To those of ancient times it was forbidden to kill; Jesus prohibits even being angry. To those of ancient times adultery was forbidden; Jesus prohibits even lustful looks; and so forth. The sixth antithesis, then, confronts the old commandment, "Love your neighbor," with Jesus' commandment, "Love your enemies."

After what has been said so far, however, we have to ask, Can we speak of a *commandment* to love our enemies? Of course, the grammatical form of the imperative suggests that we can. Yet we have to determine whether this imperative is preceded by an indicative (even though it is not expressly quoted here), or whether the imperative is given without such a preface. We will look for the answer in the context of the thesis and the other antitheses that have come down on us.

In our example we are surprised first of all by the thesis. For the commandment to love one's neighbor we can refer to Lev. 19:18, for example, but there is no evidence of the conclusion "and hate your enemy" in any of the Old Testament scriptures. Had this really been said to "those of ancient times"?

Again, we have to make a distinction between what was said to those of ancient times (and can be established from the Old Testament scriptures by historical exegesis) and what was understood in Jesus' time. Originally the "commandments" were understood as offers of Yahweh to humanity. They were meant as aids to the people. If the people relied on these offers, they could lead what we might today call "a life worth living." The sabbath regulation, for example, was really given "for humankind" (cf. Mark 2:27). Yet in Jesus' time people either did not know that or did not understand it anymore. And they no longer practiced it in this way. The words were kept, but now they were understood as a law that was given by Yahweh and was to be obeyed under all circumstances. This was in part due to a new theology; people talked of their God differently. The God who intended his offer as a help had become the God who insisted on the strict observation of his commandments and made this the condition for the communion with himself.

The commandment to love your neighbor—now really understood as a commandment from God that must be obeyed—had to lead to casuistry. Usually only fellow Jews were considered neighbors to whom the commandment applied. This thought, logically developed, posed the question of how to treat non-Jews. One could assume that they did not have the law. Hence they did not do the will of God stated in the law—nor could they do it. Yet God could not be pleased by those who did not do his will. Such people were enemies of God. Hence, did the Jews not do God's will by hating God's enemies? They had to be hated, for doing anything else would mean to make a different judgment of the enemies from that made by God. Insofar it was indeed true that those of ancient times had been told (as was understood in the time of Jesus!): You shall hate your (i.e., God's) enemies.

> From the Qumran texts we know that this conclusion was expressly reached by that community (in Jesus' time). They referred to themselves as the "sons of light" and to those who did not belong to the community as the "sons of darkness." It was stated as a commandment to be observed that they were to "love all sons of light . . . and hate all sons of darkness."

So it is not only possible but also mandatory to interpret the thesis carefully. The second clause that demands hatred not only clarifies how we must understand the first clause, namely, as a commandment to be strictly followed, which defines the circle of neighbors casuistically. It also makes explicit which theology—that is, which image of God—is presupposed.

If we now assume the same image of God in the antithesis as in the thesis, we must understand the antithesis as follows. The the old commandment with the old content is to be replaced by a new commandment with a new content, which is to be observed as strictly as the old one was supposed to be. God has remained the same, but now he demands something different.

This is the way the antitheses are often understood today. Yet this misunderstanding is old. We can find it even in Matthew, as shown by the third antithesis (5:31-32), which Matthew composed himself. The old commandment reads, "Whoever divorces his wife, let him give her a certificate of divorce." This commandment is crossed out and replaced by a new one prohibiting divorce except under one precisely defined condition. Through this composition of his own Matthew shows how *he* understood the other antitheses as well, namely, as changes in the *content* of the commandments.

Yet a mere comparison of the contents of thesis and antithesis gives an indication that the (pre-Matthean!) sixth antithesis had a different purpose. The commandment to hate the enemy is turned into its opposite. It now speaks of love of enemy, while love of neighbor is no longer mentioned at all. This can hardly mean that the love of the neighbor is not required anymore and people only have to love their enemies.

Now a look at the other antitheses will show that it is a misinterpretation to understand them as new commandments that are to be observed *instead* of the old ones. In the case of the fourth antithesis (5:33-34) we could still assume that it is supposed to express a fundamental prohibition of swearing. Yet it cannot be understood simply as a commandment to be observed, either, as we can see from those antitheses that do not contain imperatives (as we would expect) but statements.

The first antithesis (5:21-22) begins by quoting the commandment: "You shall not murder." This is followed by the threat of judgment for violators. This means theologically that if we presuppose this God, then we sin when we do not observe his commandments. Accordingly, we must expect punishment from this God. The antithesis takes up the idea. *If we presuppose this God,* then whoever is angry will be punished, and that means everyone. Anger is not prohibited in the antithesis. There is no imperative here (although interpreters keep reading one in).

Such a commandment would also be meaningless, since it would be impossible to observe. Rather, it is asserted that whoever is angry will be liable to judgment, which means, however, that *everybody* will be liable to judgment *if* (we must stress) one presupposes this God and then assumes one could be righteous before him by observing his commandments. Such attempts will always fail, for before *this* God no one is righteous.

The same is true for the second antithesis (5:27-28). The commandment prohibits adultery. Yet if we (like the Pharisee of the parable in Luke 18:9-14) think we can be justified before God because we observe this commandment (among others), we are not just given a stricter commandment here, namely, not even to cast a lustful look. Again there is no imperative formulated to advocate an ethical rigorism that would enable people to make even greater efforts and still reach their goal of being justified before God. Rather, the assertion is that whoever looks lustfully violates the commandment and is guilty in the eyes of *this* God. So here too we have to say, *everybody* is guilty.

We can see the point of the antitheses only if we understand them in a precise theological way. They force us to examine the image of God and then introduce a critique of this image. If we are oriented towards the demanding God, we are always guilty. Yet that can be understood only by someone who is really serious about *this* God. But that is not the case with those who pick from the many commandments some that they consider especially important, or who make the commandments practicable by means of casuistry. Here they are challenged to take their God really seriously. Then they must see that in his eyes they can only fail. And from this failure there is no escape.

Therefore to see in the antitheses intensification of the commandments would be to misunderstand them. This would be tantamount to an attempt by humans to secure a way out of their failure before God. They would have to make a much greater effort than they had to with the commandments given to "those of ancient times." But with the required effort the failure could still be avoided. Yet the antitheses are formulated so as to make clear that as commandments to be observed they are not observable.

The antitheses are likewise misunderstood if we see in them instructions that promote a new ethic. We might be able to design an ethic this way that could be called Christian in the popular sense, but by no means a truly Christian ethic. Rather, the antitheses show that *every* human attempt to settle our account with *this* God has to fail. Yet this is only the one side.

We can see the other side if we consider the aspect of the eschatological existence. No one can live eschatological existence by his or her own efforts. For this reason alone it cannot be commanded. Eschatological existence is the life we will live at God's table in the expected kingdom.

In those days people had a very concrete image of this, and even today we can have a very concrete image if we use the content of the antitheses to visualize it. Then it becomes immediately apparent. At God's table there will be no anger and no lustful looks. People will say the truth; swearing will be unnecessary. When former enemies sit together at God's table, they will of course no longer treat each other as enemies. Such a life at God's table will be possible, because people will live in communion with God.

In modern terminology, at God's table people live a world made whole. And this does not happen, because the people at the table were so commanded; rather, they are living a whole world because they have become whole themselves. Whole people are people living in communion with God.

So here the doers of the deeds are again brought to the forefront of our attention. Because they have changed, they are capable of the new way of doing now. Yet they are capable of this only *if* they have changed.

At this point we should consider the widespread usage of the terms *sinner, sin,* and *to sin,* and define them more precisely.

It is very common to start with deeds and classify a certain deed as a sin. From the deed conclusions are then drawn about the doer. Whoever violates commandments (or other rules) is sinning and hence is a sinner. And people who follow the commandments (or rules) do not sin. Are they therefore not sinners? If we base our reasoning on deeds, we have to draw this conclusion.

Yet if we start with the doer, we must say that anyone who does not live in communion with God is a sinner. *Everything* that such a person does is "sin." This does not mean that sinners cannot act in an exemplarary way; they certainly can. Yet even if they succeed in loving their enemy, their love of enemy remains the deed of a sinner. By no action and by no effort, however great, can they—all by themselves—work their way out of their existence as sinners.

Especially in the language of the church, therefore, a deed should not be labeled a sin. This can lead to the misunderstanding that we simply have to correct our actions, whereas the first and crucial point has to be that the doer, the sinner, must do an about-face.

In describing *eschatological* deeds the antitheses presuppose that the doers have become different people. They are sinners no more; in the terminology of our previous section, they have become *neighbors,* that is, they have let themselves be turned into *neighbors.* From this standpoint, we can now interpret the intended meaning of love of enemy.

First, we have to define the enemy to whom this must refer. An enemy is a person who in some way—through words, behavior, or action—has taken and is taking a position *against the doer.* It can never be the other way around, namely, that the doer has something against the enemy, for *neighbors* cannot have enemies.

Next we have to see that loving means active deeds directed towards enemies and intended to reach them. We cannot call a mere passive toleration of the enemy's activities *love* of enemy.

This becomes clear in some segments of tradition that originally circulated separately but then ended up near the antitheses. For instance, "Love your enemies" is immediately followed by "and pray for those who persecute *you*" (Matt. 5:44). Luke (6:27-28) adds: "Do good to those who hate *you,* bless those who curse *you,* pray for those who abuse *you.*" Another example of such concrete practice of love of enemy appears in the fifth antithesis (Matt. 5:38-39). Those of ancient times were told, "An eye for an eye and a tooth for a tooth."

Originally this saying was supposed to limit uncontrolled retaliation. If we practice "poetic justice" (*ius talionis*), we can achieve a calculable coexistence. In *this* world we can live with that. And even if today these punishments have been replaced by more humane measures, our penal code is still based on this principle.

This is opposed by the antithesis, "Do not resist [at all] an evildoer." In isolation this looks at first like passivity. Yet it paves the way for a "change of gods." The evil done by our enemy should not become our "god" in that it now determines our action as reaction. Instead, the recommended action is, "If any one strikes you on the right cheek, turn the other also" (Matt. 5:39).

Of course, this is misunderstood again if we take it as a commandment to be observed exactly in this way. Rather, the *neighbor* looks at enemies in love and asks how they can be helped out of their enmity. One possibility may indeed be to offer the other cheek. Of course, this is not done with the intention of provoking enemies to strike again. This supposed "loving" would only reinforce their enmity. Those who love their enemies cannot want this. Offering the other cheek can be an act of love of enemy only if it is done in the hope of bringing enemies to their senses. Only then can enemies experience love and indeed a love that aims to change them. For if they receive love, they as loved people will themselves be free to love.

*Neighbors* can never know beforehand whether they will reach their goal through this concrete way of acting. Hence it may be that an entirely different concrete deed is necessary to change an enemy. How that will be can never be determined in advance.

Eschatological existence always has the character of risk. This character would be lost, if a commandment to be concretely followed were established for the love of enemy. The doers would obey a rule whose observance promised success. And if they did not reach their goal, they could put the blame on the one who gave the commandment. In eschatological existence, on the other hand, the responsibility for what is concretely done always rests with the doers. Therefore there is always a double risk. First, the *neighbors* have to assume the risk of deciding exactly what to do in a specific case. Out of a number of possibilities, they must choose one. In this they also run the risk of being responsible for the consequences even though they cannot foresee them ahead of time. Whether *neighbors* can take such a risk is determined by their theology. In Matt. 5:45b we read of the God who makes his sun rise on the evil and on the good, and sends rain on the just and on the unjust. This is the God who, to put it in modern terms, is unbiased. He offers everyone the opportunity to put their trust in him.

The antitheses clearly show that any human attempt to settle accounts with God by doing his commandments has to fail. In the theology formulated in Matt. 5:45b we are offered a chance to rely on the God who loves all his children without distinction and condition, both those who fail and their enemies.

We can describe this more precisely in regard to love of enemy. If we presuppose the God who makes observance of the commandments a precondition for communion with him—as was done in Jesus' time and is still done even today—then all those who do not meet these conditions are not only *sinners* but also enemies of God. His will, after all, is laid down in particular commandments. If, however, God makes his sun rise also on the evil (and hence on all people) and sends rain also on the unjust (and hence on all people), then God loves his enemies. And when he is experienced as one who acts as a *neighbor* himself by loving his enemies, the enemies of God become enemies loved by God. His will is that his enemies, as enemies loved by him, become *neighbors,* just as he is a neighbor himself. Neighbors are liberated to love their enemies and can see that their enemies are also enemies loved by God. Therefore they can now be neighbors to their enemies. Briefly stated, in the loving their enemies, neighbors live their God for their enemies.

This brings us to the christological aspect. Jesus was experienced by his disciples as someone who in his work lived his God for them. And this changed people. For them love of enemy is not something they are ordered to do by commandment and therefore must do. Love of enemy is something they do because they can.

Yet we must still ask why in the sixth antithesis love of enemy is given as an imperative. This could at least create the impression that it is a commandment to be observed after all. Since the grammar allows this understanding, it has often been understood in this way. Yet even this imperative must be interpreted in the context of eschatological existence.

We have to start with the question: Who, basically, is a *neighbor*? The answer, for all we can see, is no one.

> In the context of the discussion above, we can state this more precisely. Nominal Christians are, for all we can see, not genuine Christians. So we have to consider whether we can develop an ethic for nominal Christians and what it would have to be like. It could be an ethic that lets nominal Christians remain what they are. In the aspect of eschatological existence, however, it is important for them to become authentic Christians, but this is something that must happen over and over. Nominal Christians become real Christians when they become, again and again, what they were once before.

> This gives the imperative a different character. It no longer has the form of a commandment to be observed, but is an invitation to a way of acting that is bound to a promise. Accepting this invitation remains a risk. But those who are willing to run the risk can experience the freedom to be *neighbors*. No one can really *be* a neighbor; we can only *become* neighbors over and over again. This is stated in the continuation of the sixth antithesis as follows. "Love your enemies and pray for those who persecute you, so that you may be children [Greek: sons] of your Father in heaven" (Matt. 5:44-45a).

> The term *son* has to be understood in its Semitic-Hebrew sense. It expresses the idea that one belongs to a kind, a power, or a realm. If someone is called, for example, a "son of poverty," "son of faithfulness," "son of joy," he is characterized as someone who is completely determined by

that particular quality. Hence a "son (or child) of God" is someone whom God has taken over completely.

So if we accept the invitation to love our enemies, we are promised that in doing so we can experience being children of God. That is, we can experience that our doing is not really *our* doing but God acting as a neighbor through us as his children.

If we express this in the usual grammatical terminology, we can say that we cannot separate the indicative from the imperative. They coincide in our actions.

Yet we can enter this indicative-imperative context in different ways. It is possible that the indicative, that is, our theology (our relying on the Father, who loves all his children), is leading us into our actions. Ethics is indeed an aspect of theology. Or it may be that when we accept the invitation to act, we realize as we act that it is the Father who accomplishes these deeds. In that case we experience our God in our actions and can formulate our theology.

The fact that the imperative is followed by a promise, however, also means that this promise may or may not be fulfilled. Thus it may well be that our (remarkable!) actions remain our own accomplishment. There is no reason whatsoever to discredit this accommplishment in some way. Yet these actions are not eschatological existence.

Finally, the idea that *neighbors* as *children of God* are not doing their own work but in reality that of their Father is stated most pointedly in the bit of tradition in Matt. 5:48: "Be perfect, therefore, as your heavenly Father is perfect." It goes without saying that this imperative does not give a commandment to be observed. It would again be impossible to fulfill, since humans can do no more than strive for perfection, and that would not be fulfillment of the commandment. Here we are really talking about perfection and nothing less. Hence this imperative is only another invitation to participate in the Father's perfection.

For eschatological existence is always perfect existence. It happens through people and hence concretely and visibly in this world (i.e., in the old aeon). Yet this existence is not "of this world." In this world, however, it is not apparent that such existence is *not* of this world. To this extent we must talk of ambiguity, for the doing remains subject to misunderstandings. Is a human being active here who strives and thereby accomplishes extraordinary things? Or is God active through a human being? (Cf. the Baptist's inquiry, pp. 77-81 above.)

*(4) Christological interlude: Jesus' activity in word and deed.* The same misunderstanding was also possible with *Jesus' activity,* that is, his work *in word and deed.* One could think that Jesus intended his deeds as examples, and thus his actions were indirect imperatives that were supposed to challenge others to imitate his deeds. These imperatives then stood side by side with the direct imperatives that were handed down in many individual sayings. Or one could see in the same actions eschatological existence that happened through Jesus himself and to which Jesus was inviting others. We have to realize that *both* viewpoints can be stated christologically, and the resulting ethic will be an aspect of that particular Christology.

If we interpret Jesus' work as exemplary, we can call him (christologically) one of "the greats" of humanity or, if we like, "the greatest." Therefore we must emulate his example by trying to do what he did or by behaving as he did in similar situations. And since Jesus was one of the really great ones, through his imperatives he could give people directions on what to do in order to carry out God's will. Hence he could be called (christologically again) the "new lawgiver."

If, however, we understand Jesus' work as eschatological existence, that is, if we see in his *work* a special quality, then we can classify him (christologically) as someone who relied on his God and did his Father's work. If we want to express this with a title, we can call him *Son of God.* In this case it is not, first of all, a matter of looking at his *deeds* in order to carry out God's will by copying these deeds. Rather, we are first asked whether we want to rely on this Son of God, which means whether together with Jesus we want to rely on Jesus' God. We are asked whether we, as sinners living in the old aeon, want to submit ourselves to transformation by the Father. For God's will is aimed at sinners and is intended to turn sinners into *children*. And if we let the Father turn us into *children*, we no longer have to be commanded to act: now we *can* act. For this reason the imperatives are not intended as commands but as invitations.

As we can easily see, the second way of understanding Jesus' work is the less obvious one. So it is understandable that it is not immediately apparent and, what is more, is also overlooked as a possibility and thus not even examined. Instead, one is content with the first possibility and holds to what is visible to the eye (the concrete deeds of Jesus) and what is present in grammatical form (imperatives to be followed). And so the ethic is developed on the basis of the great human model and the teacher of God's new law. For this undertaking the synoptic tradition offers an abundance of material, and therefore "evidence" can always be found in the texts to substantiate this ethic and pass it off as Christian.

We must ask, however, whether this (generally very demanding) ethic, for which we can point to Jesus, is a genuinely Christian ethic for this reason alone. Is it not genuinely Christian only if we abandon the superficial and examine what is less obvious? It will, to be sure, no longer be practicable in a simple way, but can this be a criterion? Let us attempt, therefore, to contrast the two and in this way bring to light some of the special characteristics of what is peculiar to the less obvious (and hence genuinely Christian) approach.

Today we often hear that Jesus engaged in social action. Therefore some say that Christian action must be social action. Did Jesus not devote himself to the poor and lowly, the oppressed and persecuted? Did he not invite sinners and tax collectors to his table? Did he not denounce the rich and speak out against possessions when, for example, he told the rich young man to sell everything he had and give the proceeds to the poor? Did he not say that it is easier for a camel to go through the eye of a needle than for a rich man to enter the kingdom of God? Did he not receive women—for whom society then had little or no respect—into his inner circle? Did he not embrace and bless children, whom his disciples did not even want come near? Did he not take the side of the woman who was caught in adultery and protect her from her accusers and judges? Did he not let his feet be washed by a sinful woman? We could easily multiply these examples, but what do they mean?

With such a catalog we can paint an impressive picture of Jesus' work; we have to remember, though, that it is a picture painted subsequently (cf. p. 60 above). Perhaps it can give us an idea of how to imagine life in the kingdom of God more concretely. It is not very graphic just to say in summary that love will reign there. Yet if we say that at God's table there will be room even for the disadvantaged and that even sinners will be invited because God loves them too, the image becomes much more concrete. Yet can we derive instructions for an ethic directly from such a compilation?

Those who try this will soon see the problems. They would like to write a concrete ethic, and thus they seek instructions for individual cases. In order to find them they must first disassemble the picture once again into the components from which it was made. This is done in two steps.

First, the (general) "commandment" to love is made more specific: it means love of the poor, the lowly, and the weak. But this already raises the question: Only them? If we do not want to admit this expressly, we dodge the question. Instead of "only them" we say "especially them." Then, however, we have already opened the door to casuistry. In the second step we go through this door. For now the picture is divided into its parts again, and they become the points of departure and points of reference.

If we look closer at these points and take the Jewish environment into consideration, we come to a surprising conclusion. Almost every example that is used to gain ethical instructions has parallels in contemporary Judaism. In the life of the church this problem receives little attention, although it has often been pointed out—recently even by Jewish experts. J. Klausner, for instance, notes that in all the Gospels there is "*not even one* ethical maxim" that has no parallel in Jewish literature (*Jesus von Nazareth,* 3rd ed. [1952], 534). If this is true, we can hardly avoid the conclusion that there is a continuity from the ethical demands of contemporary Judaism to those of Jesus, and as far as ethics is concerned, Jesus stands entirely on Jewish ground. But is it true?

Since the vast majority of cases cannot be disputed, people start looking for exceptions in order not to merge Jesus completely into Judaism, and at least two things are named. They refer to Jesus' (supposed) absolute prohibition of divorce, an obvious contradiction of Jewish ethics, which expressly sanctions the writing of a certificate of divorce. And they refer to the prohibition of swearing, for which there is no evidence in contemporary Jewish literature (at least none has been found so far). Apart from the question whether tradition has been correctly analyzed here (more about that shortly), we must consider whether these two commandments (out of a vast number of others) are enough to claim a fundamentally special status for Jesus' ethics. After all, they merely represent modifications in detail.

Since these points seem (with good reason) to be insufficient, people often quote the words "but I say to you" with which Jesus introduces the antitheses. Such a claim of authority over what "was said to those of ancient times" is indeed unparalleled. Yet here too we have to ask how this is to be understood. Is it a radicalization of the law given through Moses? Or is it a general polemic against this law?

If Jesus' claim is understood as a radicalization of the law, then this has great import for the formulation of *specific* instructions. *In principle,* however, it means nothing at all, since even a radical interpretation remains within the context of the law. In this case Jesus would have "explained" the law (as they said), which is basically nothing different from what the Torah teachers of his time did. They too began with the law and interpreted it casuistically. They looked at the customs of their time and tried to make the law practicable. They regarded the resulting "explanations" as modern statements of God's will. The people who wanted to do God's will were required to go by these "explanations" in their actions. There were, of course, differences of opinion. The school of Shammai had strict views; the school of Hillel was much more lenient. With his rigorism Jesus would have represented the strict or an even stricter school, saying that the law of Moses has to be explained quite radically, for only then will God's will truely be done. Examples of this can be found in the individual traditions. But are we really on the right track here? In fact, there are also counterexamples.

First, however, let us examine the repeatedly alleged rigorism. We really have to ask here whether this is not going too far. The strict observance of law found in Judaism only in rare and exceptional cases is found in Jesus in extreme concentration. Do we not have to agree with J. Klausner (*Jesus von Nazareth,* p. 564) when he states that such an extremely radical ethic can lead to a "deterioration of ethics"? Or with another Jewish scholar (P. Lapide, *Er predigte in ihren Synagogen* [1980], p. 51), who calls Jesus' ethic the "superhuman idealist ethic of a supermoralist"? For if God's will, which the people have to do, is laid down in the law, and if the radicalization of the law's commandments makes them impossible to obey, then the people can no longer do God's will at all. Then they look for a way out and in doing so already fail to do God's will. They do the best they can, which means whatever they themselves think is the best they can in the given situation. In this way they make the radical demands practicable for themselves through casuistry.

They accomplish this by taking their bearings from individual traditions. From the many bits of tradition they select those that seem to fit their particular situation. It is not hard to find something appropriate, for there are many differences and occasional contradictions between these traditions, as far as practice is concerned. To give an example concerning the "ideal of poverty," did Jesus *always* oppose possessions, and did he *always* (in a biased way) take sides against the rich?

Yet there is also the saying that we should make friends for ourselves even by means of dishonest wealth (Luke 16:9). But people who sell what they have and give to the poor (Mark 10:21) miss out on this opportunity. And did Jesus not also accept the company of the rich by inviting tax collectors to his table, that is, people who gained power over others by leasing their offices and obtained riches through injustice? Was Jesus impartial after all, since he *also* accepted such people?

To interpret "but I say to you" as an expression of Jesus' claim of authority to radicalize the law by making the commandments more strict is to misunderstand Jesus' "rigorism." For in this case the only people who do God's will would be those who really and fully obey these rigorous regulations without mitigation or a reduction to striving for the best possible fulfillment—in other words, no one. Rather, we have to understand "but I say to you" in a much more fundamental sense, namely, christologically and thus theologically. Then and *only* then will it really lead ethics away from the ethic of contemporary Judaism (even in its ideal form).

In these traditions Jesus was understood as someone who put *himself* in the place of the Mosaic law and therefore opposed the observance of the law on principle. This was not to criticize the law itself, however, but the *God* behind *this* law. So the polemic against the law is a theological polemic against the lawgiver. Yet it is not directed against the God who had *earlier* given the law to Moses. In Jesus' time that God is not even in the picture, for in the meantime the image of the lawgiver has changed. Instead, the target of the polemic against the law is the lawgiver who makes a person's strict observance of every commandment the precondition for granting communion with himself.

Hence we must not abbreviate the discussion of the law, as is almost always done. In such discussion God is always "implied" but rarely expressly mentioned, and the term *God* is not defined at all. The question of the particular image of God is omitted.

Yet if we include the question of God in this discussion, it becomes clear that Jesus cannot have been understood as someone who proclaimed a God who had rigorous demands instead of a God who had moderate demands (Hillel) or one with stricter demands (Shammai). Rather, Jesus was understood as someone who proclaimed the God who offered his fellowship and thus the God who invited the people to live in communion with him.

This means, with regard to the initial question of this section, that Jesus did not urge people to social action. He was understood rather as someone who invited people to a life in communion with his God. But wherever this was practiced, it could result in what we call social action.

In regard to this "change of gods" we can almost speak of a logical argumentation. The presuppositions of contemporary Judaism were taken more seriously here than by those who lived with them. Yet this is exactly what reduced these presuppositions to absurdity and proved them untenable.

> In talking *about* God, when God is understood as the one who at an earlier time gave the law, then in the present people are dealing only with the law and not directly with God. (This is not changed by the fact that people sometimes talked about God's being present in the law.) If we logically think through this concept of God (who is being talked *about* when he is called the lawgiver), then (for the sake of this God) his law must be incapable of fulfillment by human beings. Faced with such a God, people can only be subject to judgment. Hence this God, who is being talked *about* (and about whom we must then talk *logically*), cannot be the God of the people. He is and remains separated from them. With the things that follow "but I say to you," *this* God is reduced to absurdity.
>
> Hence "but I say to you" expresses a theological claim of authority. This expression does not simply replace the law, it replaces the lawgiver together with his law. This alone creates immediacy. But immediacy with Jesus is at once by its very nature immediacy with the God of Jesus. Now we are really dealing with theology, that is, with talk *of* God. And we arrive at this theology through Christology. So we can say that Jesus was understood as someone who tried to change contemporary talk *about* God back into talk *of* God.

Thus the real issue is a different God; this must not be overlooked when we discuss the problem of the law. We are no longer dealing with a God who makes demands, but with one who offers eschatological existence and invites people to accept his offer (that is, to believe in him). Since people cannot achieve eschatological existence by themselves, they can be helped neither by concrete commandments that they must observe nor by prohibitions that they must not violate.

*(5) Mark 10:2-9.* This is the very point that is usually overlooked in the discussion about divorce. It is true that the bit of tradition in Mark 10:2-9 closes with the saying, "Therefore what God has joined together, let no one separate." This supports the understanding that here we have an absolute prohibition of divorce.

This understanding is already very old and is reflected in various segments of tradition. The author of Mark 10:10-12, for instance, wanted to expand the prohibition of divorce that he saw in Mark 10:9. Though in the Jewish world only men were able to divorce their wives (apart from negligible, complicated exceptions), women had the same right according to Hellenistic and Roman laws. So the author of Mark 10:10-12 believed that divorce should not only be forbidden to men but also to women.

The same understanding (general prohibition of divorce) is also found in Matthew. This is clear from the third antithesis, which was composed by the Evangelist (Matt. 5:31-32). Yet Matthew already sees the difficulty that arises if this prohibition is observed as a generally valid prohibition. In order to solve the problem he resorts to casuistry by specifying an exception. The prohibition does not apply in cases of "unchastity" (5:32, 19:9). A prohibition of divorce seems to be impracticable without casuistry.

Yet can we really speak of a prohibition of divorce? The text of Mark 10:2-9 itself shows that this result comes only from a superficial examination. Here again the real issue is eschatological existence.

Jesus is asked by Pharisees whether a man is allowed to divorce his wife. The text states expressly that they are doing this in order to test him.

This question cannot have been asked out of the blue, as it were, for it was the usual and undisputed practice that a Jewish man could send his wife away. So if the narrator has the Pharisees ask this question, we can assume that somehow the problem of divorce has been discussed before and has been connected with Jesus. Therefore Jesus was open to attack. If he really did forbid divorce, they could accuse him of opposing a regulation laid down in the law. So the test was to find out whether Jesus was opposed to the law.

Jesus does not give a direct answer but starts a discussion about the law by asking for Moses' *commandment*. Yet instead of citing this, the Pharisees state that Moses *allowed* a man to write a divorce certificate and send his wife away.

> Yet according to Deut. 24:1-4, there is no "allowance," but even there an existing practice is presupposed. One is only required to write a certificate of divorce. This is commanded.

It is noteworthy that in his answer Jesus in no way opposes Moses' commandment, but rather points out why and under what conditions this commandment was given. And here something happens that we have mentioned many times before. Attention is directed away from the actual deed (writing of the certificate of divorce) and toward the doer, toward the men's hardness of heart. This is what made the commandment necessary. And, indeed, if such hardness exists, this commandment gives crucial help to the woman. Only if the husband writes her a certificate of divorce does the wife have the right to remarry.

Let us translate this. In the old aeon there is hardness of heart. People who live in the old aeon are sinners, and they are always dealing with sinners. This constantly endangers coexistence, but this danger can be met with rules. In the social situation of that time, the requirement of writing a divorce certificate was a good rule. Modern divorce laws can give better rules, but it is still a question of rules written for the hardness of heart, that is, for sinners, for people living in this old world.

Jesus criticizes the law by directing attention away from the deed and towards the doer. Anyone who observes the law always does the will of the God who gave the law. But the will of Jesus' God concerns the doer. Then, however, the question is not, What do we do when a marriage fails? but rather, How can we remove hardness of heart? This cannot be done by directing concrete action. For this reason that question is not answered; instead, an alternative image is drawn.

At the beginning of creation (mythologically: in paradise) things were different from the way they are in this fallen aeon. The people were different. In paradise the man and the woman lived in communion (together with God!). But when they live in this community of three, that is, when the man and the woman are not sinners, a divorce of the man and the woman is inconceivable.

Let us translate this again. The present aeon commenced with the fall of humanity. The people living in this aeon are sinners and will be sinners until the turn of the aeon. The kingdom of God, expected thereafter, will be identical with paradise in its content; people will live in communion with God again. This is the point of departure that must be presupposed. Not only is the present time taken completely seriously, but also the people living in this present time and the possibilities they have in this present time. They can live by (good) rules, and they can only be encouraged to do so.

The gospel that is proclaimed (in this piece of tradition also) is an announcement of time. The kingdom of God (paradise) will come to the people in the form of God's lordship. When a man and a woman let this happen to them, a broken marriage can become whole again. Then no man will separate what God has joined and holds together. So the image of life in paradise can only be understood as an invitation. There is no command to hard-hearted people to live in the old aeon by the rules of paradise.

It is only on the surface that this segment of tradition contains a prohibition of divorce. If we were to interpret it in this way, it would mean that through the observance of this prohibition people could create paradise themselves. And they could do this because they would be able on their own to free themselves from their hardness of heart through their own doing (or not doing). This, however, would be an attempt by sinners at self-redemption.

*(6) Mark 12:13-17.* A discussion about an entirely different topic (but still with a very similar argumentation) shows that

the present old aeon is taken seriousy as the old aeon and that eschatological existence is only possible as an interruption of this aeon. This is the discussion of the tax coin (Mark 12:13-17). It ends with the well-known, much-quoted, yet often misused statement: "Give to the emperor the things that are the emperor's and to God the things that are God's." Even though this saying is the gist of the discussion, we must not use it in isolation.

It has sometimes been assumed that originally this saying actually circulated independently. Then the discussion would be an "ideal scene" that was formed around the saying. Would that not give us the right to treat the saying in isolation? This, however, would only seem to be the case.

We have to assume that this saying originated in a concrete situation. (The same applies, by the way, to a number of other sayings that we can reconstruct from the Gospels as independent sayings.) Since this situation is no longer known, the saying has become ambiguous in isolation from its context; hence an exegesis is no longer possible.

We have to proceed from the prior discussion, secondary or not, in order to determine how Jesus' activity was understood. It follows from this that we can use the saying (today) at our discretion and for different arguments if we disregard the preceding discussion. Therefore we cannot really base anything on the saying.

Since the final saying forms the climax of the discussion, we will approach the problem from there. The real problem is the word *and*. Does it express a coordination? Then we could be talking about two (separate?) realms. The people have duties (e.g., political ones) towards Caesar (the nation) and are admonished to do these. Also, they have (at the same time or in addition?) duties towards God.

This understanding (or a similar one) was no doubt often in favor. While referring to this saying, the government could demand loyalty from Christians. Similarly, as citizens Christians could use this saying to explain why they obey the present government (often with reservation, but nonetheless): we simply have to give to the emperor the things that are the emperor's.

Yet how does the second clause fit in with the first? Is there in addition a duty to God? Then we would really have two realms. Or is the second clause supposed to restrict the first one? But who determines the boundary? It would make sense to render to God the things that are God's, but what are they?

In any case, the conspicuous thing about this saying is that even if we assume the coordination of two different realms, there is a crucial difference. From the context (and only from the context) we can see unambiguously what specific obligations are owed to the emperor: the taxes have to be paid. But what exactly are one's obligations toward God? They are not specified. Thus the second clause is incomplete. It cannot refer back to the first clause. God may not be used as an argument if we are talking about duties toward the nation.

The dispute begins with this very problem. People sent by Pharisees and Herodians approach Jesus "to entrap him in what he said." They start with compliments, saying that Jesus is "sincere," shows "deference to no one," does "not regard people with partiality," and teaches "the way of God in accordance with truth." Then they ask two questions. The first one is basic: "Is it lawful to pay taxes to the emperor, or not?" The second is specific, for now the speakers ask for themselves. "Should we pay [the taxes], or should we not?"

We must see the introductory compliments and the two questions as a unit. Then we will understand that these people want a *theological* answer to a *political* question. Thus the questions really have to be understood as follows: "Does *God* permit the paying of taxes to the emperor?" "Are we doing *God's* will if we pay taxes?"

We must pay attention to the context in which these questions are asked and in which they become possible and make sense, namely, within the concept of theocracy. The law of God is at the same time the law of the state. This is relatively unproblematic if the religious and secular authorities are either identical or work so closely together that theological decisions (e.g., by the scribes) are binding on the executive branch and are also accepted by it as binding. It becomes a problem, however, if these authorities (in modern terms, church and state) are separated. This was the case in Jesus' time (at least in part) because of the Roman occupation. The question then was whether the theocratic ideal could be realized anyway. The people would have liked it. Yet it would necessarily have created many conflicts with the Romans.

Now it is characteristic that Jesus does not deal with the first (and basic) question at all, but begins with the specific one. Here again we find what we have seen a number of times already. Attention is directed from the deed to the doers. They are requested to take a denarius out of their pockets and then are asked about the image and inscription on the coin.

At that time the denarius bore the image of the emperor and the inscription, "Tiberius, Caesar, son of the divine Augustus, chief priest."

Now the deceit of the question is revealed. The questioners have a denarius and say themselves that it bears the emperor's image. With this they show (and must admit) that they already rely on the emperor and his money. It is insincere for them to pretend that this is a theological problem still to be resolved; they have already resolved it for themselves.

According to the theology of the inquirers (in a theocracy), the answer should have been that the taxes must not be paid, least of all with this coin, for they were not even allowed to touch it. Yet anyone who gave this answer in public could count on being denounced to the Romans. Now, however, the "theology" of the inquirers has been revealed. They do not hold to the God who they allege is their God.

So for the questioners it is not really a theological issue. In theory they would not admit this, but in fact they must. Their pretended theology (as talk of God) turns out to be talk about God. They have already removed the God they are talking about from the problem.

This is where Jesus' answer is to the point. The inquirers live without God and thus in the old aeon, and it is only fair that they go by the rules of this aeon. If they accept advantages from the emperor (i.e., the state)—and money is one of them—then they should behave properly toward the emperor (the state).

We must note that the inquirers are criticized neither for having a denarius nor for having this particular, most scandalous denarius. Yet there is no concession that they may possess denarii. Nor are they granted permission to operate in this old aeon. Rather, Jesus simply states that this is the way it is in this world. In *this* world. Contrary to what the inquirers pretend—but prove wrong by owning a denarius—this has nothing at all to do with God.

If Jesus now tells them to give to the emperor the things that are the emperor's, he does not say that this is how God's will is done. God did not command the paying of taxes to the emperor. This was worked out by the people among themselves and cannot all of a sudden be given theological dignity.

Yet even if the questioners have joined a humanly devised order by using the denarius, they are not spared the question of God. To live in this world (*really* to live in this world) does not have to mean becoming a slave to this world. Yet this danger exists, and it is especially acute when we are able to live in this world by practicable rules. When that happens, we forget about God. We no longer realize that God wants to come with his lordship. This is the reason for the final clause, which really goes beyond the boundaries of the discussion: "And [give] to God the things that are God's."

So this clause does not restrict the first one. In the old aeon the first clause has its validity, and it will remain valid until the end of the old aeon. But the people who are not only living in the old aeon (everyone does that) but also know that they are living in the *old* aeon are asked to give God what belongs to God. And this is exactly what they are doing when in the old aeon they count on and wait for the lordship of God to break in again and again through them.

A theory about the relationship of Christians to the state (if there is such a theory at all) cannot be based on this dispute in Mark. Even the situation is entirely different today. Our state is not a theocracy (much less a theocracy threatened by an occupying power). Yet this dialogue could perhaps warn us against a danger from the opposite direction, as it were: we must resist the temptation to argue theocratically (which is not at all so rare). This happens whenever Christians give to the state (which understands itself as a secular state) specifications that are called God's will and demand that the state turn them, and *only* them, into laws that apply to *all* citizens. If this is what we understand by "political theology," then we are standing side by side with those who asked Jesus about taxes. This kind of political theology is only possible in a theocracy. Do we want this? With this dialogue we can argue against it.

As we have seen, Jesus' answer does not elaborate on what it means concretely to render to God the things that are God's. The second clause only keeps the question of God open and thus says nothing other than what is asked for in the second petition of the Lord's Prayer, "Thy kingdom come." People who live in this old world ask this, for they know they live in this *old* world. In other words, it is the prayer of all who are sinners. As sinners they cannot do God's will at all, because they are always doing their own. Even the best that *they* can do will always be the deeds of sinners. Hence *sinners* can only endeavor to organize their coexistence as well as possible.

Several individual traditions confirm that people (as sinners) can indeed be successful at this. For example, sinners love those who love them in return; sinners do good to those who do good to them; sinners lend to other sinners in order to receive from them (Luke 6:32-34; cf. Matt. 5:46-47). Even those who are evil (i.e., sinners) know how to give good gifts to their children (Luke 11:13; Matt. 7:11). The old aeon is misrepresented if we assume that the people who live in it only act unjustly.

When sinners, however, *believe* that they are sinners, they pray, "Thy kingdom come."

Luther explains exactly what they are asking for here: God's kingdom will indeed come by itself without our prayers. But with this prayer we are asking that it also come *to us*.

Yet wherever God's kingdom breaks into the sinners' world in the form of God's lordship, sinners turn into *sons of God* and render to God the things that are God's. Since, however, this is always beyond the people's control, they can never determine beforehand exactly what has to be done to make eschatological existence happen. In several bits of tradition, however, we do find expressions (even if in varied form) of the particularities of eschatological existence.

*(7) Luke 16:1-8.* The parable of the dishonest manager (Luke 16:1-8) tells about a manager who had deceived his employer, a rich man. Now the employer announces that he will check the accounts. Before this happens, the manager falsifies the promissory notes in favor of his employer's debtors, so that they will take him in when he is fired. The story culminates with the statement, "His master [i.e., Jesus] commended the dishonest manager because he had acted shrewdly; for the children of this age [Greek: *aion*] are more shrewd in dealing with their own generation [= their kind] than are the children of light."

We must pay close attention to the point of comparison. The dishonest manager is, of course, not praised because he added one more instance of cheating to his record. Rather, he is praised because he quickly and resolutely did the right thing in a situation that was difficult for him. And he did what he did based on his own assumptions, that is, as a "child of this aeon." But this poses the question, Will the "children of light," based on their assumptions, do as quickly and resolutely what is right for them in a difficult situation? Or will they act as children of the old aeon and resort to the means of the old aeon? This inconsistency can be found more frequently with the children of light than with the children of this aeon.

Thus one characteristic of eschatological existence is in the concrete situation to rely quickly and resolutely on the God who offers his communion. What is important is the now: to recognize this now as the now of God and act with "shrewdness." For when this moment arrives, it is not prudent to ally oneself with the old aeon. Do the children of light resist this temptation?

*(8) Mark 12:41-44.* In this moment it is really all or nothing. This is illustrated by the story of the "widow's mite." In the Temple court many rich people put a lot of money into the treasury, but the widow gives only two coins of little value. Jesus' saying interprets the situation with a comparison. The widow gave more than anyone else: the others contributed out of their abundance; the widow, by contrast, gave everything she had.

At first glance we could give the following interpretation. The widow was a model of giving. Whoever imitates her will not, of course, achieve what she achieved, but with comparable effort may perhaps at least get close. Yet this misunderstands the story, for it is not a question of "a little bit more" but "everything." Nor may we develop the story further, as it were, and ask who took care of the destitute widow afterwards. For then we would be looking—however subtly—for something like reinsurance.

How much more the widow gave cannot be calculated quantitatively; the point, rather, is the quality of her action. This is immediately underlined by the remark that she gave her whole *bios*. The Greek word has two meanings, "life" and "subsistence." She gave herself completely, and this is precisely what matters in eschatological existence. Those who rely on it give themselves up totally. It is not a question of something that people have (even if this something is all they have), but of nothing less than the people themselves.

Thus we indeed have here a christological statement, even if an indirect one. Jesus is presented as someone who points to the widow. But the author's presentation points to Jesus. He was experienced as someone who again and again gave himself completely.

*(9) Mark 11:27-33.* Only people who involve themselves can give themselves completely. Only in this way is discipleship possible. An illustration of this is the traditional question about Jesus' authority (Mark 11:27-33). Chief priests, scribes, and elders (i.e., representatives of contemporary Judaism) ask Jesus about his authority and who gave it to him. They expect a direct answer (as did the Baptist in jail; cf. p. 78 above). After it is given, they can consider it and then decide one way or the other. First, however, Jesus asks them a counterquestion: "Did the baptism of John come from heaven, or was it of human origin?" This choice is awkward, for both answers have consequences for the people who are asked. If they say "from heaven," they must admit their own failure, because they did not listen to John. If they say "of human origin," they must fear the people, who consider John a prophet. They avoid the issue by saying, "We do not know." Jesus' response is surprising, for at this point he closes the door, as it were, and breaks off the discussion, saying, "Neither will I tell you by what authority I am doing these things."

So the chief priests, scribes, and elders do not learn by what authority Jesus acts and who gave him this authority. The discussion reveals them as people who do not want to commit themselves or get involved. They want to keep their distance. But with this attitude they can never learn the source of Jesus' authority, because this can only be learned by relying on Jesus. People who instead first demand a legitimation from Jesus, in order to verify it, are not ready to commit themselves and get involved as committed persons, without considering the consequences. These people will never know the lordship of God. For only those who accept the risk of eschatological existence can experience eschatological existence as *eschatological* existence.

*(10) Summary.* Our examples exhibit one common feature: if we analyze the individual tradition in a "dogmatically guided" way (cf. p. 90 above), that is, christologically, based on the *one* image of Jesus or, with regard to ethics, on eschatological existence, we always find the same pattern. The obvious inquiry into the deed is pushed aside; instead, we take a look at the

doer. In the first place it is not a matter of *what* should be done, but of *who* is doing it.

Is it a *neighbor?* Is it people who expect the coming of God's lordship among themselves? Is it people who have let themselves be changed by God? Is it people who let their hardness of heart be taken from them? Is it people who are ready to get involved now and completely? In sum, are the doers *Christians?*

We can see now that the question about people must first be answered before we can discuss their deeds. But are we not in danger (at least according to the discussion so far) of concentrating our interest on people and completely forgetting about deeds? Since it is indeed important to do something, we may defer, but not dismiss, the question of *what* should be done. Yet can it be answered? And how can it be answered?

We will try to pursue this problem with a few systematic reflections.

### b) Excursus: Orientation Models for Sinners

Since the crucial point is always the connection between doer and deed, we cannot treat the deed in isolation. That means, however, that no deed can be called Christian in itself if Christian means eschatological existence. Otherwise anyone could copy the deed or be told to copy it. And then eschatological existence would be within the power of human beings.

It is possible, of course, for people to observe or experience an action and see in that action an eschatological event. Yet this is their statement of faith, and they can make it because they know about eschatological existence themselves. Here they see "God at work." This may even be the case if the doer of the deed does not realize this. We will not elaborate this point further, however, since our topic is ethics.

Hence we cannot speak of "Christian" action, "Christian" politics, "Christian" upbringing, and the like, but only of Christians who act, who are politically active, who raise children, and so forth. If we understand this, we should also use the language accordingly.

At the same time we have to see the problems here. The first question is whether, after all we have said so far, we can state that someone *is* a Christian. Is it not always true, rather, that we can only *become* real Christians ever anew, since being a Christian is not a permanent condition? Then if we are talking about the actions of a real Christian, we have to explain *when* they are possible. The other problem arises when we not only look at the people who act but also (in connection with them) at their action. It cannot be arbitrary, after all. Hence we must also ask again what genuine Christian actions are. Yet are we not going in a circle here? Can we break out of it?

We will try to do this through a definition: A nominal Christian as a sinner who is waiting to become a real Christian.

Of course, we must not understand this in the pharisaical sense that permeates our language. In this sense *sinner* is always a negative qualification because the term is applied to people who have violated commandments that must be observed. But if instead we define a sinner as one who lives in this old aeon far from God, then there is also a positive aspect. For now the only people who can call themselves sinners are those who know that they have already experienced the repeated inbreaking of God's lordship into their lives. They know what happened during this inbreaking of Jesus' God into their lives. They know that *then* they were able to be neighbors, and they know how this was realized concretely in their deeds. They know that then the hardness of their hearts was taken away, and how that resulted in concrete action, which they can now describe (in retrospect!). Only because they know these things is it at all possible for them to say that they are sinners. Since they could not maintain the *kairos,* they are left with *kairoi* that could not become permanent. These people must understand their present situation as lacking, yet it is not totally lacking. Since in the past they experienced the inbreaking of Jesus' God into their lives, as sinners they have a well-founded hope that in the future they will also be able to count on such experiences. They have this hope only as sinners!

This is illustrated, for example, by the tradition of the transfiguration of Jesus (Mark 9:2-8). Jesus' companions could not see from his human appearance who he really was. Now, for once, the curtain is drawn back from their eyes. They see the transfigured One, the one through whom God comes to them. Peter would like to seize this moment and build dwellings, for "He did not know what to say." He expected something impossible. Such a *kairos* cannot last in this old aeon, so the curtain closes again. From heaven, however, they hear a voice that invites them to renewed listening.

If "former Christians" are thus now sinners again, they must still act and continually make decisions. What guidelines can they follow?

In order to answer this question we will make a distinction that may seem somewhat odd; it is not very precise, either, but it can be helpful. We will distinguish between *sinners* and *children of the world*. The two have in common that they live apart from God. The difference is that sinners suffer from this separation, while children of the world have somehow accepted it. Their two situations are by no means the same. Yet the distinction is not an evaluation but only a description.

The term *children of the world* does not refer to people who have become, so to speak, indifferent toward God. It is just that they are not thinking of him at the moment. Apparently people cannot suffer continually from their separation from God; hence they do not always think, in regard to what they are doing, about the fact that they are doing it apart from God. Thus not everything that they do apart from God is an "immoral" action. Children of the world know that it is sensible and indispensable for coexistence in this world to live by certain rules, including those that are customary among them and conform to their order. This is a sphere of life that has often developed through long tradition, and most of the time we live in it without even being aware of it. Hence it is wrong to try to relate decisions in *this* sphere directly to God. When we do that, we always run the danger of identifying moral action with doing the will of God. Acting morally almost always means acting according to human conventions. These can change in the course of time, very often from one generation to the next.

Yet from time to time God is noticed; then (and only then!) a child of the world will realize, "I am a sinner." This sentence is always a confession that a person makes in a specific moment.

> Hence this confession is totallly different from the occasional statement, "We are all sinners." This sentence is understood mostly in a pharisaical sense: we all keep violating the commandments. And in this way it can even be used as an excuse for our obvious failure. Human beings, after all, are not perfect.

Yet if in a concrete situation people admit that they are sinners, they reach this conclusion by way of comparison. They compare their present situation with the one they were in when they accepted the God's lordship and the God of Jesus came into their lives. From their experience at that time they know that he is always ready to come to them. Yet he does not come, and his coming cannot be forced.

For this reason sinners are suffering from God's absence. We must be precise here: they are not just saying that they are suffering; they are really suffering. They are calling out to God.

Children of the world who confess, "I am a sinner," have become nominal Christians. They could become nominal Christians because they look back to when they became real Christians a number of times before. And now these nominal Christians (the sinners!) are waiting to become real Christians again. And this is precisely what cannot be forced.

Yet they still must act. But what are they supposed to do? Since the God of Jesus is not at their disposal, they need orientation models.

> This does not mean what is often found in the question, "What should (or must) a Christian do?" This question usually presupposes that the term *Christian* is unambiguous. Yet since this is clearly wrong, we get different answers. It is not wrong, however, because we cannot agree on exactly what to do but because we do not give enough attention to

the doer. We have to realize that a nominal Christian who is preparing for action is a sinner who is waiting to become a real Christian.

Hence such sinners are looking for orientation models. Where can they find them?

The first (provisional) answer is: in their own past. For sinners now remember the experiences they had when they became involved with the God of Jesus. These experiences occurred in concrete actions, and the sinners can now describe and portray these actions.

Yet one's own experience is always limited; younger people have less than older people, but they can still help each other, for example, through what we call pastoral care. Among Christians pastoral care refers to the sharing of experiences with God. Pastors can uncover such experiences in those to whom they are giving pastoral care. Or they can share other experiences. These do not have to be their own, though it can be helpful to use one's own experiences. A pastor, however, is also the mediator of others' experiences, such as those that his contemporaries had when they got involved with God or those of people in earlier times, going back to the people who formed the old Jesus images.

For the Jesus images that speak of concrete actions express experiences that people had earlier when there was an inbreaking of God's lordship into their lives. And sinners then have to consider whether to act according to these Jesus images and to use them as orientation models.

We should note carefully that they are orientation *models* and nothing more. There are two reasons for this.

First, we have to remember that we are just dealing with the final stage of a coherent process. The entire process goes as follows. The lordship offered by God breaks in in a person's turning around and is realized in a visible action. We can see this action only in its concrete, visible form, which we may not isolate and try to copy.

For if we take our bearings from the concrete actions that we can see directly in these Jesus images, we end up with a law. And this law is then called God's will, and the doing of this will is termed Christian action. If we proceed in this way, we unknowingly change the image of God and turn the immediacy back into indirectness.

People who are guided by God act with immediacy. But people who act in the same way that a person guided by God acted in a concrete situation are no longer acting with immediacy to *God* but are guided by an *action* that has already occurred.

We now have these actions in writing; that is, we have texts. And guidance by a text may not be equated with guidance by God. This error is widespread, but people disguise it by calling the New Testament God's word. As a consequence, an action based on the New Testament (or the Bible) is called a Christian action. In reality, however, a text has now taken the place of God, as was the case in the Judaism of Jesus' time, when people talked about God's presence in the law.

Since the key to eschatological existence is immediacy, we must not understand the actions we see in Jesus images as instructions, but always as orientation models. As such they are helpful, but we must not overburden them.

And there is a second reason. If, in the context of these models, sinners decide upon an action, it does not mean that this action causes God's lordship to break in. Any such claim would be an attempt to gain control over God. Hence no action can force the coming of God's lordship—not even one based on the orientation models. They are certainly a help, but it is sinners who use this help.

If we remember this, it will be easier to deal with two problems that especially today are hard to overcome.

The first problem is ambiguity in ethical decisions. People who consider their concrete actions on the basis of these orientation models have to decide between different options. But other people have the same problem. Hence it is not only possible, but will actually happen, that people will make different decisions again and again. They will discuss their decisions and hopefully really talk with each other.

And now it all depends on whether they know the kind of person they are as they talk, namely, sinners. As sinners they suffer from the fact that by their efforts they cannot live with God, although they would like to. They do not control him. Hence they know why unambiguous decisions are not possible. Each person tries as well as possible to be guided by the available orientation models. But they do not write each other off because of different decisions. They know that they are sinners.

If they assume that they *are* Christians, their communion is immediately in danger of breaking up. For if someone is of a different opinion, the question arises whether this person can still be called a Christian. The claim to *be* a Christian often proves to be destructive for the communion. (The problems between denominations are a case in point.) Sinners, on the other hand, can maintain a communion, even though it is the communion of sinners.

So we may ask whether discussions within our church (for instance on political issues) are often unpleasant and awkward because we almost always discuss different opinions of what has to be done (which we claim to be God's will). And we do not take into consideration the fact that *every* decision is a decision of sinners.

Sinners will not be divided by the realization that there are no clear decisions in ethical matters. A sinner must always be prepared for the possibility that the decision of another person could be right. And yet each must make his or her own decision and be responsible for it.

This brings us to the other problem, the conflict of duties. It arises especially when we consider not only what should be done (on the basis of the orientation models), but also what consequences our actions could have. (Here we will ignore consequences for the doers themselves, which will be treated in the following section.)

Usually the orientation models give us various options for concrete actions. In our choice we must look not only into the past, in which the orientation models originated, but also into the future. Thus we necessarily face the question, What consequences will a specific action have? And the answer to this question will determine our decision. Therefore we can and must make various judgments, but will they be correct? Who can predict future consequences with the necessary certainty?

A very simple example is telling the truth to people who are sick. Usually the question is, Should a terminally ill patient be told the truth? Yet in this general form (once again the question concerns only the doing itself) the question leads us very quickly into casuistry. And no one is confronted with this general question anyway, for it is always particular people who face this problem. So the question should read (for example), Should I tell my sick father the truth about his condition, and should I do it now?

If we look for orientation models, we will quickly find (at least) two options. (1) Since in the kingdom of God yes is yes and no is no (cf. Matt. 5:37), I can count on the lordship of God occurring (perhaps) most likely if in this particular case I let yes be yes and no be no. Will this not be doing God's will? (2) Since in the kingdom of God the greatest person is the one who is everyone's servant (Mark 10:43), I can count on the lordship of God occurring (perhaps) most likely if I now do whatever serves my sick father. Will this not be doing God's will?

Yet at this point we are already in the middle of the problem. Am I really serving my sick father when I tell him the truth? Or am I serving him when I turn yes into no and no into yes? But then my actions are clearly contrary to the first orientation model. Does that model not correspond to God's will? Or not always? But when does it? I must decide.

Is my decision also binding for others, for example, for physicians or nurses? Here too, everyone must make an individual decision in each case.

Thus it is totally impossible to designate a certain decision as God's will. For God's will cannot be concretely determined. Yet people who consider themselves Christians are especially inclined to make this very claim for their decisions. Sinners, on the other hand, realize that in this old aeon they are not in a position to state God's will unambiguously and specifically. However they decide, they always decide as sinners. Hence all of their deeds are done in sin, and they must accept the responsibility for the consequences. A hopeless situation?

Not for sinners! For they can look back on the experiences they had when they got involved with the God of Jesus; miraculously, God's lordship occurred. For this reason sinners have orientation models from their own past and from the experiences of others. These models can help them make concrete decisions. The more they have followed these models in their lives, the easier it will be for them to make their decisions.

Sinners know of course that they cannot take a decision they have made with the help of the orientation models and immediately understand it as God's will. Therefore these models are not imperatives to be followed in the name of God. Rather, they are invitations. Since God's lordship occurred in these concrete forms earlier, sinners can hope that the very same thing will happen again.

This does not neutralize the risk of a decision, but for sinners it is a trusting risk. Sinners trust the God of Jesus even when they run the risk of a wrong decision. But since they have not made the decision lightly, they can hope that the miracle will happen again: in the deed they learn that they have acted as real Christians.

## c) The Consequences of Eschatological Existence

When people act, they are pursuing a goal. In doing specifically what they are doing, they would like to reach that goal. Only when they have reached that goal can and will they talk about success. The goal sought after generally lies in the future. Can it be reached?

If we base our actions on "orientation models for sinners," we may possibly be successful. We always have a variety of options from which to choose. In our selection we consider the final goal and choose the course that has the most promise of success. Yet is this also true for eschatological existence?

This question can be answered only in the context of Christology, and as a start we can state it rather simply. Did Jesus succeed in his actions?

Even in answering this question we must make a christological decision. We can see this right away if we understand the problems in many contemporary reflections on Christian ethics. If, for example, we understand Jesus as someone who tried to establish justice or peace on earth, we have to say that he did not reach his goal. His work failed in his time and remains a failure today. So our conclusion would be (if we agree with the goal) that Christians now have to finish what Jesus tried but unfortunately failed to accomplish. Yet is this not too big a task? And why do we call this a task specifically for Christians? All people of good will are striving for this goal.

There is no doubt that in the design of such an ethic we can appeal to individual Jesus images in the synoptic tradition. In our discussion thus far, however, this has turned out to be problematic. We must instead take our bearings from the summaries or the overall picture, which shows that Jesus' way ended on the cross. In view of what we can see, this means that Jesus did not succeed but failed.

*(1) The cross of Jesus as an ethical problem.* If we include the cross of Jesus in our discussion of Christology and thus of ethics, we must pay attention to two diverse lines of tradition that must not be confused. This can easily happen if we talk indiscriminately of a theology of the cross. This term is too ambiguous and, if used indiscriminately, too dangerous, because misunderstandings then become almost inevitable. By making distinctions we will try to clarify this problem as much as possible.

*(a)* It is correct to say that Jesus' way was a way to the cross. We must remember, however, that this statement could only be made in retrospect, for during his earthly activity Jesus' way into the future was still open. There was no telling in advance how it would end. Theoretically, many possibilities were conceivable. Hence we have to distinguish between two assertions: that Jesus was active and on his way, and that Jesus' way ended on the cross.

(*b*) Only after Jesus had been crucified was it possible to look back and say that his way was a way that ended with his death on the cross. Yet even in retrospect we still have to make a distinction. One can look at Jesus' entire way to the cross, as the Gospels do. Or one can look only at the cross and then ask, How could this man Jesus have ended up on the cross? This was the case in some pre-Pauline traditions and also in Paul. Here Jesus' way plays no role, but only the cross, which is now interpreted as "salvific event." So we can interpret both Jesus' way and the cross.

(*c*) In the texts this distinction corresponds to the two lines of tradition. The interpretation of Jesus' death as a dying "for many" is found, as we said, only in the line of tradition to which Paul belongs, and throughout this line. (The significance of this for ethics will be discussed later in the context of Paul's ethics.) In the synoptic material (i.e., in the "Galilean" tradition) this motif does not appear, except for Mark 10:45; 14:24. So we may assume that it was not originally a part of this tradition. It is a foreign element that was imported into these two places from the line of tradition represented by Paul.

(*d*) The difficulties arose when the two themes were later mixed. Since Jesus' death was understood afterward as a salvific death, this interpretation was added to Jesus' way. Because of this Jesus was seen as someone who consciously directed his way toward the cross and thus intended to die on the cross. For his work had only one aim: to accomplish through his expiatory death the reconciliation of the people with God.

> This Jesus image is widespread at least in the consciousness of the church. It is reflected in many passion hymns and reinforced by singing these hymns (and often by imprecise language in sermons). We rarely think of the consequences. Does it not make Jesus' activity before his crucifixion unimportant? Its only remaining significance is preparation for the crucifixion as the real climax.
>
> Thus this dogmatic construction, which resulted from combining the interpretations, must be untangled once again.

If we look only at the synoptic tradition, we must assert that Jesus was understood as someone whose work had its own significance and did not need later expansion or completion. Thus he was not understood as someone who wanted death and whose work received its real and deepest meaning only through his death on the cross.

Looking at the summaries of the individual traditions, we can indeed say that Jesus was understood as someone who wanted to reconcile the people with God, but *through his activity,* and who therefore wanted people to be able to live and act as people reconciled with God. He was understood this way even before his death (and without any reflection on the possibility of death).

Only when Jesus' activities could be seen as a whole and presented in order as his way, was the end of this way also included in the presentation. Only then did the cross become a christological and thus also an ethical problem in this line of tradition. The cross could have been regarded an unforeseen, abrupt termination of the work, as a misfortune. Yet this did not happen. Rather, on the basis of the cross, Jesus' work, which in the end led to the cross, was interpreted in a more comprehensive fashion. People realized that expressed here was a characteristic aspect of Jesus' activity that they would not have seen without the cross, or at least not with such clarity.

For the time being we can reduce this aspect to a short formula. Revealed in this Jesus image was the risky nature of eschatological existence. Jesus had accepted the risk; therefore discipleship was not possible without accepting the risk.

*(2) Discipleship on the way to the cross.* If Jesus (according to Mark's summary) was regarded as someone who lived the lordship of God in the middle of the old aeon, this means that he opposed the old aeon and thereby provoked the old aeon's resistence to his activity and thus to himself. This resistance had different levels of intensity.

Here we must first mention the *disputes.* Jesus' healing on the sabbath has to disturb those who consider it God's will that all work, in whatever circumstances, must cease on the sabbath. Jesus' leniency or even negligence regarding fasting has to offend those who believe that people must do something to create communion with God, such as fasting or strictly observing the purity laws. It is unheard of for Jesus to invite to his table rich tax collectors, who are working for the occupying power, and at the same time sinners, that is, those who do not try hard enough to observe all the commandments earnestly. People who are serious about God do not do what Jesus does. People who are serious about God have to be biased (as we say today). The fact that Jesus is not puts him at odds with popular opinion.

So the protectors of the "divine order" turn against him. Yet we always have to remember that from their standpoint these people are right. Two "conceptions" confront each other here. On the one side are the representatives of an order that has developed during the course of a long history. For those on the other side, however, it is not a question of being oriented toward the law and toward an order determined by the law; they are concerned about orientation directly toward God.

These two conceptions are now in collision. In general, people who get involved with God and live the inbreaking of his lordship are tolerated. Perhaps they are called fanatics or firebrands or people especially committed to religion. Yet they become a problem when they question the view of others that an orientation toward Christian custom is in itself an orientation toward Jesus Christ; or, in Jesus' time, if they question the view of those who take their bearings from the law and believe that they are thereby dealing with God.

These examples should prevent shortsighted argumentation. For if we say that Jesus was understood as someone who lived the lordship of God in the middle of the old aeon and thereby provoked the resistance of the old aeon, then the old aeon is all too easily regarded as a (morally) corrupt world throughout. Yet the old aeon is not simply a world in which everything is a total mess, in which there is nothing but murder and killing, robbery and adultery, lies and deception. There is no question that such things *also* exist, but to describe the old aeon in this way is a caricature.

Rather, the old aeon is a world in which people can and do live in a quite orderly fashion. And if order in the old aeon is violated, the old aeon is able by itself to limit such problems and restore order. Things get dangerous only if decent, orderly people in this old aeon claim that this life is in accord with the will of God and others counter that this life has nothing to do with God. Now we have a dispute. People disagree about God. Who defines God correctly?

The disagreements begin verbally and argumentatively, and examples include the disputes in the Gospels. Here Jesus is presented as someone who risks the quarrel. And the large number of the disputes shows that he did this over and over again.

If we compile these disputes we can show that the quarrels got worse and in the end became more than disagreements. An example of this is Mark 2:1-3:6 (which probably goes back to a pre-Markan compilation). At the end of the disputes we read in 3:6 that the Pharisees went outside to hold counsel with the Herodians on how to destroy Jesus. The cross comes into view.

Since it is a quarrel over theology, however, the question is, Who defines God correctly? The answer is christological. Based on Jesus' activity in these disputes, which is understood as an eschatological activity, Jesus is qualified as the Son of man. The Son of man has the authority on earth to forgive sins (Mark 2:10). The Son of man is lord even (!) over the sabbath (2:28). Hence it is the Son of man whom the keepers of the law and of order want to destroy in the name of *their* God.

The fact that eschatological existence can lead to quarrels cannot be used as an argument against such activity. If we exist eschatologically, we run risk such quarrels, and we can accept the risk because the Son of man accepted it.

This idea is further developed by Mark in the so-called passion announcements. "Then [Jesus] began to teach them that the Son of Man must undergo great suffering, and be rejected by the elders, the chief priests, and the scribes, and be killed, and after three days rise again." (Mark 8:31; cf. 9:31, 10:33-34)

> To speak of "passion announcements" here can be misleading at least to the extent that one might think that Jesus' death was announced as a salvific death, but this is not the case. Instead we have an outline of Jesus' *way:* passion, rejection by the authorities, death, resurrection.

Jesus' way is interpreted twice. It is a road that he travels under God's command. Those who live God's lordship in the middle of the old aeon place themselves in opposition to the old aeon. Thus they must run the risk that the old aeon will rise up against them. At the same time the quality of this way is interpreted as qualifying Jesus on the basis of this way. It is the Son of man who follows this way. These interpretations complement each other.

Yet this Christology also has ethical implications. If we, like Jesus, travel this way, we must run the risk that our way will lead to what has the outward appearance of disaster. And yet God is with us on this way, for it is the way on which the work of the Son of man, eschatological existence, happens. Thus, contrary to all outward appearances, it is a glorious way. This is indicated by the prospect of our goal: resurrection.

The composition of Mark explicates the ethical aspect of Christology. Immediately after the first passion announcment comes Peter's protest; he rebukes Jesus (Mark 8:32). His protest is understandable, since it is really the most obvious reaction. Do people who follow God's way not have to be able to count on success, even for themselves? Yet this very thought is now revealed as a temptation by Satan, for if we think this way, we are not thinking like God but like human beings (Mark 8:33).

The conclusion is that if we want to follow Jesus on his way, we have to deny ourselves and take up our cross (Mark 8:34). Only in this way we can follow him. This is the consequence of eschatological existence. And we must not ignore this consequence when we discuss Christian ethics. Yet I fear that this is done much too often nowadays. We may be able to write a nominally Christian ethic in a way that promises success. For a genuinely Christian ethic, however, this will not work.

> For this reason a genuinely Christian ethic is ill suited for use, for example, in politics. What party could afford to recommend a political program that states openly that every person who adopts this program runs the risk of personal failure?

The only "success" promised to those who exist eschatologically is that they will have the opportunity to experience working with the God of Jesus in their very existence. At the same time it raises the possibility that other people will recognize this and be encouraged to accept the risk of eschatological existence for themselves.

And *this* was in fact the success that Jesus had.

# B. The Ethic of Paul

*a) Preliminary Considerations on Order*

After what was said in the previous chapter, we would have good reason to treat Paul's ethic under the heading of Part II: "Developments and False Developments." For Christian ethics began as ethics oriented toward Jesus. So we should ask whether or not Paul's ethic was faithful to this beginning. In any case, the Pauline ethic cannot be a norm for judging whether an ethic is Christian—at least not directly—because the apostle was already living in the Christian tradition and was not himself a part of its beginning. Nonetheless, there are four basic reasons for treating the ethic of Paul in Part I.

*The first reason* is a literary one. The oldest (extant!) documents come from Paul's pen.

*The second reason* is that we find a different Christology in Paul. Unavoidably the problem of Easter comes to our attention here, whereas it played no role at all in the Jesus images of the early synoptic tradition, even though they were written after the date(!) of Easter. We have already demonstrated that the entire ethic derived from those Jesus images can be developed without drawing on the Easter motif at all.

Yet we must stress the *motif!* For we can indeed ask whether the thing referred to by the motif was not there long before but was expressed quite differently. We are not yet able to discuss this point, but it should at least be suggested with an example. If Jesus was experienced as someone who even now lived the kingdom of God expected after the turn of the aeon and lived it repeatedly as the lordship of God, then this could also be expressed in Easter teminology by saying that Jesus

142

was experienced as someone who lived the life after the resurrection of the dead even now and repeatedly. Be that as it may, the resurrection of Jesus, as expressly stated in literature, is found for the first time in Paul.

Subsequently this special Christology represented by Paul became almost the only Christology accepted in the church. And this raises the question whether this different Christology also brings with it a different ethic.

*The third reason* results from the first two. With his letters Paul forms the starting point of a line of development that is reflected particularly in the epistolary literature of the New Testament. The apostle was influential not only in regard to literary forms but also through certain ideas. In short, since Paul without doubt presupposed what we call the resurrection of Jesus, this resurrection was often generally and fundamentally presupposed for anything that people have usually called Christian (even today). This poses the question whether there could be a (competing?) definition of the term *Christian* that is different from the one we have developed thus far and how these definitions relate to each other.

*The fourth reason,* finally, is Paul's self-understanding. He realizes, of course, that he cannot be counted among the "first generation," because he first persecuted the (already existing) church. Nevertheless, he claims that his apostleship has the same origin as that of the other apostles and substantiates this with his having "seen Jesus our Lord" (1 Cor. 9:1; cf. 1 Cor. 15:3-11). Is this only a defensive statement against the attacks of opponents? Or can we verify and substantiate this claim?

Thus it is advisable not to present Paul prematurely as someone already living in the Christian tradition. Even if this is doubtless the case, we will first present him as one who embodied a beginning.

### b) *Preliminary Considerations on Dividing the Material*

The seven extant letters of Paul form the point of departure for our presentation of the apostle's ethic. This observation is only apparently self-evident; only by remembering it can we avoid a premature systematization. For letters are not treatises that discuss a subject "academically" but communications in concrete and distinct situations. Thus all of Paul's comments on ethical issues are "incidental." They are incidental because they deal only with questions that are acute and are posed from the outside. And they are also incidental because they are discussed and substantiated in the way that Paul thinks necessary and appropriate in each particular case. This raises the question, How can we organize these at times seemingly disparate comments? In other words, is there a common center from which we can understand them?

There are two possible ways to find such a center. We can start with the letters and on that basis try somehow to sum up Paul's message. Or we can look behind the letters and try to determine the point from which the apostle makes his statements and from which these statements—however diverse they may be in concrete situations—can still be understood in a unified way.

The Protestant tradition has often preferred the first way, regarding the so-called doctrine of justification as the center of the Pauline message. Yet since, on the one hand, there is no consensus about this doctrine and, on the other, there is no agreement that justification can be called the center of Paul's message, this way would be burdened not only with many uncertainties but also with prejudgments and prejudices.

So it seems to be more obvious to go behind the letters and look for a center there. This draws our attention immediately to what is usually called Paul's "Damascus experience." It is indeed true that Paul himself connects this crucial turning point in his life with Easter (cf. 1 Cor. 9:1; 15:8). But he does not identify the two. Therefore we should not be too quick to do this either, for we run the risk of reversing the sequence. In our examination we will pass through the Damascus experience to Easter, and this will form our starting point and the basis for our argumentation.

We often find formulations such as this: "The point of departure[!] and basis[!] . . . of the ethic of Paul is the eschatological salvific event of Jesus' death and resurrection" (W. Schrage: *Ethik des Neuen Testaments* [Ethics of the New

Testament], p. 161). Yet this formulation is in many respects unclear, first in the language, then also in the content. Can we call death *and* resurrection the eschatological salvific event? First, we would have to determine whether and why a plural is formulated in the singular. Of course, there is no doubt that Paul presupposes both Jesus' death and his resurrection. But if we do not want these words to remain empty formulas, we have to fill them with content. Then, however, we immediately face a choice: Should we first determine the content of Jesus' death and resurrection and then presuppose this content as Paul's view? Or should we ask on the basis of Paul's letters (and *only* on this basis) how *the apostle* understands Jesus' death and resurrection? Only by following the second course can we avoid unnecessary errors.

If we look behind Paul's letters, however, we first encounter the Damascus experience. And we can show that all the apostle's work (including the work he did through his letters) is a development of this experience.

On this basis we will structure our presentation. First, we will reconstruct the center from which Paul's work must be understood. Since the churches drifted away from this center in different directions, we will then show how Paul tries in his letters to lead them back to this center. Finally, we will discuss some individual problems paradigmatically.

## 1. The Center: The Damascus Experience

If we want to reduce the Damascus experience to a short formula, we can say: The Pharisee became a Christian. Quite obviously this happened not in a gradual process but abruptly. The point of departure for understanding this "conversion" is that this Pharisee turned Christian had earlier persecuted Christians.

### a) The Persecutor

We may assume that if a man persecutes a group of people, he does it because he is not only highly offended by the opinions of these people but also for some reason considers these opinions dangerous. It follows that Paul must have known something about what the Christians believed even before his Damascus experience. Hence he knew the Christian message or at least some of its essential elements, and these elements incited him to persecution.

For the interpretation of the Damascus experience this means that the apostle's experience did not convey to him any new content of faith; rather, he now surrendered himself to the same beliefs he knew already. In short, knowledge became faith.

This problem requires fundamental clarification. The contents of a faith can be learned. We can know (and then describe) what "Lutheran faith," "Reformed faith," "Catholic faith," and so forth are like. And we can describe what "Christian faith" is like if we substantiate our description with appropriate use of the New Testament scripture. In each case we are dealing with historical theologies. Then we can compare these different contents of faith and find agreements and differences. All this belongs in the realm of knowledge.

It is an entirely different question whether one of these contents of faith becomes *my* truth. It becomes my truth when I totally surrender to this faith, and that means when I live this faith.

Interest often focuses on the question of how it came about that Paul's knowledge became faith. And frequently there is an erroneous view that by desribing the process we can prove the truth of the faith of the (Christian) Paul. Now it is not possible in any case to prove a faith true, because a proven faith would no longer be faith, and, what is more, we cannot really reconstruct what happened to Paul near Damascus.

The apostle provides only meager information and in various formulations. From 1 Cor. 9:1; 15:8 we could infer a vision. This became the predominant idea because the "vision" was later graphically embroidered and supplemented by the motif of audition (cf. Acts 9:1-6; 22:6-11; 26:12-18). In Gal.

1:16, however, the apostle talks only generally about a revelation, without further specification and in 2 Cor. 4:6 about God's having shone light "in our hearts." Thus we cannot reconstruct the events of the Damascus experience.

We can, however, discuss the only question that matters here. What did Paul know about the content of the Christians' message?

*(1) The message of the persecuted.* There is no doubt that the Pharisee Paul persecuted the Christians because of their position toward the law. For whenever Paul mentions his activities as a persecutor and provides content in this connection, he also mentions his own zeal for the law (Gal. 1:13-14; Phil. 3:6).

Earlier it was sometimes said that Paul persecuted Christians because they worshiped Jesus as messiah and even as a crucified messiah. Yet Paul never mentions this as a reason for his activities as persecutor. Furthermore, that would not even have been a crime worthy of persecution. In contemporary Judaism there were various groups that put forth some "prophet" or other as messiah. Those, however, were considered curious sects, and a crucified messiah had to seem downright ridiculous. People who held such a view were derided but not persecuted.

The crucial question is why the Christians' position toward the law was so dangerous in the eyes of the Pharisee Paul that he had to become a persecutor. We can understand this only if we realize that this is a theological problem in the precise sense of this word.

Very often people argue too shortsightedly here. They look only at the law itself and determine that Christians were "critical" of it. But what does this mean? It is said, for example, that Christians did away with the cultic commandments but continued to observe the "moral" commandments. We cannot, however, talk of a merely lax obedience of the law. It was normal for people not to observe all the commandments. If they were too liberal about the law, they were subject to contempt. The Pharisees separated from these "sinners" (the "country folk") by renouncing communion with them. But they did not persecute them.

Rather, the Christian's critical attitude toward the law had a fundamental character. And this made them blasphemers in the eyes of Paul, who still considered them Jews.

One is not permitted to disrupt the continuum God-Israel-law and treat one of these entities in isolation. God had given the law, and he had given it only to Israel. For Israel this was both an honor and an obligation. It was an honor because only Israel knew God's will. The Gentiles did not know it, and therefore they were unable to please God. So Israel took delight in the law despite the obligations connected with it. For God's sake these obligations were taken quite seriously. This led to the scribes' casuistic explanation of individual commandments. Life was regulated down to the smallest detail. We may smile about this, but we should not. For behind it was the immense seriousness with which God's will was sought. And the Pharisees distinguished themselves by striving with utmost strictness to hold to the law even in its smallest details.

Not only did they strive for this, but they often succeeded in their efforts, as becomes especially clear in the case of Paul. It is a common error to think that Paul had in time come to believe that people could not keep the law. Quite the contrary! Even as a Christian Paul still maintains in retrospect that he was "blameless" with regard to the law (Phil. 3:6). And there is no reason to doubt the apostle's autobiographical statement. In his opinion people can keep the law and its commandments.

That only a few people achieve this in reality is a whole different story. But this is no reason to postulate the impracticability of the law.

And if Paul, the (successful!) zealot for the law, then encounters a group of Jews who are critical of the law, it has a particular meaning for him. By removing one element from the continuum God-Israel-law, these people destroy the whole thing. Thus criticism of the law is merely a symptom of a much deeper illness. For if Jews believe they can do without the law, they are thereby attacking God, who gave the law and demands its obedience. At the same time they are destroying the foundations of Judaism, which loses its particular character and privilege as God's people. This loss poses a mortal danger especially to the synagogues in the diaspora, for the Jews there become equals of the Gentiles. And that is precisely what makes the persecution of Christians understandable.

So for the Pharisee Paul absolutely everything was at stake, but most of all his God. Therefore we should not mention only the critical attitude of Christians with regard to the law as the reason for Paul's persecuting activities, because this easily results in a failure to grasp the whole problem. The real reason was a theological one: these (Christian) Jews were opposing his God. Paul *realized* this only when they asserted that they could do without the law. This was the part of their message that Paul knew and that offended him.

This raises two questions: How was this message presented by the Christians? And how did it originate?

*(2) The formulation of the Christians' message.* We may assume that the message of the Christians included more than this (basically negative) point that upset Paul so much. Yet we learn nothing about it from Paul himself, at least not directly. Is it still possible to reconstruct this message somewhat more fully?

We can start by considering how the Pharisee Paul learned about the Christians' critical attitude toward the law. Theoretically, there are two possibilities. He may have *observed* the activities of the Christians, or he may have *heard* them expressly voice their criticism. We must rule out the first possibility. By observation we can perceive only that people are lax about the commandments of the law, maybe even very lax. But we cannot infer from this a total rejection of the law. Furthermore, we can hardly imagine the Christians as a group of people who continually violated commandments. So only the second possibility is left. The Christians must have *said* that they regarded following the law as unnecessary and hence the law itself as superfluous.

Yet this seems rather unlikely, at least at first glance. For if Christians had said such things aloud in Jerusalem (or Judea), they could not have survived for a moment in that surrounding. They would have been driven out immediately.

Now we know from the Acts of the Apostles that such an expulsion had already occurred quite early. Yet this event did not involve the Aramaic-speaking Jewish Christians, but only the Greek-speaking, the so-called Hellenists.

The information in Acts was written down at a later time. What is told there can hardly have happened the way it is related. It is unimaginable that during the great persecution that arose against the Jerusalem church *all* Christians were scattered over the countryside of Judea and Samaria *except for the apostles* (Acts 8:1). One does not persecute the followers and leave the leaders unmolested. Thus the information in Acts has to undergo historical criticism.

The result is more or less the following picture. There were frictions in Jerusalem between "Hellenists" and "Hebrews" (Acts 6:1). These frictions must have become public and come to the attention of the Jewish authorities, who took note of the Christians and intervened. One of the Hellenists, Stephen, was put on trial and stoned. (It may also have been a lynching.) Afterwards the Hellenists were run out of the city.

We can gather from the indictment against Stephen why the Jewish authorities proceeded against the Hellenist Christians. The accusations were that he spoke "blasphemous words against Moses *and* God" (Acts 6:11), he "never stops saying things against this holy place and the law" (6:13), and he claims that "this Jesus of Nazareth will destroy this place and will change the customs that Moses handed on to us" (6:14). These are the same charges made by Paul against Christians, and they are made in the same context of God-Israel-law. In this situation the Jewish authorities in Jerusalem also had to step in.

So there were two groups of Christians. The Aramaic-speaking Jewish Christians could practice their faith in Jerusalem and were tolerated as a Jewish sect. The Hellenists, on the other hand, could not be tolerated because they overstepped the boundaries of what was possible within Judaism. They expressly stated that they rejected the law.

For our purposes we can conclude that it was Hellenist Christians whom Paul persecuted, because only they gave radical expression to their critical attitude toward the law. And this means, conversely, that since Paul later adopted the faith of the people he persecuted, he first became a Hellenist Christian through his Damascus experience. Only later did he seek an accommodation with the Aramaic-speaking Christians—and also achieved it, at least in part.

These two "Christianities" existed side by side for a long time. Not until the Apostolic Council (cf. Gal. 2:1-10) did Paul succeed in convincing at least the "pillars" (2:9) of the correctness of his law-free gospel. Yet there had to be a division of responsibility (Paul became responsible for the Gentiles, Peter for the Jews). This is an indication that in a Jewish environment one had to be considerate. To abandon circumcision (which placed one under the law; cf. Gal. 5:3) would have resulted in the Jerusalemites' being expelled from the city and the land. The incident in Antioch (Gal. 2:11-14) shows how hard this was to practice. When Peter arrived there, he ate at first with the Gentile Christians, thus behaving in accordance with the agreements of the Apostolic Council. Then James's people (from Jerusalem) pointed out to him that he, as one of the Jerusalem leaders, endangered the Aramaic-speaking Jewish Christians in the capital through his law-free behavior. So he (along with Barnabas and other Jewish Christians) gave up their table fellowship. Thus, in Max Weber's terms, he placed the ethics of responsibility above the ethics of attitude. Paul, on the other hand, wanted only the "Hellenistic point of view" to be accepted in Antioch, but did not succeed.

The coexistence of two "Christianities" poses the question whether the Hellenists created a new Christianity out of the old. In other words, did the Christianity that Paul first adopted and then advocated turn into something entirely different from what people had experienced earlier in the presence of Jesus? This has been frequently claimed, and since later Paul's theology largely prevailed in the churches, the apostle has sometimes been called the "real founder" of Christianity. This, of course, he certainly was not. But the question remains whether the designation can be applied to Hellenistic Christianity.

For there is no doubt that Hellenistic Christianity came out of Jewish Christianity and in some way further developed it. Whether this development was inherent in Jewish Christianity or is an alteration of it can be determined only through a reconstruction of the Christianity of Aramaic-speaking Christians

There are, however, some uncertainties. They have to do with time and with place.

Without doubt Hellenistic Christianity arose at a very early time, before Paul's Damascus experience, say, within three years after Jesus' death. In view of our sources, however, it is very difficult to get more detailed information about the faith and life of the Aramaic-speaking Jewish Christians of that time. Furthermore, we do not even know where Hellenistic Christianity developed out of Jewish Christianity. It could have been in the diaspora and perhaps under the influence of Galilean churches. But we cannot completely rule out the possibility that it happened through Hellenistic Jews staying in Jerusalem and encountering Aramaic-speaking Christians.

In the first case we could reconstruct the Jewish Christianity that was further developed by the Hellenists on the basis of material in the early synoptic tradition. But this should also be possible in the second case. For even if it is unlikely that the Jerusalem church was the source and vehicle of the synoptic texts (cf. pp. 45-46 above), we may still assume that the people who formed the core of that church were people from the company of Jesus, who then (after *Easter;* see pp. 175-80 below) were still or again living as they had lived with Jesus and as they had seen Jesus living.

So we have to start with the question, How did people see Jesus deal with the law? and at the same time be aware of the fact that this question is asked from the standpoint of Hellenistic Christianity, that is, as a matter of principle. If, however, we do not ask as a matter of principle, we can assume that the everyday lives of the Jews were indeed regulated by the law and its commandments, but that the people who lived these everyday lives usually were not aware of their living "according to the law." It was simply usual not to work on a sabbath and to follow custom in questions of diet and purity. Real reflection on the law occurred only in borderline cases, and then only if people were willing to see them and recognize them as borderline cases. Then people resorted to casuistry, which was pursued by the scribes (with varying results). And reflection on the law also occurred when someone deviated drastically from the norm.

It may thus be appropriate to describe the things that the people saw Jesus do as follows. His life was normal, but every so often in his normal life he would do something "against the rules," and he often did it quite consciously and conspicuously. The Jewish Christians probably lived the same way. They were living in a Jewish environment and lived what was a normal life in this environment. Their sons were circumcized, their work ceased on the sabbath, and they observed dietary and purification laws. Yet from time to time they probably also ventured an action against the rules, as they had seen Jesus do. Whether in each particular case they thoroughly considered what they were doing, why they were doing it, and what assumptions allowed them to do it cannot be determined, but it is rather unlikely. They may have asked what Jesus would have done in a given case. And if they saw a parallel between his time and theirs, they may have risked the same exception they had seen Jesus risk. In this environment, however, they would hardly have had a fundamental discussion of their position on the law, because the determination of their everyday life by the law was taken for granted, and what was taken for granted was hardly given any consideration.

By contrast, the Greek-speaking Jews in the diaspora were in an entirely different situation. The environment in which they lived was not oriented toward the law. Yet these Jews had to abide by it and probably did abide by it to a large extent. For that reason they started much earlier reflecting on how they had to live differently from their environment.

The Jews gathered around the synagogue were inevitably an exclusive circle vis-à-vis their environment. If this circle displayed its elitist aspect too clearly, it could create hostility that now and then resulted in persecution. Conversely, exclusivity could also be appealing and could lead people in the vicinity to want to join the synagogue, especially since they could come into contact with God there in a unique way. So the Jews then also tried to convert Gentiles to God. Yet Gentiles could really come to God only if they became proselytes (through circumcision or baptismal immersion) and thereby became Jews. Yet if they did that, they were obliged to keep the law, and this was a nuisance. For if they oriented their lives toward the law, they left the society in which they had been living. Because of dietary and purification laws alone, they could no longer sit at table with Gentiles. Well-to-do people could lose their social position this way, and for this reason many Gentiles did not take this last step. They did not become proselytes but as "God-fearers" maintained a somewhat looser contact with the synagogue. These people were genuinely interested in the God of Israel. Yet the law was a barricade that blocked the way to him, for this God was simply not available without the law.

So the law had to become a fundamental problem in the Diaspora—actually the only place where it could be a problem. For in the coexistence of a minority of Greek-speaking Jews and a majority of Gentiles there was always a latent question: Do people really need the law in order to stay with God or come to God fully? Now, it is clear that the problem of the law is a theological problem. Gentiles could come to God only if they adopted the law. And Jews could stay with God only if they adhered to the law—as hard as that might have been for them, especially in this environment.

If Greek-speaking Jews met a group of Aramaic-speaking Jews who in their environment usually lived "by the law" yet occasionally dared to transgress it and (while referring to Jesus) were still convinced that they would not lose God and indeed even did it in God's name, then this situation had to amaze Greek-speaking Jews and make them think. One theological deduction seemed obvious: if people do not lose God despite (occasional) violations of the law, then observing the law can no longer be a basic condition for coming to God and is no longer required for communion with God.

This deduction, however, does not change what Aramaic-speaking disciples of Jesus practiced in a Jewish environment but only carries it to its logical conclusion. Stated more precisely, *the Hellenistic Jews thought through to the end the theology of the Aramaic-speaking Jews.* For these Jewish Christians were living (through Jesus!) with the confidence of being with God already and not just on their way to him. If God is the Father who gives himself to his children in communion, then he cannot *at the same time* be a demanding lawgiver who is ready to have communion with people only if they first follow the law. So the criticism of the law formulated by Hellenist Christians is on the surface indeed a criticism of the law, but only on the surface. In reality it is a thinking through of the Jewish Christians' theology to its logical conclusion.

Rejection of the law as the salvific way to God, however, could not remain the only consequence of this thinking through. Going hand in hand with it was a critique of Israel's special status. For belonging to Israel could no longer be a precondition for communion with God either. And the accusation against Stephen (Acts 6:13-14) shows that the Jews necessarily understood this as an attack against them as well as an attack against God. Yet if God is indeed the Father, he can only be the Father of *all* his children, of Jews *and* Gentiles.

Understandably, the Aramaic-speaking Jewish Christians in Jerusalem did not draw these conclusions on their own. So tensions developed between them and Hellenist Christians. The latter's conclusions went too far for the Jewish Christians, who could hardly afford to draw them if they wanted to remain in the Jewish environment in Jerusalem.

Now we can also correct historically the puzzling presentation in Acts 8:1. Not just "the apostles" escaped the persecution that arose against Hellenist Christians in the city in connection with the stoning of Stephen but Aramaic-speaking Jewish Christians in general.

Not until a decade and a half later were the Jerusalemites again confronted with this problem, and then through the Hellenistic Jewish Christian Paul. At the Apostolic Council he succeeded in getting even Aramaic-speaking Jewish Christians to accept the conclusions drawn by the Hellenists, at least in principle, even though they could not be put completely into practice (cf. Gal. 2:1-10). The incident in Antioch (cf. Gal. 2:11-14) shows how hard it was to practice such a life-style.

As a result we can say that it was Hellenist Christians who first formulated the Christian message that confronted Paul. It originated when the Hellenists took what the Aramaic-speaking Jewish Christians—inspired by Jesus—were already practicing implicitly, though more or less unconsciously, and explicitly thought it through to its logical end.

So in another area the same thing happened at least formally that we observed in the history of the traditional synoptic material (cf. pp. 59ff. above). At first glance, the individual texts offer a somewhat disparate picture. In his beginning summary in 1:14-15, Mark provides a "center." In the same manner the Hellenistic Jewish Christians explicated what they saw the Aramaic-speaking Jewish Christians do from time to time and in very different ways. The thinking through and summing up were done with the help of different concepts and different linguistic expressions. Nevertheless, in content there was agreement.

## b) The Content of the Damascus Experience  (Theology and Ethics)

Paul gives only brief indications of what actually happened during his Damascus experience, and he uses various terminology (cf. pp. 146-47 above). Even so, we learn very little about the content of this experience.

According to Gal. 1:16, Paul knows from the beginning that he has been sent sent to proclaim the Son of God among the Gentiles. That the apostle emphasizes mission *among the Gentiles* can be explained from the context of the Letter to the Galatians (cf. 2:9). Whether this mission focus was really new for him is at least uncertain, for he had probably undertaken missions in the Diaspora earlier to convert Gentiles to the God of Israel.

Such missions were undertaken with different emphases. Their purpose might be to lead proselytes to the synagogue. Since this was difficult because of the law, however, missionaries could also be content (for the time being at least) to win God-fearers.

So if Paul had already been such a missionary among the Gentiles, the field of his activity did not change, but its content did. According to Gal. 1:16, this content was now the Son of God. What does Paul mean by this formulaic expression? He states this a little more clearly in 2 Cor. 4:6. It is a new image of God, which he has been proclaiming since his Damascus experience. He wants to let shine "the knowledge of the glory of God," which has appeared "in the face of Jesus Christ." Yet in what does this glory of God consist? In this verse also, the information does not go beyond the formulaic.

We can learn more from two other texts from Pauline letters, which do not expressly mention the Damascus experience but still give information about its content.

In Phil. 3:3-11, in the context of arguing with opponents, Paul contrasts then and now. Here he clearly indicates that he is referring to the crucial turning point in his life. First he lists the privileges of which he could and did boast by virtue of his birth into the chosen people: "Circumcised on the eighth day, a member of the people of Israel, of the tribe of Benjamin, a Hebrew born of Hebrews; as to the law, a Pharisee . . ." As a Pharisee he persecuted Christians and boasted that he had observed the law blamelessly. But then came the turning point: "Yet whatever gains I had, these I have come to regard as loss because of Christ . . . because of the surpassing value of knowing Jesus Christ my Lord." For his sake Paul suffered the loss of everything, of pride and of glory. Now he can only regard the past as rubbish. Paul sums up this contrast: earlier his concern was gaining a "righteousness of my own that comes from the law"; now he is striving for "one that comes through faith in Christ, the righteousness from God based on faith."

The same terminology occurs in Rom. 10:1-4. Here too the Damascus experience is not mentioned; Paul does not even talk about himself. Yet his own turning point forms the backdrop of his statement.

> The Letter to the Romans was occasioned by the situation in Rome, which Paul did not know first hand, but he had heard about it. In the capital of the empire there had been quarrels between Gentile and Jewish Christians that led to disturbances. So in A.D. 49 Jews (and Jewish Christians) were expelled from Rome through an edict of Claudius (cf. Acts 18:2). After the emperor's death (A.D. 54) the edict was relaxed. The banished could return. Paul then tried to prevent the old quarrel from starting again. For this reason he tells the two groups to talk to each other. Especially in chapters 9-11 he promotes the understanding of the Jewish Christians among the Gentile Christians, using Jewish history for clarification.

In Rom. 10:1-4 Paul explains what must happen and does happen when Jews become Christians, namely, exactly what happened to him near Damascus. His heart's desire and prayer to God for his fellow Jews is "that they may be saved." This will not happen to them as Jews, although "they have a zeal for God," as Paul expressly verifies, because their zeal lacks the real knowledge of God. "For, being ignorant of the righteousness that comes from God, and seeking to establish their own, they have not submitted to God's righteousness. For Christ is the end of the law so that there may be righteousness for everyone who believes."

The Greek word *dikaiosyne* used here can easily be misunderstood if we translate it "righteousness," for in English the word usually refers to a state of being morally righteous *by human standards*. But this is not what it means here. Rather, it is a forensic expression, a judicial term, and this immediately brings the theological aspect to our attention. It is a question of the judgment that God passes on people: "You, human being, are accepted by me." The question is, when and under what conditions does God pronounce this judgment? Here the Pharisaic Jewish view and the insight Paul received at Damascus diverge diametrically.

*Paul the Pharisee* argued (and according to Rom. 10:2-3 other Jews still argue) that God has given the law, and therefore people are obliged to obey it. If they follow the *law* in their actions, they act righteously in *God's* eyes.

Thus the law is the standard for righteousness. People have no room for their own decisions if they do not want to forfeit their righteousness. If the law demands, for instance, that one not keep company (especially not at table) with unclean persons (i.e., Gentiles) or with sinners (especially the "country folk"), then those who refuse company with such people are acting righteously, even if the result is behavior that we would call antisocial. It is the law.

At the end of the ages there will be judgment. The books will be opened. If they show a positive balance (that is, if a person has acted righteously most of the time), God will pronounce his verdict, "You, human being, are accepted by me." Only these *righteous* will then enter the kingdom of God.

It is always *God* who pronounces this verdict, yet Paul still calls it the person's *own* righteousness. The reason is easy to see. This verdict was earned by people through their own accomplishments. Moreover, in his verdict God is dependent on the individual's observation of the law.

This is where the real theological problem arises for Paul. Is *this* God really still God if in his verdict he makes himself dependent on human beings? If so, God's sovereignty is at risk. And since it is a question of the deity *of God,* Paul later calls this way a way that lacks genuine knowledge of God. So the issue is a theological one: Is my God a being whose judgment on me I can manipulate through my own actions? If so, it would be up to *me* to decide *God's* attitude toward me. Thus the problem of the law is not really a problem of the law and should never be treated as such in isolation. Rather, the problem is the image of God. Is God a being who demands that the people observe the law so that he can then (and *only* then) pronounce his verdict on them?

The image that Paul draws of his fellow Jews is often countered with the objection that there were also other groups and currents in contemporary Judaism that had a completely different image of God. This is indisputable but irrelevant for Paul's argumentation. Presumably because of his Pharisaic past, he has one image in mind and considers it typical of the Jews. Certainly this image did exist, and it is *only* against this image that Paul polemizes. The fact that his polemic does not apply to other groups and currents in Judaism at that time (and maybe not today either) is no argument against *this* polemic against *this* image of God.

*Paul the Christian* realizes that the way of one's own righteousness is the wrong way. He now relies on "God's righteousness." We have to note that this genitive is a *genitivus auctoris:* it stresses that God is and remains the sovereign, the sole author of judgment. He does not make himself dependent on human beings in any way, not even in his verdicts. Yet if God does not want to be dependent on humans, there is nothing they *can* do to influence God in his verdict on them. This defines God as the loving One.

If the sovereign God decides to love his creatures, human beings, then he will love them whether they want his love or not. But then the law can no longer have any importance, at least not in a way that would give people a chance to earn a good verdict by observing the law. Furthermore, if people now try to win God's love by obeying the law, that would be blasphemy. For anyone who tries to earn a gift after the fact (even if only in part) shows disrespect for the giver.

It is again obvious that we cannot understand the expression *God's righteousness* (or *God's justice*) in the way our language usually suggests. For the God whom Paul recognized at Damascus passes his favorable judgment on all people, even on those who have not observed the law. His love is truly toward all people and has no end. Yet according to human standards that love is really unjust.

The question now is, how does Paul substantiate this new image of God? Is it merely an assertion? Rom. 10:4 suggests an answer. For those who have faith Christ is the end of the law. Yet this is only an empty formula. How can we fill it?

According to 2 Cor. 4:6, the glory of God has shone "in the face of Jesus Christ." Here Paul first points to the past: since that time people no longer need the law to attain God's righteousness. In other words, Paul the *Pharisee* waited for God's judgment at the end of the world. Paul the *Christian* assumes that favorable judgment has already been passed: in Christ.

The difference can be illustrated as follows.

The way of Paul the Pharisee:

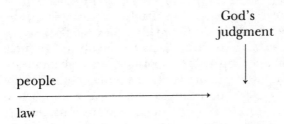

The way of Paul the Christian:

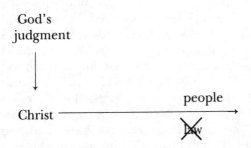

How favorable judgment has already been passed in and through Christ is explained by Paul in his Christology. In his Jesus images he uses different concepts to illustrate God's action. Despite differences in language the statements are identical. Paul always wants to show how and why people can live even now on the basis of the judgment of God already passed. We will note three examples of such christological concepts.

The best known is the statement that Christ died for us. It occurs very often in Paul's letters. The apostle adopted it from tradition (cf. p. 168 below) and then varied it in many ways on his own. The favorable verdict pronounced on humanity is illustrated here with the concept of vicarious atonement: Christ's death achieved the reconciliation of humanity with God. People can now live as persons reconciled with God; they do not need to do anything themselves for that reconciliation and are not even allowed to try it.

The second christological concept is connected with another sentence that Paul adopted: God raised Jesus from the dead (on the formula itself cf. pp. 175-80 below). In Rom. 6:4, for instance, we can clearly see how Paul takes up this theme: ". . . so that, just as Christ was raised from the dead by the glory of the Father, so we too might walk in newness of life." To "walk in newness of life" simply means to live in reconciliation with God, to live not in anticipation of God's verdict but under the assumption of a judgment already passed. Thus the resurrection that happened in the past is understood as and used to illustrate the enabling of the new life.

In his third christological concept Paul uses as an illustration what we now call the incarnation. "But when the fullness of time had come, God sent his Son, born of a woman, born under the law, in order to redeem those who were under the law, so that we might receive adoption as children" (Gal. 4:4-5). God's favorable verdict appears here in the image of redemption from slavery. The coming of the Son effected the emancipation and the adoption of human beings "as children." Again this means nothing different from what is expressed in the other images and in different terminology. If we live as children, we walk in newness of life, are persons reconciled with God, and so forth. None of this, however, is something toward which we must strive with the help of the law; rather God has accomplished it by sending his Son.

For understanding the Christology, it is important to see that Paul looks back three times and in these retrospectives he focuses on three different points in the past. He can illustrate God's favorable judgment with concepts that are connected first with the coming of the Son, then with the death of the Christ, and finally with the resurrection of Jesus. And in every single case he is saying the same thing.

Of course, we cannot turn the whole thing around now and arrange it in a so-called history of salvation. This would necessarily raise the question, exactly when was God's favorable judgment on humanity passed? Already at Jesus' coming? Not until his death? Or not until his resurrection? Otherwise we would have to assume a gradually increasing process, or we would have to add things up because only the sum would produce the whole. Paul, however, looks back and asserts the whole idea at each indvidual point.

(Here we can see how problematic it is to state that "the point of departure[!] and basis[!] . . . of the ethic of Paul is *the* eschatological salvific event of Jesus' death *and* resurrection" [emphasis added]—cf. pp. 144-45 above.)

These Christologies, which are quite different in regard to the concepts used in them, thus have the function (each in itself) of demonstrating clearly how in the past God's verdict was pronounced. Yet Paul is able not only to use different images without changing the content of his statement but also to omit the images altogether and simply use Christ as a symbol. He can say, for example, that God "reconciled us to himself through Christ" (2 Cor. 5:18) or that "Christ" is the end of the law for those who believe (Rom. 10:4).

So we can expand our diagram as follows:

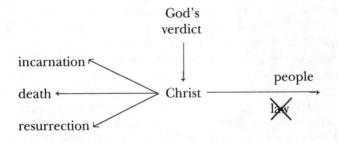

Now the question remains, how do things that happened in the past "in Christ" affect people today? It is answered by the final precise, defining remark in Rom. 10:4. Paul does not simply say, "Christ is the end of the law" (as is unfortunately often alleged by this abbreviated quotation); rather, Paul goes on to give the reason: ". . . so that there may be righteousness [through God's judgment] for everyone who believes." This means, however, that God's judgment affects all who accept it, who trustingly rely on it *in their everyday existence*. In short, whoever lives it, believes it. So the formula *faith in Christ* has a very precise content. This content is stated inadequately if it is formulated as a *conviction* and expressed with the words, "we believe *that* God in Christ has already pronounced his verdict on humanity." If faith is the expression of a conviction, then it refers to knowledge. According to Paul, however, we can speak of faith in Christ only when believers pattern their *lives* on the basis of the pronounced judgment.

Thus believers are changed by this judgment of God in which they believe. Paul has many ways of making this point. He can call the people changed by God's judgment reconciled people, free people, people come of age, people living as children of God, or people guided by the Spirit. He can refer to them as a new creation, people who have left the old creation behind if they are "in Christ." The terms Paul uses come from different contexts and have different origins in the history of religion. Paul can switch terms and choose from the multitude of possible means of expression those he considers most appropriate in each context of argumentation. From this, however, we must not infer differences in content. He does not care what these expressions once meant in earlier contexts. Rather, he always adopts them in order to say the same thing. He always has "believers in Christ" in mind, which means people changed through God's judgment who are living their life *as changed people*.

Therefore we can say that at Damascus Paul "came to faith." Yet we must fill this empty formula, for Paul the Pharisee would never have admitted that he did not believe in God. In Gal. 3:23-25 Paul suggests how the brief formula can be filled. Here he states very tersely that faith came with Christ—and of course not until Christ. But this immediately becomes a theological problem. Before this faith came, people were imprisoned. The law was their *paidagogos*, which does not mean "schoolmaster" or "custodian" but "disciplinarian." The Pharisees were given to this disciplinarian and surrendered themselves to it. Law the disciplinarian was their God. But after faith came (that is, after Christ came), those who believe no longer live under the disciplinarian law; now they live as people on whom God has already passed his favorable judgment. As believers they are changed: the prisoners have become free people.

So we can sum up Paul's Damascus experience as follows. Paul experienced a change of gods (on this terminology cf. p. 8 above). Paul's "conversion" consisted in turning away from the God who demanded from people observation of the law as a precondition for his verdict and in surrendering to the God who appeared to him "in the face of Jesus Christ," the God who, because he loves *all* his children, has already pronounced his judgment without first demanding achievements from them.

> We should not try to avoid the term *change of gods* by assuming only the *one* God. If we do, we must say that at Damascus Paul realized what God is *really* like. Yet this obscures the problem. It is true that when Paul the Pharisee was speaking Greek, he referred to his God with the word *theos* and that Paul the Christian still refers to his God with the same word. So there is an identity between the Pharisee's God and the Christian's God, but only in the *word*. When the same word is filled with contradictory contents (judgment *is still to be* pronounced versus judgment *has already been* pronounced), it is more than just problematic to speak of an identity of two entities only because of the identity of the words referring to them.

Thus before and after Damascus we are dealing with two fundamentally different theologies. And since ethics is an aspect of theology, the ethic of Paul the Pharisee and that of Paul the Christian are also fundamentally different. Their differences can be perceived most easily if we look at Paul's opposition between *work* and *fruit* (cf. Gal. 5:19, 22).

Characteristic of the Pharisaic ethic is the fact that it is *work*. Here the (old) humanity is left to itself and thus alone. People have the law; they have rules and regulations toward which they try to orient their lives. They are convinced that the law came from their God, but now they do not have this God with them and therefore have to strive by themselves. They do this in two ways. First they must try to know the will of their God as precisely as possible. This leads into casuistry. Then they must endeavor to do what they know as God's will. They can have great success, and even Paul the Christian can still point to such success without calling it into question. In fact, Paul the Pharisee has good reason to be proud of his success and can boast of it. Hence it is a common mistake among Christians to disqualify the Pharisaic ethic as an "inferior" or even "bad" ethic. What makes it theologically problematic is the obligation under which it always stands, which is a *theological* obligation. The Pharisees' God first demands works, specific actions as well as specific abstentions. And he promises the people that he *will* justify them *if* they do these works.

Characteristic of Paul's ethic after Damascus is the fact that it is *fruit*. This fruit is really produced. In the practice of life it becomes visible again and again. Yet the people who act here do not belong to the old humanity anymore, to the people who, alone and dependent on themselves, still must struggle to find their *existence*. No, the people who act here are changed people who have already received their existence through Christ. Therefore whatever they do is "fruit of the Spirit." Insofar it is not really they who act, although they shape their own actions. The real agent is Christ or the Spirit. So it is no longer possible for people to boast of their deeds.

Thus the crucial difference between the two ethics lies in their fundamentally different points of departure. This becomes especially clear if we ask, what do we do if the ethic does not work? Doing Pharisaic ethics may not work if we either do not know the will of the God of the Pharisees precisely enough or do not try hard enough to do the will of this God. In the first case the situation can be remedied by finding out and determining as precisely as possible what must be done or not done according to this God's will, and in the second case by intensifying one's efforts. In the ethic of the Christian Paul, the action will not work if people do not base their lives on the prevenient gift of the God who has already pronounced his verdict on them in Christ. Then they are still the old, unchanged people. Only changed people can bear fruit. This situation can be remedied only by having faith, by being reconciled with God.

In short, in Pharisaic ethics people must *change their ways* in order to accomplish works. In the Christian Paul's ethic people must *let themselves be changed,* so they can bear fruit.

## 2. Excursus: Jesus' Cross and Resurrection

One might ask whether it is necessary for the presentation of Paul's ethic to go yet another step behind the Damascus experience and in that context expressly discuss Jesus' cross and resurrection. There are three reasons why this step would seem appropriate.

(1) According to widespread opinion, Paul's theology and ethic presuppose Jesus' cross and resurrection. Even though this cannot be doubted, there remains the question, How is this true in Paul's case? Does he begin with cross and resurrection? That seems to be presupposed in statements such as, "The point of departure and basis . . . of the ethic of Paul is the eschatological salvific event of Jesus' death and resurrection, in which God acted eschatologically and finally for the salvation of the world" (cf. pp. 144-45). Or does Paul ascribe his Damascus theology both to the incarnation and to the cross and resurrection of Jesus?

(2) Does Paul's talking of the crucified and resurrected One change the content of what people experienced when they encountered Jesus? Or is it a readoption or new adaptation of the old content? Paul himself does not touch on these questions, but they are of interest nonetheless.

(3) Paul gives us at least a hint in this inquiry by connecting his Damascus experience with an experience of earlier followers. He has "seen Jesus our Lord," as others had before him (1 Cor. 9:1), and this common seeing (before Paul but also through him) is brought into the context of Jesus' resurrection (1 Cor. 15:8).

Since in this excursus we want to treat Jesus' death and resurrection only to the extent to which we can see it in Paul's ethic and to which it is relevant there, we will start with the literary findings.

Frequently the Apostle uses preformed material in his letters. In our context we can mention three groups of formulas that are found repeatedly. In part they are adapted to the context but can be traced back to these basic forms with sufficient certainty:

(1) a formula that refers to Jesus' death: We believe that "Christ died for us" (Rom. 5:8 etc.);

(2) a formula that refers to Jesus' resurrection: We believe that "God raised [Jesus] from the dead" (Rom. 10:9) and also occurs as a predication of God: God is the one who raised Jesus from the dead (cf. Gal. 1:1);

(3) a combined formula that refers to Jesus' death and resurrection: "We believe that Jesus died and rose again" (1 Thess. 4:14), or in more detail: We believe "that Christ died for our sins in accordance with the scriptures, and that he was buried, and that he was raised on the third day in accordance with the scriptures, and that he appeared to Cephas..." (1 Cor. 15:3-5).

Here one speaks of "pre-Pauline" material, and for this very reason we have to be careful in dating it. We must not infer that these formulas already existed before the Damascus experience. This is possible but not necessarily the case. At this point it is only certain that Paul knew these formulas when he wrote his letters, that is, from A.D. 50 on. The date of their origin in the previous twenty years (approximately) is unknown.

In a relative chronology, however, we can assume that the combined formula was constructed by joining the other two, and thus is later. This point should be noted especially in the case of the formula in 1 Cor. 15:3-5. It contains so many reflections that there is very little likelihood that it originated within the first three years after Jesus' crucifixion (that is, in the time before Paul's Damascus experience). Thus, contrary to what is often maintained, this is not a very early formula, but a relatively late one.

So the process of origination and development of these formulas was simultaneous with Paul's activities.

Thus we can ascertain that when the apostle wrote his letters, he knew that people were saying, "We believe that Jesus died for us." He also knew that people were saying, "We believe that God raised Jesus from the dead." It is important to see that Paul knew the two statements independently as self-contained statements. So he could adopt them separately and use them separately. Yet Paul also knew that there were people who could combine the two statements, and he adopted such combinations (1 Cor. 15:3-5). But he also made combinations of his own and used them in his argumentation (cf. Rom. 5:6-11; 6:3-4).

Yet we can observe a certain shift in emphasis here. First we have formulas that are introduced with the phrase *we believe*. We must take this quite literally, as we will see shortly. People are asserting what they base their lives on. The phrase *we believe* also occurs in the short summary in 1 Thess. 4:14, but there the content of faith has started to become independent in the sense of a presentation that interprets past events as a process. This is also the case in the formula Paul adopts in 1 Cor. 15:3-5. Here the *direct* connection of this past to our lives in the present is beginning to fade. In order to describe this shift of emphasis, we can say in short that "believing *in*" becomes "believing *that*." In other words, the earlier content of faith becomes knowable. In this way it can be used as material for argumentation. Apparently Paul stands in the middle of this process, yet we can hardly say that there is much reflection on the process itself.

If we retrace the path indicated by literary criticism, we eventually find two separate formulas, which we will now discuss.

### a) *Christ Died for Us*

This sentence, which originated as a statement of faith, is frequently repeated word for word even today. Its content often creates problems. An attempt is usually made to treat these problems by pointing out that we are dealing with a statement of faith. Yet this hardly offers help in understanding it.

If we want to understand the statement, it makes little sense to focus immediately on its content. We must first determine how the statement originated. That sometime after Jesus' death someone uttered this sentence for the first time cannot be disputed. When we repeat it today, we must remember that we are not merely repeating the words of a sentence. Rather, we are repeating a sentence with which someone once stated his or her faith. Since the origin of the sentence is a constituent part of its content (and thus must not be omitted under any circumstances), we must answer two questions: (1) What did the person who first formulated this sentence mean by it? (2) How did that person happen to formulate this sentence in just this way? (Was it a bold claim? Or is that claim somehow understandable?) We will discuss these two questions one at a time.

*(1) What did the person who first formulated this sentence mean by it?* This is precisely the question of historical exegesis. In order to answer it we must not only know but also remember that this person was a person of that time who in this sentence used concepts that were familiar in that environment. Without these preconditions the sentence would not have been understood at the time it was written.

The concept was that God demands a sacrifice for human sins. This sacrifice should properly be the people themselves, for it is they who deserve death for their sins. Yet God can be satisfied with a vicarious sacrifice, an animal that is slaughtered in the temple. So this animal is sacrificed *for the people* (= in their place), so that God can be reconciled with them. This is the context in which "for us" belongs. With this phrase we are in a realm where concepts of sacrifice were familiar as expiatory and vicarious sacrifice. And it is *God* who *demands* this sacrifice as a precondition for reconciliation.

The person who first expressed the sentence, "Christ died for us," meant that the death of Jesus was such a vicarious, expiatory sacrifice for us.

If we read the statement in the context of its time, we see that it destroys the then familiar concept, and it does so by using the very same concept. For there will be no more sacrifices in the future. In other words, God is redefined: he is no longer the one who really wants the death of sinners but settles for a sacrifice; rather, God is the one who wants to live reconciled with the people without any prior achievement through sacrifice.

The individual who formulated this sentence formulated it as a personal statement of faith. Thus that person believed that he or she could live as a person reconciled with God. This faith was substantiated by using a contemporary concept and interpreting an event of the past, Jesus' death on the cross, as a vicarious, expiatory sacrifice. The people of that time could immediately understand.

We must now consider whether this statement can still be understood today. In our consideration we must distinguish strictly between the content of faith and substantiation of the content.

The idea that the central content of Christian proclamation is the announcement of the reconciliation with God accomplished "in Christ" is not only expressly stated by Paul (cf. 2 Cor. 5:19-20); it also can and must be repeated today. But can we substantiate in the same way the reconciliation that occurred? As we saw above, Paul was by no means dependent on substantiation by interpreting Jesus' death as a "death for us"; he could refer just as well to the sending of God's Son without having to "balance" cross and incarnation. The two stand side by side unconnected and equal. And since Paul was a child of his time, he could also use the concept of vicarious, expiatory sacrifice.

Today, however, this could create problems. For if we use this concept to interpret Jesus' death, we presuppose the image of God according to which a sacrifice is required for his reconciliation with humanity. Do we not thereby revoke the new definition of God? In any case, we must face these problems and deal with them before we simply repeat that old statement of faith as our statement of faith.

Now there is no disputing the fact that someone substantiated his or her faith by interpreting the past event of Jesus' death as a vicarious, expiatory sacrifice. This raises the question of whether this interpretation was justified.

*(2) How did that person happen to formulate this sentence in just this way?* The event of the crucifixion itself did not show that an expiatory death was taking place. Therefore there was an interpretation, and there are two possibilities for the origin of the interpretation. Either it was a contingent and thus not a deducible assertion, or it was a deducible and therefore an understandable assertion.

If it is a contingent assertion, its adoption poses almost insurmountable difficulties.

The assertion cannot be verified in any way. We cannot determine whether it was simply this person's idea or whether the claim was based on revelation or on something else.

If this is the case, we cannot bring in faith and call the content of this sentence an expression of that person's faith. In this case faith does not concern the content of the sentence at all but rather the assumption that that person was able to give an appropriate interpretation of Jesus' death. How that person was in a position to do so remains unknown, because there is no way to tell. Only if we assume this ability and are satisfied with it can we repeat the sentence for ourselves. It all depends on the judgment of the person who formulated the sentence for the first time. This is what our faith is built on. If we are certain of this faith (and only then), we can logically accept the content of this sentence. Thus a faith today(!) that declares Jesus' death as a "death for us" stands or falls with that person's judgment. But can we even discuss that judgment?

We can avoid these difficulties only if we can make the origin of this sentence understandable. Actually, that is relatively easy.

When encountering the active Jesus, this person experienced him as the Reconciler, because Jesus' God was a God who offered reconciliation to the unreconciled—and without demanding works (or sacrifices) first. Furthermore, this person experienced Jesus as someone who took a risk by living this God for the people around him. Yet neither the enmity nor the persecution that Jesus underwent prevented him from living the reconciliation of his God for the people. Thus the visible destiny of someone living such reconciliation is no counterargument. The living of reconciliation still really happens. But could Jesus' death on the cross be a counterargument?

This is precisely what the originator of the sentence is protesting against. In order to express this and communicate it in an understandable way, this person uses the concept that was available at the time: the vicarious, expiatory sacrifice. At the *end* of Jesus' life, as a kind of summary, the author of "Christ died for us" asserts what he or she had experienced again and again when meeting the *active* Jesus.

> Later Paul expresses it this way: "All this is from God, who reconciled us to himself *through Christ,* and has given us the ministry of reconciliation" (2 Cor. 5:18). Here we must note two things.
>
> First, Paul is of course familiar with the sentence, "Christ died for us." Yet he does not restrict God's reconciling activity to the crucifixion event. Instead, he substantiates the accomplished reconciliation in a very general way with God's act in Christ.
>
> Second, the ministry of Paul (and of Christians) consists in preaching the accomplished reconciliation in order to free reconciled people for reconciling deeds. This brings us to the point of departure for ethics.

It is certainly a pointed expression—but not wrong in content—to say that reconciliation came *through Christ,* not through the cross. For "Christ died for us" does not really interpret the *event* of the cross; rather, it asserts by the example of the cross what was experienced in Jesus' activity. It was the understanding of Jesus' *activity* that caused that person to explain Jesus' *death* (*even* his death) as death for us.

Paul places this exemplary statement of the salvific meaning of the cross right beside the other (also exemplary) statement in Gal. 4:4-5 that God accomplished the redemption from slavery under the law by *sending* his Son.

So it is very problematic to make the cross the center of attention, as almost always happens. What is true for the history of the synoptic texts is also true for the other lines of tradition in which Paul stands. The crucifixion event was by no means the goal and culmination of Jesus' activity. It was, however, the extreme consequence that *can* happen when reconciliation is practiced in an unreconciled world. Yet after this consequence has occurred, it is somehow understandable that interest was now focused on this extreme point.

Through the cross thus interpreted, Paul could bring to bear an important feature of his ethic—again, by the way, in parallel to the synoptic texts: "If any want to become my followers, let them deny themselves and take up their cross and follow me" (Mark 8:34). Paul expresses this with the so-called *theologia crucis* (theology of the cross), which is understood correctly only if seen in the context of his disputes with his opponents, who in turn represent a *theologia gloriae* (theology of glory). These are ethical categories. For (by human standards) there is really no reason why the practice of ethics provides no guarantee of success for the doers themselves. Those who carry on the ministry of reconciliation in this world, who preach and practice reconciliation, always run a risk: the risk of the cross.

This indicates that Paul's ethical instructions are hardly suited for people who are not ready to run this risk.

Finally, we should once again make the following point. The sentence, "We believe that Christ died for us," is a self-contained statement; it does not require expansion by a statement on Jesus' resurrection. Hence we can indeed say that this sentence is already a statement on *Easter*. For we are looking back on the completed work of Jesus in such a way that this work opens up the future. That God has reconciled the world to himself *in*

*Christ* is said *also* of the cross. From now on we can proclaim that God has reconciled the unreconciled world to himself. Whoever accepts this message by relying on it can live from now on as a reconciled person.

> That these people then "walk in the newness of life," and that *this* is based on Christ's resurrection (Rom. 6:4) is only the other side of the same coin and not something added to it.

### b) God Raised Jesus from the Dead

To understand this second statement of faith, we must answer the same two questions: What was the person who first uttered this sentence trying to say? And how did this person happen to make such a claim? This time, however, we must reverse the order of the questions because of the content of the sentence.

> We can clarify this with a consideration that is admittedly hypothetical but at the same time demonstrates how closely we must observe the use of the language. A man who is guarding the grave sees the dead Jesus come alive: he sees him *rise*. If this man now says that God *raised* Jesus from the dead, he deduces the author of the event from the event that was before his eyes, and at the same time he switches verbs. The sentence, "Christ died for us," mentions an event and adds an interpretation. In the sentence, "God raised Jesus from the dead," however, the wording itself is an interpretation. The event (Jesus' rising), which we hypothetically assumed to have been experienced by this man, is no longer mentioned.
>
> Now since there are no witnesses to this event (and no preserved text says that there were any), we must first ask how this "interpretation" came about.

This context brings an entirely different question to our attention: What exactly does this sentence interpret?

*(1) How did someone happen to formulate this sentence?* This question would be relatively easy to answer if the sentence had come from Peter.

It was later claimed that Jesus had appeared to Peter after the crucifixion or that Peter had seen Jesus (1 Cor. 15:5; cf. Luke 24:34). If this is true, he could have first said, "I have seen Jesus." The sentence, "God raised Jesus from the dead," would then be an interpretation of this seeing. This interpretation would have been obvious, for according to Jewish ideas, God was to raise the dead at the end of time. This would have happened to Jesus ahead of time. The sentence would then explain how this seeing was possible: through the intervention of God.

It has never been asserted, however, that the statement that God raised Jesus from the dead goes back to Peter, and there is also no indirect reason for such an assumption. Therefore the sentence must have come from someone else. Nevertheless, we can state with relative certainty where this person is to be found. He or she lived in a group of "Jesus-followers" who had reunited after Jesus' crucifixion. They were centered around Peter.

If someone had asked persons from this group why they were still living as followers of Jesus, they would have pointed to Peter, who had gathered the scattered people together again. The gathering by Peter was based on a "vision" he had experienced. And then some day someone in that group formulated for the first time the sentence, "God raised Jesus from the dead." So the retracing of this sentence goes back through three stages: from the group through Peter as the gatherer of the group to Peter's vision itself. The intention of the sentence is to interpret the beginning of life in that group.

A comparison with what was discussed in the context of Paul's Damascus experience shows that in the beginning this sentence did not formulate new content (cf. p. 145 above).

As a persecutor, Paul already knew what was important to the persecuted Christians. Likewise, those who had accompanied Jesus to Jerusalem and experienced there his death knew what they had lived under his influence and in communion with him. As a persecutor, however, Paul did *not yet* live his knowledge. And the followers of Jesus—deprived of their Lord by the cross and thus now confused—*no longer* lived their knowledge.

In his Damascus experience Paul surrendered to the things he had known before. Likewise the Jesus-followers reunited by Peter surrendered *anew* to the things they had known before.

Thus in both cases it is not a matter of new content; rather, already known content is (re)applied to life.

During his work on earth Jesus had started the life of that group. They had learned that only under his influence and in communion with him could and did they succeed with this life. Yet since the group gathered by Peter was concerned with living the same "thing," Jesus was and *remained* the one who started it. *In living* the same thing, this group became certain that Jesus still really comes today. And since he still comes today, his "thing"—what Jesus represents—continues.

How the new start happened could be answered by referring to Peter's vision. The identity of the Initiator was then discerned.

Following this (or maybe simultaneous to it) someone at some point formulated, "God raised Jesus from the dead." With this sentence that person (once again) thought it through to the end: From the experiences the group had in living "Jesus' thing," this person could say that Jesus is still at work and express this with a then familair concept and in the language of that concept.

We can even mention two "life situations" that might have produced such a formulation: paraclesis and apologia.

The paraclesis could become necessary within the group. Since its members lived without the bodily presence of Jesus as if he were with them, the question could arise, with what justification could this actually still be done? People tried to assure each other: When we live what he accomplished in us, he is still with us, for God raised him from the dead. In other words, the *extra nos* (outside of us) is perceived.

The same question could also come to the group from outside. Why are they living a life into which they had been led by a failure? The answer: God raised Jesus from the dead.

And these explanations have already essentially answered the other question.

*(2) What did the person who formulated this sentence mean by it?* Let us remember that the entire wording of the sentence is interpretation. So the thing that is interpreted is a basic component of the statement that the person made. Contrary to what we assumed in our ficticious example above, however, it is not the event of Jesus' resurrection that is interpreted. Rather, it is the faith instilled *by Jesus,* which this person is living in the community of Jesus-followers after Jesus' death.

We must be very careful to observe the whole context of this interpretation. Without the precondition of the lived faith this interpretive sentence would never have come about. Hence we must never separate the interpretation from what is being interpreted. For such a separation would fundamentally change the character and thus the content of this sentence.

Yet this is exactly what had already happened in the time of the New Testament. The breach point for this interpretation was possibly a modification in the wording, although at the time this modification was probably not considered as significant as it appears to us today.

This modification probably happened in the following way. Originally the sentence read, "God *raised* Jesus from the dead." The intention of this sentence was to give a reason why this person and his or her group were still living the faith into which Jesus had once led them. Later this sentence became, "Jesus has *risen.*" How this second sentence *arose* is clear. First, the interpretative sentence was isolated, then it was reworded, and finally it resulted in a statement that at least *could* be understood so as to state an "event" that happened in the past. It is absolutely clear that this was not the original author's meaning. And it is just as clear that the interpretative sentence does not provide a basis for postulating such an event.

> Nonetheless, it is easy to see that this could happen. It probably had also to do with the second life situation mentioned above (the apologia). If the sentence, "God raised Jesus from the dead," was used apologetically, *for the*

*speakers of this sentence* it was an interpretation of the faith they were living. *Outside hearers,* however, did not have this presupposition. So they could only understand that the Christians were asserting Jesus' resurrection as an event that happened in the past. Yet this understanding also arose among Christians. This can perhaps be seen most clearly in Matthew. In order to counter the accusation of a theft of Jesus' body, he constructs the story of the guards at the tomb (Matt. 27:62-66; 28:11-15). Hence even Matthew must have already understood the resurrection of Jesus as an event. We will not discuss here the developments leading up to and proceeding from this point. Yet it forms the point of departure for the still ongoing discussion of whether Jesus' resurrection was an event (in history) or not.

Thus everything depends on preserving the interpretative context within which the original sentence arose. The sentence is a *consequence* of the lived faith. It is not itself a *credendum,* an assertion that as such requires faith, which must be "accomplished," in order (subsequently!) to draw conclusions from it.

Yet the New Testament scriptures, even as early as Paul and before him, talk of the raising and rising of Jesus without any noticeable difference (cf., e.g., 1 Cor. 15:4 with 1 Thess. 4:14).

Today, in the wake of Enlightenment thought, we often ask whether Paul understood Jesus' resurrection as an actual event. Especially because this is *our* question, we must be careful with the answer. How Paul *conceived* what he expressed with the terms *raising* and *rising* we cannot tell, since he does not talk about it. We can only determine how he uses these terms, namely, never to designate a single event but always in an interpretative context.

Now this is by no means some special thing but the only thing possible. For if we understand the sentence, "Jesus has risen," as the designation of an event, it (quite literally) says nothing. Outside of stating a fact, it has no content. This statement of fact, however, will at once provoke questions— about the content.

If we now say that in the resurrection God declared himself for Jesus or confirmed Jesus through the resurrection, then these are also formulas waiting for a content. *As who* did God declare himself for Jesus, and *as whom* did he confirm Jesus? Only after we have answered these questions do we see content. And then we could say, for example, that God confirmed Jesus as the one who inaugurated life in reconciliation with God. The confirmation would mean that what Jesus *brought* can and shall *continue* to be brought.

In other words, the sentence, which originated in an interpretative context, can only make sense if used in an interpretative context. Only if we today rely on what Jesus brought (i.e., only if we believe), can we say that Jesus lives. And conversely, in saying that Jesus lives, we make sense only if we rely on what Jesus has brought. Without this context the sentence, "Jesus lives," is meaningless.

The interpretative contexts in which Paul talks about Jesus' raising or rising are manifold and cannot be discussed here in detail. (Yet we must warn against taking individual sentences from their contexts and arguing with them.) They all have a soteriological aspect in common. The important thing is the present salvation (and present hope) that God has given "in Christ."

By preserving the interpretative context, Paul adopts what the person who first formulated the sentence, "God raised Jesus from the dead," meant to say.

### 3. Indicative and Imperative—Imperative and Indicative

Rudolf Bultmann set the course with his famous essay, "Das Problem der Ethik bei Paulus" (The Problem of Ethics in Paul; *Zeitschrift für Neutestamentliche Wissenschaft* [1924]: 123-40; rpt. in R. Bultmann: *Exegetica* [1967], 36-54). Since then it has been common to characterize the nature of Pauline ethics (and Christian ethics in general) with the two terms used in the title of this section. They are supposed to express the idea that there is a tension that cannot be resolved through logic. Hence there are also difficulties in the presentation of this paradox or antinomy. This is seen especially in the discussion that has continued to follow Bultmann's fundamental explanations. Most critics think that one of the two sides of the paradox has not been sufficiently accentuated, and therefore they believe more emphasis must be put on that side. Yet when such a correction shifts the weight to that side, there is a risk of upsetting the balance in the opposite direction. Presumably any presentation of this paradox will be open to misunderstanding.

The problem we are dealing with here is easy to demonstrate (after our previous discussion). If, incomprehensibly, God has already passed his favorable judgment on humanity (indicative)—which Paul obviously presupposes after Damascus—what significance can be given (theologically) to the imperatives that we often still find in Paul's letters? Does Paul think that God *requires* these imperatives to be carried out? If this is the case, is there not a danger that everything will again depend on a person's deeds? Do such deeds required in the name of God through imperatives not at once become *works*? And does that not mean a reversion to Pharisaic ethics? Yet if the indicative is taken seriously as *God's* indicative, then the imperatives are disturbing, because they seem to take back the indicative. Do we not, therefore, have to accuse Paul (theologically) of inconsistency for not dispensing with imperatives?

Yet we can also ask conversely whether dispensing with imperatives would not mean that the indicative would be diminished and hence misunderstood. For if God "in Christ" has already pronounced his favorable judgment on humanity and *if the people believe this* (that is, if they rely on it), then this changes every person *entirely*. No one is the "old" person anymore; no one is a sinner anymore but "a new creation" "in Christ" (2 Cor. 5:17). New people, however, are new people only if their deeds are new deeds. For if justified people do not live their justification, they are not in truth justified people. So if the actions of the justified are not visible as something inevitably and necessarily connected with their justification and are not expressly mentioned, then faith will remain an intellectual conviction, or it will wither away to become a matter of a pious heart or private intimacy. So we have to talk about people's deeds and hence about the imperative, if God is really to remain the God who gives *to the people* and the indicative is really to remain the indicative. Thus the paradox cannot be resolved.

Yet the persistent problem is how to present this paradox, as well as how to live it. We can illustrate the problem with the process of speaking and then also with language. We should really speak of the indicative and the imperative, of the imperative and the indicative at the same time and in such a way that both are expressed in *one* term. This term would have to be chosen so that both sides of the paradox are summed up in one word. Is there a suitable term? Later (following Pauline terminology) we will make a suggestion, which, however, will not solve the problem completely (cf. pp. 190ff. below). There is probably no entirely satisfactory solution. And this is due to the fact that we live in this old world in a history that is winding down, whereas life as a "new creation" (eschatological existence) is not of *this* world and thus "timeless," even though it is *in* this world that such life is lived and is supposed to be lived, is supposed to be lived and is lived. So we have to speak *successively* of the indicative and the imperative *or* of the imperative and the indicative. This inevitably creates an order, and this order involves the danger that the thing first *named* will also receive first priority.

We can see this in an alternative that is found again and again even today. In opposition to a so-called dogmatic faith it is asserted that the most important thing is a so-called practical Christianity. And if one sees people who reject "dogmas" altogether or are not even familiar with them but still live what is considered practical Christianity, they are dubbed "anonymous Christians." Apart from the fact that people are thereby rather arrogantly characterized and thus judged, we must say that here Christianity is on the verge of deteriorating into *mere* ethics. Yet those who (justly) protest against this are often content to limit their protest to a shift in emphasis. The practical aspect, of course, is not disregarded here. It is declared indispensable, but its absence does not jeopardize the "possession" of the indicative of faith—at least not fundamentally.

We have the same problem in the coexistence of the disciplines of dogmatics and ethics. Traditionally they are mentioned in this order, thereby raising the danger that two things will be separated that we can indeed distinguish but must never separate. This continually creates problems for students (but not for them alone). At one time one discipline is treated (and studied and examined); at another time, the other discipline. The statement is always made, of course, that the two belong together, and "references" are made accordingly. Yet a really comprehensive presentation of both disciplines is rare. Yet separation ruins *both* disciplines.

We can maintain the paradox only if we do not establish an order or give emphases of different weight. Since we are simply "condemned" to *name* the two sides of the paradox in succession, it is natural in our case to begin with the imperative.

### a) *Concrete Ethics?*

We will start with one side of the paradox, the imperatives, which demand quite concrete action. The question mark in the title already points to a problem. Perhaps we can see it most clearly if we proceed from the present.

In the church we often find a great deal of uncertainty in ethical questions. The topics are diverse: the Christian and the state, political decisions of Christians, the establishment of social justice, marriage and divorce, the role of women in the church, and so forth. Accordingly people often demand that "the church" (who is that?) finally speak a clarifying word on this or that issue. This clarifying word is supposed to be as specific as possible, so that Christians will know as precisely as possible what they have to do according to God's will. (The Roman Catholic church, of course, can speak such a word because of its understanding of church and office.)

Yet can we make such a demand? Expressed differently, is it possible to pass off very concretely defined action as

Christian action? Here too people like to point to Paul. He gave his churches concrete instructions through imperatives. When those are adopted (modified, of course, and adapted to our present situation), such "apostolic directions" are introduced into Christian ethics.

Yet can we, in Paul's view, call a very concrete action a genuinely Christian action? There are two strong arguments against this: a literary one and a factual one.

*The literary argument.* The documents at our disposal are letters. This, of course, states what is obvious, and it is not enough merely to confirm the obvious. The letters of Paul are not "testimonies of church-founding proclamation" (as Martin Kähler once said of the New Testament scriptures). Rather, Paul's letters (like all other New Testament writings) are testimonies of church-*sustaining* proclamation. Hence no single New Testament writing can be the foundation of what is genuinely Christian.

With his letters Paul tried to bring the churches back after they had somehow strayed from the course on which he had set them at their founding.

The only exception is the First Letter to the Thessalonians. Here Paul encourages a church to stay on the road it is traveling. This is the special attraction of this oldest of Paul's letters, which is generally given far too little attention. Yet even this letter was written to sustain an already existing church.

Yet since the individual problems in the churches were different, and since in the case of several letters to the same church the problems changed (at least in regard to their focus), Paul had to respond in entirely different ways. With his specific ethical instructions he tried to deal with the difficulties that were immediate. Thus we can say that the more concrete the imperative is, the more situational it is and the less suitable it is for presenting and understanding the character of the Pauline ethic. Hence the imperatives in the letters are useless for resolving concrete ethical problems. We will illustrate this with two examples.

When in Rom. 13:1-7 Paul urges the Christians *in Rome* to "be subject to the governing authorities," he is adopting ideas that were expressed repeatedly in the Hellenistic Judaism of the time. They are not specifically Christian, and Paul does not try to give them some sort of Christian foundation. Thus he is not discussing here the topic, the Christian and the authorities (or the Christian and the state). His letters give no indication at all that he ever thoroughly examined that topic. Paul's writing of these verses to Rome has to do with the concrete situation there. Of course, that situation can only be reconstructed, and on this point there are different opinions. If the situation cannot be reconstructed with certainty, we must not attempt to explain the text apart from it. For this pericope cannot be analyzed at all *as a statement by Paul* apart from the situation, because it is an imperative *to Rome*.

Paul probably knew about a previous intervention of the Roman authorities into quarrels within the church. According to Acts 18:2 Jews had been expelled from Rome at that time: their strife had disturbed public order. After the return of the Jewish Christians, the quarrels threaten to erupt again. Paul wants to prevent this if possible.

Such specific instructions are misused, however, if they are generalized.

The same thing can be said of the discussion of women in the church. According to 1 Cor. 14:34 women should be silent in congregational meetings. Whether this word comes from Paul or whether 1 Cor. 14:33b-36 is an addition by a later scribe (which I believe is probable) can well be left undecided, for this issue does not affect the basic problem. If Paul orders (or is supposed to have ordered) that women remain silent, he does not mean women in general but the women in Corinth who created disorder with their enthusiastic ecstasies. If "orderly" conditions prevail in a church, Paul can easily assume that women pray in public. In his view, order in those days included women praying with their heads veiled (1 Cor. 11:5). How situational such specific instructions are can be seen in the fact that Paul could write (to the Galatians and for entirely different reasons) that "in Christ" there is no longer male and female (Gal. 3:28). That this is no statement of fact (even in church gatherings) is shown by the context: "in Christ" there is neither Jew nor Greek, neither slave nor free. As a matter of fact, these differences do exist even in the church; only "in Christ" do they no longer exist.

If we want to present Pauline ethics, we cannot take the content of specific imperatives and then summarize them according to topic—certainly not if we want to make statements about Christian ethics today. The documents we have before us, after all, are just letters.

*The factual argument.* After Paul has given the Romans advice in Rom. 13:1-7 on how to deal with the authorities (on account of the situation in Rome), he proceeds in 13:8-10 to a discussion of fundamental issues.

The transition is clearly marked in 13:8: "Owe no one anything, except to love one another." The preceding obligations, for instance the paying of taxes, can be fulfilled. Love, however, is a "debitum immortale" (an immortal debt; Bengel). It has to be practiced ever anew, for we can never be finished with it.

Paul quotes a few commandments from the Decalogue. Their fulfillment always results in concrete action. Then he designates the commandment of love as the common denominator of all the commandments and substantiates that by saying that when we love, we will do our neighbors no wrong—that is, we will do precisely what the commandments demand.

It follows that when we see a concrete action, we cannot tell from the outside whether the doer is governed in this deed by love or is obeying the commandments (and thus is following the path of Pharisaic ethics). For the concrete action is the same in both cases. Hence the genuinely Christian nature of an ethic cannot be based on a concrete action but only on the doer.

This shows clearly once more that the Christian ethic is not a "better" ethic than the Pharisaic but a different one. The difference is theological.

Since the genuinely Christian character of an action is never decided by the concrete action, Paul's ethic cannot be grasped by deriving it in isolation from the specific imperatives in the apostle's letters. We have to look at the doer.

So even if we start with the imperative, we are soon confronted again with the question of the indicative, more precisely, with the question of Christology. Of course, the particular nature of Pauline Christology must be taken into account here.

Paul's Christology is misunderstood if it is seen as a "known" Christology and thus as the expression of a conviction. Such a Christology could be examined and presented. Yet as an examined and presented Christology it would remain apart from the person who is speaking. Naturally, it could be *about* an action of God in Christ in the past. Yet this would not affect the person talking *about* this action of God. Such a "known" Christology would be at best a "Christology on call": those who had it could employ it whenever and wherever they chose to or needed to.

We can succeed in comprehending Paul's Christology only if we present it strictly as theology (as talk *of* God). Not only may the speaker be *named,* but he must himself become *visible* in the presentation. Only then does it become clear that the past has really affected Paul. He describes what has affected him as coming from the past, but he can fill the descriptions of that past with various contents.

Paul has become a child of God because God *sent* his Son. Paul lives as a person reconciled with God, because Christ *died for him* on the cross. Paul lives in newness of life, because God *raised Jesus.* Paul lives as a person justified by God (and therefore no longer under the law), because *Christ* is the end of the law for believers.

Only if Paul's Christology is understood as theology (as *one person's* talk of *his* God) does it imply action. For Paul's Christology always talks at the same time about a change in the person. The Pauline imperatives are not intended just to invite people to act: they are addressed to *changed* people. Therefore they do not simply presuppose a "known" indicative; they presuppose an indicative that has *affected* people.

This is exactly what must not be ignored when we appeal to Paul today in Christian ethics. To quote a paradigm, we are called to be reconciled with our enemies. If we accomplish this imperative, we are without doubt doing something that deserves high recognition. Yet it is wrong to call this a specifically Christian action, for we are still looking only at the deed and not at the doer. Only when *reconciled* people practice reconciliation can we talk about a Christian deed.

We should consider the implications of these reflections. One consequence is that those who *can* practice reconciliation as reconciled persons should not look down on others who accomplish reconciliation (not "by faith" but) by their own effort, nor should the latter (conversely) be claimed as "anonymous Christians" because of their exemplary actions. Another implication is that in the church we should not issue the call to reconciliation itself as a Christian imperative. If we do not address potential doers regarding the indicative that has *affected* them, we have missed the crucial point.

So we cannot present Paul's ethic by taking our bearings from his imperatives. Even if we start with them, we are soon referred to the indicative—and thus to the paradox.

### b) Paradoxes

First we will illustrate with a few examples how Paul can formulate the paradox with various concepts and various terms.

*(1) Examples.* The so to speak classic passage (which is also quoted repeatedly in Bultmann's fundamental essay) is Gal. 5:25: "If we live by the Spirit, let us also be guided by the Spirit."

The context shows that Paul intends to offer a summary here. In 5:1 he already had the indicative, "For freedom Christ has set us free," followed by the imperative, "Stand firm [in it], therefore, and do not submit again to a yoke of slavery." And in 5:16 he formulated the imperative, "Live by the Spirit."

In Gal. 5:25 it is obvious that there is no imperative, at least not grammatically, but an exhortation. This is a slight shift of accent, which, however, really expresses his intention better. He is not talking about an obligation in the sense of an ordered duty but an "enabling obligation," with the ability to fulfill it given to us first. This makes us wonder whether Paul's imperatives in general are closer in character to exhortations such as "let us _____" and "we will try to _____" even if their grammatical form is imperative.

In Rom. 6:2 Paul states in an indicative that "we . . . died to sin." Yet in Rom. 6:12 admonishes his readers not to let sin (to which they have died!) exercise dominion in their mortal bodies. In analogy to Gal. 5:25, we could say, "If we have died to sin, let us also not live in sin."

In 1 Cor. 5:7 Paul expresses the paradox with an entirely different concept (which he also uses in Gal. 5:9): "Clean out the old yeast so that you may be a new batch, as you really are [already] unleavened." In this case the imperative does not follow the indicative but precedes it. So the order is apparently reversible. It is characteristic of the indicative here that the characterization is included in the designation of the "doers": *they* are the unleavened ones. Again following Gal. 5:25, we could say, "If we are unleavened, let us also clean out the old yeast."

Another concept with which Paul expresses the same paradox is that of putting on the *kyrios*. In Gal. 3:27 he substantiates the indicative by reference to the received baptism: "As many of you as were baptized into Christ have clothed yourselves with Christ" (RSV: "have put on"). The appeal to lay aside the works of darkness and put on the armor of light is summed up by Paul in Rom. 13:14: "Put on the Lord Jesus Christ." And once again we can say in analogy to Gal. 5:25, "If we have put on the Lord Jesus Christ, let us also put on the Lord Jesus Christ."

Here we should at least mention in passing one problem whose solution created difficulties later on. Paul can express the origin of faith and with it the reception of the indicative in two ways. He can (e.g., in Gal. 3:27) refer to the received baptism and talk about the Spirit in connection with baptism (1 Cor. 12:13). He can also say (e.g., in Rom. 10:17) that faith comes from the message that is heard, and he can likewise trace the reception of the Spirit to what is heard in the proclamation of faith (Gal. 3:2). It is important to observe closely the direction of this statement. *In retrospect* Paul can refer to the received baptism *or* the heard proclamation. *To this extent* we can indeed say that he does not reflect on the relationship between word and sacrament. Apparently he sees no problem in the coexistence of the two.

Yet we cannot simply reverse the direction of the statement. Paul never talks programmatically about baptism. Nowhere does he say what will happen to those who are baptized in (future) baptisms in the churches. If, however, we interpret Paul's statements on *completed* baptisms as statements on *ongoing* baptisms, we not only misuse them but also risk losing the paradox. We would make the indicative (the completed baptism) an issue in itself, to which the imperative is added. We would then, of course, also have to assert of (today's) proclamation that it "bestows" the Spirit.

Such a misunderstanding had apparently already happened in Corinth. Paul quotes the "sacraments" that the ancestors had in the wilderness (1 Cor. 10:1-6). Yet since they had not integrated ethics into the sacrament, "God was not pleased with most of them." Thus, according to Paul, baptism in no way bestows a *character indelibilis* (indelible character). This is true for ongoing baptism. But baptized persons can refer to the baptism they received *or* they can trace their faith to the word proclaimed to them (without saying anything different here).

Apparently the temptation to resolve the paradox is great. We will now explain the character of this temptation with another example.

*(2) The shaping of the shaped.* Paul uses the words *typos* and *mimetes* several times, individually as well as together. They occur in the indicative (1 Thess. 1:6-7; 2:14; 1 Cor. 11:1; Phil. 3:17b) and in the imperative (1 Cor. 4:16; 11:1; Phil. 3:17a).

*Typos* is usually translated "model" or "example"; the noun *mimetes* in most cases is used in a verb construction meaning "be(come) an imitator." These English translations, however, do not render Paul's concern adequately, for they are easily misunderstood to mean a kind of imitation: we should look at the behavior or action of the model because we can learn from it how we should behave or what we must do. For ethics this means that the model is an imperative, since its example calls for imitation. An indicative is missing.

> This is an ancient misunderstanding. Just a few years after Paul, the author of 2 Thessalonians succumbed to it when he composed his writing as a letter "of Paul" (often slavishly adhering to the wording of 1 Thessalonians). The (unknown) author says that he has learned that there are some among his readers who are living "in idleness" (3:11). Thus they have deviated from the "example" Paul has given them (3:9). In 3:8 he describes this example for them, copying 1 Thess. 2:9 almost word for word, and urges them to *mimeisthai* (imitate) Paul's example (3:7, 9). Thus he intends to correct this idle life with an imperative: "Imitate the example of Paul!" An indicative that would enable his readers to follow the imperative is missing. This is true not only here but throughout the letter. This deutero-Pauline scripture lacks all the indicatives that belong to the many imperatives we find in it (cf. pp. 250-55 below).

Yet with these words Paul is not referring to imitating the behavior seen in a model. He makes this clear especially by the indicatives that substantiate the imperatives. It is not simply "people" who are ordered to follow the imperatives; instead the imperatives are always given to "changed people." They already bring with them what is expected of them.

In Phil. 3:17 Paul urges his readers to become his *mimetai*. He and those who live like him are a *typos* for the Philippians. The reason why they are a *typos* (and can be in the first place) is mentioned by Paul in the preceding verse, "Only let us hold fast to what we *have* attained" (Phil. 3:16). He can invite the Corinthians to be his *mimetai* because he *has* become their "father through the gospel" (1 Cor. 4:15-16). And he can do this only because he himself is a *mimetes* of Christ (1 Cor. 11:1).

What we find here in scattered utterances of the apostle had already been stated earlier in a coherent text. He writes to the Thessalonians that by holding to God's gospel in all their distress and affliction they have become *mimetai* of him and thus of the *kyrios*. And as such *mimetai* they have themselves become a *typos* for all believers in Macedonia and Achaia (1 Thess. 1:6-7). So now we can see a chain. The *(arche)typos* is the *kyrios*. Paul is a *mimetes* of the *kyrios,* and as such he is a *typos* for the churches. The churches are then *mimetai* of Paul (and of the *kyrios*). And if this is what they are (and Paul exhorts them to be what they are), then they are a *typos* for others.

Typical here is the paradox that determines Paul's self-understanding. On the one hand, Paul is indispensable; on the other, he is totally unimportant. Paul is indispensable because the churches would never have become *mimetai* without the *typos* Paul. At the same time he is unimportant because the churches that became his *mimetai* did not really become his *mimetai* but those of the *kyrios.*

This chain is set to continue, although in Paul (in the "second generation") we can see only its beginnings. This creates problems in a history that (inevitably) continues. The real issue, however—even in the tradition—is always immediacy to the *kyrios.*

The question now is, what does it mean that Paul (and through him the churches) are *mimetai* of the *kyrios*? In other words, in what sense can we call the *kyrios* the archetype?

By no means may we point here to the earthly Jesus, to his behavior and deeds, and quote examples from the synoptic tradition. This misunderstanding has arisen at times because people have understood *typos* and *mimetes* in the sense of imitation. With this understanding, naturally, it is quite impossible to try to "imitate" the *kyrios* (as the exalted Lord) in any way. So people have then understood the behavior and deeds of the earthly Jesus as a model or example and have thereby done the exact same thing as the author of 2 Thessalonians, who took the behavior and deeds of Paul as an example to be imitated.

And if the behavior and deeds of the earthly Jesus (mostly called the historical Jesus) are understood today (not exactly seldom) as a model for Christian ethics, we must ask the same question that we ask of the author of 2 Thessalonians: Will this not result in an ethic that has only imperatives, that ignores indicatives and even thinks it can do without them?

For Paul the *kyrios* is always that *kyrios* who met him near Damascus. Yet if he looks back to the earthly Jesus (which happens seldom enough), Paul always sees him from the perspective of the Damascus experience. The *kyrios* is the one "who loved me and gave himself for me" (Gal. 2:20). In other words, whenever Paul talks of the *kyrios* (or the Son of God or Christ), he is giving a summary of his Christology or, more precisely, a summary of the Christology that he *received*.

This becomes clear if we understand the terms *typos* and *mimetes* in their precise meanings. Paul uses the word *typos* in its original sense of a die. The *kyrios* has shaped the person Paul just as a die leaves an impression or imprint. In this way Paul can become a *mimetes:* as a person shaped by the *kyrios* he becomes a shaper himself. Hence the term *mimetes* has to be translated "one who shapes further." The *further* is important. For only people who have been shaped themselves and pass on their received shape through their own acts of shaping are *mimetai*.

Those who, by contrast, only *imitate* someone else do so as "old" (unshaped) people to whom nothing has yet happened. The indicative is missing. They only see how someone else has behaved (e.g., the earthly Jesus or Paul) and attempt to behave in the same way.

These considerations bring to our attention an English word, *to shape,* that permits us to state the paradox of indicative and imperative in *one* expression (at least to some extent):

Indicative/imperative: Paul is a shaped shaper.
Imperative/indicative: Paul is a shaping shape.

At this point we can also understand why Paul can start with either the indicative or the imperative. What he starts with depends on the situation that he is addressing. Nevertheless, this does not resolve the paradox; it only shifts the emphasis.

If Paul starts with the indicative and works it out with special emphasis, it means in regard to the imperative that an activity is already going on, but it can be improved with a more thorough understanding of the indicative. The most striking example of this is 1 Thessalonians.

Paul addresses the Thessalonians as shaped people who already have become shapers (1 Thess. 1:6-8). In 1 Thess. 2:1-13 he vividly tells how this shaping occurred by interpreting the past as he experienced it. In 1:8, for instance, he emphasizes that his missionary work consisted not only in sharing the gospel with the church (today this is still generally considered the crucial part) but also in sharing with the Thessalonians his own life. In other words, Paul presents to the church his own shaped existence. The church has been shaped by him and hence can be encouraged to live the indicative that it is already living even better through more comprehensive understanding (cf. 1 Thess. 4:1, 9-10).

In the terminology of Gal. 5:25 we can say, "You who live by the Spirit are already walking in the Spirit, and this is exactly what you can do even better."

In writing to other churches Paul begins not with the indicative but with the imperative. He challenges them to become his *mimetai*. This raises the initial (and fundamental) question, Under what conditions in Paul's ethic can we begin with the indicative?

The clearest illustration is in Phil. 3:17. The Philippians are to become his *symmimetai* (fellow *mimetai*) and look after those who live in the same way, because they have Paul as their *typos*. Paul quickly connects his initial imperative with the indicative.

We can begin with the imperative, because in doing the imperative we soon catch up with the indicative. Those who are challenged to shape can (and should!) realize in the process that they are shaping *as shaped people.* This is indispensable for Paul if ethics is to remain Christian ethics. For the doing of a formulated imperative remains Christian ethics only if we realize while doing it that this doing does not happen as an obligation demanded by an imperative but as a capability. This capability is then substantiated christologically with the help of a Christology *that is received in the doing.* If this is not the case and this connection is not seen, the doing is our own accomplishment and a reason for boasting.

Do we give this enough consideration when we are concerned with ethics in the church today? We almost always focus on imperatives, which give concrete directions, for example, on how reconciliation is to be practiced. Occasionally an indicative is presupposed, but it takes the form of a reference, say, to cross and resurrection. To whom the imperatives are addressed remains an open question. Yet they really can only be spoken to those who have received the indicative. They can never be valid for *everybody* as the "word of the church." Yet if they are supposed to be valid for everybody, is it then made sufficiently clear that as the the imperative is done, the indicative will try to come? It can indeed happen that doers of reconciliation will realize during their doing that they can afford to do reconciliation because they risk it as people reconciled *in Christ.*

Thus we must always be careful not to resolve the paradox. This can easily happen, because this paradox is not only diffcult to formulate but also difficult to maintain. Very likely there are no formulations that are not subject to misunderstanding and therefore to the risk of missing the mark in practice.

If we express the paradox with the words *gift* and *task,* for example, and even stress the inseparable connection between the two, there is still the risk that people will think that they can "have" the gift even when at the moment they are not doing the task. The gift, however, does not come until we do the task.
    If, comprehending this, we understand the gift merely as an offer, there is a risk that we will see in it an opportunity we

are invited to seize. This is indeed true, but it can easily lead to the misunderstanding that we ourselves are the ones who carry out the imperative (here again, as our own accomplishment).

Yet another risk is that we might separate the gift from the Giver. This leads to the loss of theology (a person's talk *of* his or her God). For now we are talking *about* God, who not only remains apart but is even pushed off into the distance by this separation. The people have only the gift. They overlook the fact that God does not give something; God gives himself.

Perhaps with the help of the suggested term *to shape* we can avoid such misunderstandings somewhat more easily. Avoiding them altogether, however, will hardly be possible, and it is not hard to demonstrate the reason why this is true.

Whatever terms are used to express the paradox, it can always be reduced to the two entities, God and humanity. The concrete actions of shaped people are always the actions of these people and the actions of God, and they are both at the same time. So any concrete (!) action has two subjects: God and a human being. Yet the idea that one and the same action is performed by two different actors can only be stated as a paradox.

With his Christology Paul tells how God acts. To illustrate this we can point again to his Damascus experience. We have shown that what happened to Paul here was a "change of Gods." Prior to Damascus Paul's God was a God who had given the people the law. Yet this was talk *about* God. For Paul's real God was the law itself with its specific instructions, which the people were obligated to follow. In this ethical concept it is clearly the people who act.

When Paul realized at Damascus, however, that God is really *God* (that is, when talk about God became theology), then the one who acts could only be God, even in things the people are doing. Paul expresses this most pointedly when he uses the term *synergon (tou) theou* (coworker of God).

He applies this term to himself (together with Apollos) and accordingly calls the church God's (!) field and God's building

(1 Cor. 3:9; cf. varying translations: "labourers together with God" [KJV], "fellow workmen for God" [RSV], "God's servants, working together" [NRSV]). Paul calls Timothy "our . . . co-worker for God in proclaiming the gospel of Christ" (1 Thess. 3:2), which copyists tried to soften because it seemed to them too strong. But this is precisely what Paul means; he can even call Titus and other brothers *doxa Christou* ("the glory of Christ"; 2 Cor. 8:23). If we translate the word *doxa* as "reflection," we must emphasize that those who reflect Christ's glory are radiating this glory themselves.

In general, we can state what Paul means as follows. *Every action of Christians(!) is an action of their Lord.*

It is understandable that later people tried to master this paradox by means of some logical system, as can be seen in the history of dogmatics. For instance, they asked the question whether people can or even must play a role in their salvation. Yet every answer given to this question is wrong. It is wrong especially when salvation is placed in the future. But it is also wrong when we seek a salvation that occurs in the present.

For if we say that people can or must help effect their salvation, we do not take seriously the *kyrios* who accomplishes *all things.* If we say, on the other hand, that people cannot play a role in their salvation, we immediately run the risk that people will no longer be responsible for their actions.

So for human beings, according to Paul, Christian ethics remains an impossible possibility *as well as* a possible impossibility.

The same idea occurs in the synoptic tradition in Mark 10:17-27. The rich young man had observed all the commandments but was not ready to sell everything he had and give the proceeds to the poor. Then comes a discussion of the rich. It is easier for a camel to go through a needle's eye than for those who are rich (who have ties on earth that they neither can nor will cut) to practice the lordship of God. "For mortals it is impossible," as we read in the conclusion, "but not for God," for whom "all things are possible"—even making a mortal his coworker, to use Paul's term.

For people who are waiting to become Christians, this is hardly acceptable. They cannot even state it logically. Therefore they can only wait for it to happen anyway. But this must not lead them to try to get Christian ethics "cheaper" or to abandon hope. For while hope is determined by what is not there yet, faith is determined by what was there already.

*(3) Paul as a typos of the resurrected crucified One.* Paul understood himself in his work as a *typos* for his churches. He substantiated his authority to serve as a *typos* by the fact of his being a *mimetes* of the *kyrios*. Yet this self-understanding as a *typos* was not something that he claimed only for himself and that was therefore true only for him (e.g., as an apostle). The churches too became a *typos* for others in their work. Hence we can generally define Christian existence in Paul's understanding: it is serving as a *typos*. This happens through people, but only through people who have themselves been shaped by the *kyrios*.

We have already seen that Paul cannot be referring to the earthly Jesus when he talks about the *kyrios* in this context (cf. pp. 192-93 above). Rather, the *kyrios* is the resurrected or exalted One. Yet this designation is insufficient because it provides no content. According to Paul, without a better definition of the content, we can come to a dangerous misunderstanding. This misunderstanding can be avoided only if we make clear that we are talking about the resurrected crucified One.

As already seen, the creeds "Christ died for us" and "God raised Jesus from the dead" were originally individual formulas that existed independently. So we are dealing literally with two competing formulas. Each of them was a complete statement of faith and needed no expansion. Paul was familiar with these individual formulas as well as with the combined form, as can be seen especially in 1 Cor. 15:3-5. The combination of the two, however, is precisely where the problem arises.

There are two ways to combine the statements made by these two formulas: paradoxically and additively. We can see right away that the first way is the more difficult way. For now we must try to connect two originally competing statements in such a way that *one* statement results but still contains *two* statements. For example, "We believe that Jesus died and rose again" (1

Thess. 4:14). Here is an attempt to formulate paradoxically. The *one* faith is based on death and resurrection *at the same time.* This is precisely what constitutes the paradox and makes it hard to recognize and maintain. Therefore the easy path is to resolve it.

It may be, however, that we never get to the paradox because we simply add the two formulas. An example of this is the bit of tradition adopted by Paul in 1 Cor. 15:3-5. The contents are added and not included in each other or closely connected with each other. There is, rather, a sequence. First, Jesus' death is mentioned as the earlier event, then his resurrection.

This addition marks the beginning of a problematic Christology, which then implies a problematic ethic. Instead of formulating Christology paradoxically and maintaining this paradox as the statement of the one *faith,* the new Christology *describes* two "stages." First the cross is mentioned, but it remains in the past, for the crucified One subsequently(!) arose. This now becomes the crucial point, and the resurrected One, the one who in the meantime was exalted to God, receives exclusive attention. This has immediate consequences for ethics. If we express these consequences with the motif of the *typos,* we can say that people are shaped by the One exalted into the glory of God. Yet since they are shaped by this exalted One, the shaped people are themselves exalted by such a shaping. They now understand themselves as "exalted ones," which has consequences for their appearance and their way of life.

This very Christology was advocated in early Christianity and also made its way into Paul's churches. We can see it especially clearly in Paul's correspondence with the Corinthians. At first we might think Paul's concern was, on the one hand, to defend his claim to be an apostle of Jesus Christ against opponents who disputed his apostleship and, on the other, to denounce ethical abuses and eliminate them if possible. Of course, this is also true, but these two issues, which at first glance hardly seem to have anything in common, share the same background: the conflict over Christology.

We cannot simply see Paul's opponents from his perspective and condemn them prematurely. It is understandable that Paul goes after them with sharp words and tries to expose and depose them in the eyes of the Corinthians. Actually, however, they were not simply malicious and malevolent people whose only intention was to defame Paul and who moreover practiced and propagated ethical laxity. Instead, they were theologians (in the precise sense of the word) who had a Christology of their own and who had to be taken seriously. The real question is, which Christology can be called genuinely Christian?

Most of the time we do not realize that early Christianity (even in Paul's missionary area) was by no means a uniform entity. Paul's opponents claimed to be Christians too, and it was anything but certain which Christology would prevail. Our judgment is easily obscured by the fact that we can draw only indirect conclusions about Paul's opponents from his polemics against them, and our literary evidence comes only from Paul.

So the appearance and behavior of Paul's opponents in Corinth can be explained by their Christology. And they were indeed consistent with this Christology. Yet what can we find out (directly or indirectly) about these opponents?

First we must mention that they called themselves "ministers of Christ" (2 Cor. 11:23) who claimed that Christ spoke in them (2 Cor. 13:3) and that they had received revelations (cf. 2 Cor. 12:1). They referred to their descent from God's people (2 Cor. 11:22) and claimed to be apostles (2 Cor. 11:5; 12:11). So it was claim against claim. How could the Corinthians decide which claim was valid? The opponents had good arguments. When they came, they introduced themselves with letters of recommendation (2 Cor. 3:1). Their appearance must have been imposing, for when Paul says that they "boast according to human standards" (2 Cor. 11:18; cf. 2 Cor. 5:12; 11:12), he means that they had outward merits and emphasized them as a means of legitimation. So they were outwardly impressive. They compared themselves only with one another, formed their own standard, and were thus incomparable (2 Cor. 10:12-13). So it is no surprise that they had considerable success in their proselytizing (2 Cor. 11:20-21). In comparison to them the Corinthians must have felt very humble and had to accept that these "perfect Christians" were above them. The opponents claimed freedom for themselves and hence could live this freedom even in ethical practice (2 Cor. 12:21; 13:2).

Being absent, Paul had a hard time repelling the influence of these people; he was not successful even during a short interim visit. For this very reason he writes a letter. He calls his opponents, who are making such an excellent impression, false apostles, deceitful workers, people who only disguise themselves as apostles of Christ. In this they are doing the work of Satan, who also likes to disguise himself—even as an angel of light (2 Cor. 11:13-14). Because of their magnificent appearance Paul refers to them ironically as "super-apostles" (1 Col. 11:5; 12:11). He accuses them of proclaiming a different Jesus and thereby conveying a different spirit to those who fall for their proclamation. In short, the opponents bring a different gospel (2 Cor. 11:4).

Now, all these things are of course merely assertions, not arguments. Paul can hardly be convincing with them, especially since he must and does admit that the portrait of him drawn by the opponents is quite accurate. The opponents really make an impression, and Paul is nothing by comparison. He actually did arrive in Corinth without letters of recommendation. He lacks any legitimation that would confirm his authority. It is true that he can write weighty letters (through which he has been influential even into our time and has authority as a letter writer). But when he is present in person, he makes a weak impression and is not even a good speaker, let alone a charismatic one (2 Cor. 10:10). So it is not surprising when he behaves humbly (2 Cor. 10:1). He would not even dare to think of having himself supported by the church, as his opponents do on account of their imposing appearance (2 Cor. 11:7, 12:13). All in all, he really presents a strange image as an apostle of Jesus Christ.

Yet Paul uses this very image as an argument. He points out that long before the opponents arrived, this "weak" apostle accomplished something among the Corinthians. From the beginning, he trusted in the hope that he would be legitimized by his work. Why would he then need a letter of recommendation? The church that originated through his work was itself his letter of recommendation (2 Cor. 3:1). His work in weakness proved powerful enough to bear fruit in the church. When he came to Corinth, he really did not excel in speech or in wisdom. Rather, he came "in weakness and in fear and in much trembling." Yet in this very way he accomplished among the Corinthians a "demonstration of the Spirit and of power." In his behavior and ministry he wanted "to know nothing among you except Jesus Christ and *him crucified*" (1 Cor. 2:1-5).

Here Paul states the christological antithesis, and he does so by reversing the point of view. The opponents in Corinth (and many Corinthians under their influence) thought in "soteriological stages," which they perceived as a progression. The cross was left behind and thus became history already overcome. Now they had only the resurrected One, in whose exaltation they participated. The result was a *theologia gloriae* (theology of glory), which shaped the opponents in their appearance and behavior. Paul, by contrast, looked backward. Anyone who believes in the exalted *kyrios* today believes in the resurrected *crucified* One. As *mimetes* of *this kyrios* Paul became a *typos* for the Corinthians. For this reason he could not appear in glory, like his opponents, but only in the weakness of the crucified One. So the people who looked at Paul always saw humility. Paradoxically, however, from this humility glory is asserted because it is the glory of the *resurrected* crucified One.

People who judge by outward appearance have to regard this as foolishness, just as the "word of the cross," which Paul *lives*, is "a stumbling block to Jews and foolishness to Gentiles" (1 Cor. 1:23). Yet if the Corinthians remember what happened to them through Paul, they should be able to testify that exactly this is the power of God.

When Paul refers then to his appearance and his activity, he is referring to the resurrected crucified One and can only argue paradoxically. "We are afflicted in every way, but not crushed; perplexed, but not driven to despair; persecuted, but not forsaken; struck down, but not destroyed; always carrying in the body *the death of Jesus,* so that *the life of Jesus* may also be visible in our bodies. For while we live, we are always being given up to death for Jesus' sake, so that the life of Jesus may be made visible in our mortal flesh. So death is at work in us, but life in you." (2 Cor. 4:8-12)

If we dare to become *mimetai* of *this kyrios*, we cannot expect this to bring great success *for ourselves*. Rather, we will risk many kinds of trouble. Outsiders will always considers us losers. If we try to avoid trouble, we cease, as his *mimetai*, to be a *typos* of *this kyrios* and become unfaithful to his service (cf. 2 Cor. 6:3). The people who prove themselves as "servants of God" will only be those who maintain their lived faith "through great endurance, in afflictions, hardships, calamities, beatings, imprisonments, riots, labors . . . in honor and dishonor, in ill repute and good repute . . . as impostors and yet . . . true; as unknown and yet . . . well known; as dying, and see—we are alive; as punished, and yet not killed; as sorrowful, yet always rejoicing; as poor, yet making many rich; as having nothing, and yet possessing everything" (2 Cor. 6:4-5; 8-10).

This existence according to and with the image of the resurrected crucified One would be misunderstood, if we assumed that Paul was talking about intentional suffering (or even a longing for martyrdom). Sufferers are not distinguished by suffering as such. They are not told to endure possible sufferings with "stoic patience" because they are "free" and their "freedom" cannot be endangered by suffering. On the contrary, according to Paul only a slave of Christ is free. Hence we are dealing with the suffering of a *typos* who as a sufferer shapes other people. For as a *mimetos* of the resurrected crucified One, a *typos* knows that there is always a risk of suffering. Yet for this very reason the suffering that is endured for other people can be experienced paradoxically as glory.

These statements would also be misunderstood if we assumed that Paul had only "apostolic" suffering in mind, that is, that suffering was a peculiarity of his existence as an apostle. Paul tries, rather, to demonstrate by his own example what is true for Christian existence in general. He told the Thessalonians that they had become a *typos* for other people (1 Thess. 1:7). He urges the Corinthians to become his *mimetai* (1 Cor. 4:6), for through him they will then become *mimetai* of Christ. And if they become *mimetai*, they will inevitably become a *typos* for others—a *typos* of the resurrected crucified One.

It is legitimate to ask whether we still perceive and evaluate these connections when we reflect on Christian ethics today. The Christology of Paul's opponents—and with it their self-understanding and claim—remain a temptation for the church and its members. Do we see clearly enough, in contradiction to this Christology, that those who dare eschatological existence cannot escape its consequences? Are these consequences still named and presented *together with* ethics today as explicitly as they were by Paul in his correspondence with the Corinthian church?

If they were, many a discussion of ethical questions would probably be different. First, we would have to take a more intensive look at the doer (will we and can we dare to *become* Christians?) before we ask what Christians do or should do and discuss imperatives.

## 4. Imperatives

Nevertheless, imperatives remain a topic in ethics. But it is a question of putting this topic in its proper place.

### a) The Necessity of Imperatives

The paradox expressed by indicative and imperative is always in danger of becoming unbalanced. When that happens, it is necessary to shift the accent to the other side. Yet this must be done in such a way that the balance is really restored, rather than now leaning in the opposite direction. Whenever the indicative is overemphasized (say, in Corinth), the imperative must be stressed, without resulting in the destruction of the indicative. Conversely, whenever the imperative is overemphasized (say, in Galatia), the indicative has to be stressed, again without resulting in the destruction of the imperative. It is always essential to maintain the paradox.

Especially in 1 Cor. 5-16 we can see that in Corinth there was great uncertainty in ethical questions. Here Paul answers inquiries that the church had directed toward him; these are apparently arranged according to particular topics. There was a severe case of immorality; Christians sued each other in pagan courts; some church members gave offense by participating in meals involving offerings to idols; glossolalia (speaking in tongues) turned meetings into ecstatic happenings; common meals became carousals; etc. There was great chaos. People went by the motto, "All things are lawful for me" (1 Cor. 6:12; 10:23).

Paul counters this motto with two sentences. The theological sentence reads, "God is a God not of disorder but of peace" (1 Cor. 14:33). The ethical sentence states that "all things should be done decently and in order" (1 Cor. 14:40).

Here it becomes clear again that ethics is an aspect of theology. *If* the God of the Corinthians is a God of peace, then all things are done decently and in order.

In such a situation it is evident that imperatives are necessary. Yet when this has been ascertained, we should still take our time and not start too soon with imperatives. For if we want to judge the whole situation, we must first have a thorough understanding. This statement may sound trite, but it is not unnecessary.

For we would understand the situation very superficially if we thought that in Corinth it is a question of "dissolute Christians" who must be called to order with energetically delivered imperatives.

This premature judgment is frequently encountered. People have certain standards by which they judge, and they apply these standards to people of the past. Then it is easy to talk of failure. The more obvious question, however, has to be, Did these people, who seem to have acted so impossibly, act correctly according to their presuppositions? Precisely this may be the case for the Corinthians, as strange as this may at first glance appear to us.

For the Corinthians were by no means ethically "dissolute Christians." We could almost say: on the contrary! For these people not only considered themselves Christians but were also convinced that when they acted the way they did, they acted correctly as Christians. In their veiw, after all, as Christians they had become "free" people.

Again we are confronted with a problem we have often pointed to already. People are prematurely interested in concrete ethical decisions without reflecting on how they come about.

The whole situation becomes understandable if we consider the dualistic anthropology of the Corinthians and use it as a point of departure.

Their concept was that in a person's body lives the person's soul. (The terminology varies: instead of *body* we may read *flesh*; instead of *soul* we find *self, ego,* or even *spirit.*) Body and soul are opposites. The soul alone was in need of redemption and capable of redemption, which could happen in different ways: through mystery cults or sacraments. Or the soul could receive *gnosis* (knowledge) through proclamation.

If the soul was redeemed, however, it was saved once and for all. It did still live in the body, which could now be called the prison of the soul. But after the death of the body the saved soul would start its journey to heaven.

Thus in this dualistic anthropology everything depended on the soul and on it alone. If the soul was redeemed, the person had received the indicative. The body had nothing to do with this indicative. And since ethics was lived with the body, the saved soul could be indifferent to what the body was doing.

With this anthropological presupposition the Corinthians could then say: "I am a Christian," meaning my self, my ego, my soul *is* a Christian. For that is where redemption had really happened.

This standpoint allows us to understand, for example, the behavior of some Corinthians at their common meals (1 Cor. 11:17-22). When the wealthy came together, ate, drank (and got drunk), they could do so in good conscience, for the poor who came later did not miss anything: they participated in the sacrament that was celebrated at the end.

In this anthropology the indicative could be understood as

a "gift" and indeed as a gift that one "had." In this situation the imperative had to be stressed. This, however, was not at all easy. For the real question here (at least for the Corinthians) is, what is the soul supposed to do with an imperative?

The task facing Paul was basically to change the dualistic anthropology. But is this possible? Can Paul simply impose his (originally Jewish) anthropology on the Corinthians as the "correct" one?

Jewish anthropology is not dualistic; it sees a person as a unified whole. This is often hard to see, for we find very similar terms. We can also ask whether Paul always fully recognized these differences (from the beginning). As an example we can point to 1 Cor. 15.

Some people in Corinth held that there is no resurrection of the dead (1 Cor 15:12). Paul concludes from this that if there is no resurrection of the dead, then there is no hope for humanity (1 Cor. 15:19). Now Paul reproaches the Corinthians for inconsistency, since they practice baptism for the dead (so-called vicarious baptism; 1 Cor. 15:29). This has to be meaningless if there is no hope for the dead.

Yet from the Corinthians' point of view (and that of their anthropology), it is not meaningless at all. In disputing the resurrection of the dead, they are disputing the resurrection of the body. For them there is indeed hope of resurrection, but only for the redeemed soul. If a person whose soul is not yet redeemed dies, the soul of the deceased is subsequently redeemed through vicarious baptism, so that it can start its journey to heaven. The body, of course, stays in the grave. Thus the Corinthians are not at all without hope, as Paul maintains. Yet if resurrection of the dead means resurrection of whole persons (body and soul), then this does mean hopelessness for the Corinthians, for now the redeemed soul remains in its body, that is, in its prison. Precisely because the Corinthians have hope (even though only for the soul), they dispute the resurrection of the dead.

We cannot say whether Paul succeeded in overcoming the anthropological dualism of the Corinthians (or whether this is even possible). Anthropology was not an express issue in this dispute. We do find, however, distinct attempts at correction.

In 1 Cor. 6:12-20 Paul calls the body a "temple of the Holy Spirit" and says that the Corinthians have their body from God. Thus in contrast to the Corinthian anthropology, he tries to upgrade the body. In so doing Paul brings in the concept of creation, which is unknown in the context of dualistic anthropology. It is required, however, by Paul's concept of God. There is nothing that is not from God. In this way body and soul can be treated together. Ethics becomes possible again.

We cannot say whether the Corinthians understood this. The exegetical question, meanwhile, is what Paul was trying to achieve, and the dogmatic question is whether we can understand this and accept it with our all but uniform anthropology.

Now we must note that Paul is arguing dialectically, because he is trying to maintain the paradox. This becomes evident, for example, when he discusses the problem of freedom.

When the Corinthians talk about the freedom that they have as Christians (and hence about the indicative), and when they express this freedom with the statement that all things are lawful for them, then Paul cannot—and does not—dispute this indicative. He expressly repeats, "All things are lawful for me." In this way he adopts the thesis of the Corinthians, but he immediately continues, "but not all things are beneficial . . . but I will not be dominated by anything" (1 Cor. 6:12). Similarly, in a later context he writes: "All things are lawful, but not all things are beneficial. All things are lawful, but not all things build up. Do not seek your own advantage, but that of the other" (1 Cor. 10:23-24) So here too we find Paul's characteristic way of speaking.

In this context we often hear that Paul limits freedom: freedom may be practiced only if it does not hurt other people. This is not wrong, of course, but it should be stated positively. It is also helpful here to use the *typos-mimetes* motif. Since we are free as people shaped by the *kyrios,* we are shaping properly only if other people become free through our shaping.

Freedom is nevertheless too easily understood in a one-sided way. All troublesome restrictions are removed. Nothing suppresses people anymore. Nothing compels them or keeps them in check. They are "free."

Yet this is not the freedom that Paul has in mind. He sees it paradoxically and includes its positive aspect.

The given freedom is an effective power. The *kyrios* gave it. Hence *he* effects freedom through the people who have become free, in that these people are living freedom for others and in this way making them free. So we can (and must) say paradoxically that those who are slaves of the *kyrios* are free. And only they!

If we apply this basic pattern to the imperatives of the letter, we see that it is not simply a matter of imperatives that are to be obeyed. Rather, we must keep in mind the people in whom the actions originate and the people who are to be affected by the actions. The freedom that a person lives is always the freedom of others too.

Of course, Paul does not have in mind simply and exclusively libertines, but also people who are uneasy and feel uncomfortable with the actions of the libertines. These uneasy ones may be the very people who asked the questions that Paul is answering.

We find similar problems in the context of food sacrificed to idols. Apparently Christians in Corinth do not know what position to take on this issue. If Paul wants to resolve the prevailing uncertainty, it seems the question of what to do must be answered with imperatives, and these do indeed occur in 1 Cor. 8-10. Yet if we look only at the imperatives in regard to this problem, we can easily get into trouble, for they seem contradictory. A prohibition (cf. 1 Cor. 10:14, 21) is followed by an explicit permission, which then, however, is restricted again (cf. 1 Cor. 10:25-28). Hence at times experts have thought that the different statements had to be separated and regarded as parts of hypothetically different letters. Yet this is not really necessary, and it would not solve the real ethical problem.

First we have to see that within the whole problem field of sacrifice to idols there are two aspects, which are connected with each other but still have to be distinguished. Both deal with the eating of food: in one case within the context of *worshiping* an idol (that is, cultically), in the other, simply as the *eating* of meat sacrificed to an idol (that is, as a completely "secular" eating of the meat of cultically slaughtered animals). This alone makes it necessary to state the imperatives differently. Yet this is not the real problem.

The real issue is perceived only when we see that what is important is not the imperatives themselves but their theological (in the literal sense) substantiation. This means that we must first look not at the actions demanded or recommended in each case but at the doers, and we must inquire about their God. Which God defines them? If we see this, we recognize the similarity of the argumentation in the two cases.

In Corinth Christians believe that idols and demons do not exist. This consequence of monotheism is almost taken for granted, and insofar Paul shares this view (1 Cor. 8:4-6). The Corinthians, however, have put this view directly into practice. If there are no idols, people can freely participate in pagan worship services. For the Corinthians these were no longer services of worship but simply popular, widespread social events. Just as freely, they could eat sacrificial meat at such events, and in their homes or in the homes of others they could also eat meat bought at the market, where one never knew whether or not it came from ritually sacrificed animals. If there were no idols, there could be no meat sacrificed to idols but only "normal" meat. And it could be eaten in good conscience (1 Cor. 10:25). Actually, this should have settled the matter, but for Paul it did not settle it at all. He sees that a monotheism that is understood only metaphysically and includes the nonexistence of idols and demons ignores the anthropological aspect, if it even sees it. Yet this is precisely what counts. By bringing in this aspect, Paul makes important distinctions. Even though idols and demons are nonentities (1 Cor. 8:4-5) and hence "by nature" are not gods, they still have power over the people who believe in them (cf. the reverse argumentation in Gal. 4:8).

Therefore participation in the worship of idols is by no means a purely social and thus harmless affair. People who attend such services are exposing themselves to the influence of the idols and hence, whether intended or not, become "partners with demons" (1 Cor. 10:20). In this way Christians challenge their Lord and rebel against him, and Paul asks, "Are we stronger than he?" (1 Cor. 10:22).

With the imperative, "flee from the worship of idols" (1 Cor. 10:14), Paul issues a warning against an unpremeditated "change of gods." The Corinthians must not understand belonging to the *kyrios* as a permanent possession. They can fall out of this relationship, and they even risk doing so carelessly, when they consider the worship of idols permissible and harmless because in their opinion there are no idols. The correctness of a metaphysical (and insofar *only* dogmatic) conviction is not sufficient protection. If the Corinthians participate in such events, which are socially familiar to them and therefore considered harmless, they must not think they are really harmless. Christians must remember that behind these (and probably all) social customs there are powers that compete with the *kyrios* and try to replace him, even if these powers are nonentities. They cease being nonentities when people believe in them. For then these alleged nonentities really influence people, and they become the slaves of demons. In this way they lose the freedom that is theirs only as slaves of the *kyrios*.

The Corinthians can also lose their freedom in another way, however, if as people shaped by the *kyrios* they do not live the *kyrios*. Here that means if they do not *live him for others*. This has to be considered in the question whether one may eat food offered to idols.

People who live in the freedom of the *kyrios* are "strong" and therefore do not need to worry about eating food offered to idols. For idols are really nonentities (1 Cor. 8:4), and thus meat sacrificed to idols is like any other food (1 Cor. 10:25-27). Yet the strong can do this only when they are eating alone or together with other strong people. Here there is no problem at all. But not everyone knows this (1 Cor. 8:7). For "weak" people idols are by no means nonentities. If the weak see someone eat meat sacrificed to idols, they must think that this person is a "partner with demons" and, intentionally or unintentionally, is trying to make them partners with demons too. The nature of the food is not the real problem. Paul does not even take this into consideration. The problem is what happens in the act of eating: the strong are not living the *kyrios* for the weak; they are living demons. And they are really doing this, no matter what subjective intention they attach to it. Now the freedom of the strong becomes a stumbling block to the weak (1 Cor. 8:9), not just an offense but a stumbling block that can destroy them (1 Cor. 8:11).

So lived freedom can have two concrete forms. If the strong are with each other, they can eat sacrificial meat, because sacrificial meat does not really exist. But since in this world and in a church they are never completely alone with each other but always in the presence of the weak, freedom must always take another form. As Paul states for himself, "For though I am free with respect to all, I have made myself a slave to all" (1 Cor. 9:19). And this is what he expects from the strong in Corinth.

Yet forgoing the eating of meat sacrificed to idols—thereby making a slave of oneself—is by no means commanded as an (isolated) imperative; rather, it is suggested argumentatively. It is a question of shaping the freedom in which a person shaped by the *kyrios* lives. Yet this will be understood only by people who see that ethics is an aspect of Christology. For the *kyrios* lived his freedom in this very way.

In this kind of freedom, free people can afford to forgo things they would like to do and are even allowed to do. They can even give up their rights and not sue for them in court (1 Cor. 6:1-11). Yet does this not lead to the disintegration of all order?

Paul sees things differently. By contrast he states, "For God is a God not of disorder but of peace." (1 Cor. 14:33) This contrast is indeed surprising. If we want to replace disorder with order, we usually do this by setting up rules, by formulating imperatives whose observation establishes or reestablishes order. When Paul instead defines God here as a God of peace, he assumes that the bringing of peace is the power that creates order among Christians.

This bringing of peace carries a price for those who bring it. They are not seeking their own advantage but that of their neighbors. For the people who are seeking their own advantage are the very ones who become slaves; they are slaves to themselves. So Paul can say, "All things are lawful for me, but I will not be dominated by anything" (1 Cor. 6:12), not even by himself. The only one who rules him is the *kyrios*.

We can summarize by saying that an imperative is necessary wherever people do not see that an indicative always contains an imperative. So the imperative is never something that is added to an indicative. If we urge the following of an imperative, we have to do this in a way that makes people recognize and experience the prior indicative.

> A grammatical consideration can be helpful here. Imperatives are Christian imperatives only if they are hortatives such as "let us _____." For only then does it become clear that they are not commands to be followed, but exhortations to do what the people have already been enabled to do. The paradigm is, Let us love our enemies, for God has already covered us, his enemies, with his love. Imperatives are necessary, but they are formulated appropriately only as hortatives.

## b) *The Contents of Imperatives (on the question of concrete ethics)*

Paul had to impress upon the Corinthians that ethics is by no means unimportant, for being a Christian is not a quality that one can acquire once and for all. Rather, it must be practiced again and again and ever anew, and it must be done physically, for only through paractice can people receive a truly Christian nature. Deeds are not something added to being a Christian; rather, the person shaped by the *kyrios* does the work of the *kyrios*. Hence we can distinguish doer and deed, indicative and imperative, gift and task, dogmatics and ethics. But if we separate them, we ruin both.

Keeping this in mind, when we try to make the distinction, we must answer the following question. When the doer is shaped by the *kyrios*, is the resulting deed different from those of other doers? Nowadays this question is discussed controversially, and that is understandable when we look at the large number of imperatives in Paul.

> Here the temptation to separate what can only be distinguished is especially great. There have been frequent

attempts to arrange the imperatives by topics as a way of establishing "the ethics of Paul." We can approach this in quite different ways. We can compile Paul's scattered comments on individual ethics and social ethics. We can compile his positions on individual problems, such as man and woman, marriage and divorce, work, vocation, property, slavery, relationship to the state, etc. Often this is even done with the intention of getting instructions that can be carried over into a modern Christian ethics.

This approach is problematic in two respects. These issues, which come up only incidentally through the different situations of the addressees and are often dealt with inconsistently, now give the impression that they come from a "Christian ethics" that Paul had at hand and applied as needed. This reconstructed(!) ethics is then presupposed as "the ethics of Paul," who unknowingly becomes the creator of an ethical system and thus citable authority. Overlooked here, though, is the fact that Paul was living in a world entirely different from ours and under completely different social and political conditions. Hence his statements (including the imperatives) cannot be carried over into our time as directly as is often done on the basis of "the ethics of Paul."

So we can succeed only if we ask basic questions from the beginning und do not make separations despite the possible distinctions.

If we look over the large number of imperatives occurring in Paul, we can see that none of the contents is really new. There are many parallels to all of them in Paul's environment. He can use Jewish traditions, commandments of the Decalogue, statements from Old Testament writings, and sayings (cf., e.g., 1 Cor. 6:16; 2 Cor. 8:15; 9:9; Rom. 12:16, 17, 19, 20). He can adopt catalogs of virtues and vices, which were common in Hellenistic popular ethics (cf., e.g., Rom. 12:2; 1 Cor. 5:11; Gal. 5:19-22). Here it is easy to succumb to the false impression that the contents are specifically Pauline (and hence Christian). This is also true of the famous *hos me* ("as though not") sentences, such as, "Let even those who have wives be as though they had none, and those who mourn as though they were not mourning, and those who rejoice as though they were not rejoicing, and those who buy as though they had no possessions, and those who deal with the world as though they had no dealings with it. For the present form of this world is passing away" (1 Cor. 7:29b-31). This is a downright classic description of the Cynic-Stoic ideal of life: the "wise" man lives free from all obligations and in great tranquility; good or bad fortune cannot affect his innermost being.

We can point further to general ethical statements that Paul adopts and to his references to nature. For instance, nature itself is supposed to teach that it is degrading for a man to wear long hair but an honor for a woman (1 Cor. 11:14-15). Paul can refer to custom and hence to what is to be done. The Philippians, for example, are supposed to consider and then practice "whatever is true, whatever is honorable, whatever is just, whatever is pure, whatever is pleasing, whatever is commendable, if there is any excellence, if there is anything worthy of praise" (Phil. 4:8). We can hardly state it more generally. Above all, however, we must ask where in a Christian environment (then or now) are there people who could not agree with such ethical maxims? Decent and orderly people in Paul's pagan environment were also doing all of these things.

All this supports Rudolf Bultmann's judgment: "The ethical demand gained *no new content* for [Paul], and his ethical practice is distinguished from that of other people only by the fact that it has the character of obedience [that is, obedience out of faith]. From the justified person is demanded only whatever is good and acceptable and perfect, whatever virtues and praiseworthy things we might name (Rom. 12:1; Phil. 4:8)" (*Exegetica*, p. 51). Thus according to Paul there can be no material Christian ethics; that is, we cannot specify in detail how Christians should live their lives as Christians, so that their actions can be labeled Christian and can be unmistakably distinguished from the actions of other people.

Yet this view (voiced by many experts other than Bultmann) has also been rejected. This is at first understandable. For if we cannot name the specific contents of Christian actions, there are several dangers. Being a Christian can again be understood as merely the affair of a person's inner being, and deeds are in danger of being left up to the subjective arbitrariness of the individual. Whether this is the only alternative, and whether these dangers are real, can remain undecided for the time being. The question is whether this latter position can be substantiated in Paul.

This is what Wolfgang Schrage (for example) tries to do (*Ethik des Neuen Testaments* [Ethics of the New Testament], esp. pp. 189-92). He does concede that Bultmann made basically correct observations but still holds that there is no way that we can speak of "a wholesale identity between of Christian and extra-Christian ethics." He gives two basic arguments for his position.

First, Schrage refers to statements by Paul saying that Christians should not be conformed to this world but should live apart from it (Rom. 12:2). This should raise the question whether the contents of Pauline ethics can ever fully agree with those of Paul's environment. Yet is this a counterargument in this context? We do have to distinguish between non-Christian ethical "ideals" and the reality of the life lived "in the world," and we have to admit that it is not only non-Christians but also Christians who can fail in their actions. Christians should not be conformed to this oscillation between reality and ideal that is found in the world. And they do not need to do this either, if they let themselves be shaped by their Lord. Yet if we look at the contents of the actions *expected* from each group, those of Christians cannot be distinguished from those of non-Christians. It is always a question of "what is good and acceptable and perfect" (Rom. 12:2).

Then Schrage points out that Paul does not use the all of extra-Christian ethics but only a part of it. This is hard to dispute, but it is hardly helpful either. For now we would first have to compile the contents of the extra-Christian ethical systems that Paul knew but disregarded. And then we would have to determine the criteria for Paul's selection.

Yet we will not, in my view, be successful in finding examples of the *contents* of Pauline imperatives that go beyond what we can also find in Paul's environment. So the real difference is indeed the point made by Bultmann: the actions have the character of obedience. If we want to protect this 1924 formulation from being misunderstood, we can make it more precise. This obedience is of course the obedience of believers, that is, of justified persons who are living the justification they have experienced. So now we have a different motivation for action. It is a question of the shaping action of shaped people. This shaping might well then influence the specific form of the contents. But the contents themselves are not changed in practice in such a way that something *visibly* different results. Only if this were the case could we formulate imperatives that could be called specifically Christian. But this is precisely where Paul offers us no examples.

In this context we cannot refer to love either, although it has a central position in Paul's ethics. That love is supposed to happen concretely cannot be doubted. Therefore it is not properly understood if we take it as an attitude, as a sentiment, or even as a feeling. Rather, the person for whom love is intended should experience it as concrete action. The question is, What does this action concretely look like? Can it be formulated as an imperative? Will the doing of this imperative be visible as a *Christian* action? Here too we cannot appeal to Paul.

To begin with, this again concerns the fact that we can distinguish doer and deed, but we must not separate them. Love is a power that controls the doer. This becomes most obvious where Paul talks about the love of Christ that wants to seize people. When it has seized them, it forces them under its spell and "urges us on" (2 Cor. 5:14). We can indeed say that the love that Christians practice is lived Christology. And this also means that we can speak of the love that Paul has in mind only when Christology is lived.

On the basis of this Christology we can understand that for the doers love always means self-renunciation, but never self-realization. Yet self-renunciation as such is not necessarily a Christian act. It is indeed possible to give away all one's possessions and hand over one's body to be burned (cf. 1 Cor. 13:3), and conceivably this may even be done because of imperatives that have been issued. Yet without love—and that means without doers who are shaped by the love of Christ—this action is worth nothing (by Christian standards).

Ernst Käsemann is correct when he states, "We cannot determine once and for all what God's love demands of us in each case, because only in a concrete decision in a given situation can we know it and do it" (*An die Römer* [To the Romans], p. 315). We can draw two conclusions from this.

We cannot say today what situation we will be in tomorrow. Hence we also cannot state today what concrete action we will take tomorrow as God's will, out of love of Christ. Otherwise we would be pushing away the Lord who is guiding us. In our action tomorrow we would not let ourselves be guided by *him* but by an instruction formulated today by ourselves (or by someone else). We can always follow an instruction, even if the Lord is not driving us with his power. But if today we follow a concrete instruction given yesterday, and if today we pass this instruction off as God's will, we will get the same results that the Jews got over the course of a lengthy history with the law: the instruction will take the place of God.

We have to consider further that it will always be the concrete decision of an individual in a particular situation. Therefore the decision of one person can be totally different from that of another. They both stand or fall before their own lord (cf. Rom. 14:4)

Anyone seeking to avoid ambiguity in ethical decisions will consider this "solution" unsatisfactory. It is also unsatisfactory because there is no solution. Yet this is exactly the nature of the matter.

How hard this is to practice can be seen in an example from the life of Paul, which we can infer from Gal. 2:11-14. It shows, moreover, that not even Paul could always handle it.

When Peter came to Antioch, at first he shared in the table fellowship with Jewish and Gentile Christians. He gave this up, however, when the people of James came from Jerusalem. Paul took him to task for that—apparently to no avail. Which of the two acted correctly in this situation?

If we decide this question in favor of Paul, we are at least judging prematurely. Of course, we could state fundamentally (and then in the imperative) that Jewish and Gentile Christians belong at one table. Yet is this so fundamentally true? Before we condemn Peter, we should listen to his arguments; Paul (understandably) does not mention them in his Letter to the Galatians, but we can certainly reconstruct them. As Paul states, Peter was afraid of the Jews. This must refer to the Jews in Jerusalem. They had already looked suspiciously at the little group of Christians at the Apostolic Council (cf. Gal. 2:4). If it became known in Jerusalem that one of the "pillars" of the church (Gal. 2:9) had been sitting at table with Gentiles, these Jews would have an argument against the Christians. Thus by participating in table fellowship in Antioch, Peter endangered the Jewish Christians in Jerusalem. This is what the people of James made clear to him. So he did not give up the table fellowship because he was opposed in principle to table fellowship between Jewish and Gentile Christians, but because he did not want to endanger other people with his "correct" practice.

We have here an exact parallel to the question whether or not Christians may eat sacrificial meat (cf. pp. 209-11 above), to which Paul had answered that all things are lawful, but not all things are helpful. In Antioch, however, Paul apparently demanded an unambiguous decision. Did he not estimate the danger to be as great as was thought by Peter (and Barnabas and the other Jewish Christians that also left the common table; Gal. 2:13)? Paul does not comment on this (which, again, is understandable in the Letter to the Galatians).

In any case, Paul and Peter judge the situation differently. Hence they necessarily came to different conclusions for their respective actions. For this reason unambiguous concrete decisions are simply not possible. And they are also not possible because we must all render an account before the Lord for our own decisions. If we bow to someone else's decision, we immediately risk denying our own responsibility before our Lord.

We will come back to this problem in the next section.

Since there are no unambiguous concrete imperatives in Pauline ethics, but Christianity has to be practiced concretely in the flesh, each decision is always a risk.

The crucial help in running this risk is Christology. When it shapes people (which does not mean only when people are familiar with it), it changes them and enables them to act. What their concrete actions will be like can never be said in advance. However, even here people are not without help.

Again, we can point to Paul's imperatives. Especially if understood as hortatives, they offer an arsenal of helpful hints that we can employ in our decision-making. Yet we must be careful not to interpret them unintentionally as instructions to be followed. Rather, the things we said above in the excursus "Orientation Models for Sinners" also apply here (cf. pp. 126-34).

### c) The "Weight" of the Imperatives

Pursuant to the foregoing discussion, the problem we must now face can be stated as follows: can anyone (in Paul's view) formulate an imperative for someone else in a way that obliges that person to follow the imperative in order to make sure that his or her action is Christian? Given the nature of the situation, Paul would be the only one who could formulate such imperatives. And what we have said so far already suggests the answer to this question: it is only remotely conceivable.

But what about Paul's "apostolic authority"? Is it the authority of a leader over his followers? Does this authority involve speaking for his dependents and possibly even something like spiritual dictatorship? In Paul's writings on this problem there is a peculiar tension. On the one hand, he can emphasize his authority. On the other, he can play it down completely.

Even in his first (extant) letter Paul writes that as an apostle of Jesus Christ he has the right to act with firmness. Yet he acted gently toward the Thessalonians (1 Thess. 2:7). When his opponents deny his status as an apostle, he can defend his apostleship vigorously and emphasize that he is not ranked second behind Peter and other apostles (1 Cor. 9:1-2). To the same church, however, in which he must fight for the recognition of his apostleship, he can later write: "For we do not proclaim ourselves; we proclaim Jesus Christ as Lord and ourselves as *your slaves* for Jesus' sake" (2 Cor. 4:5). And in the last preserved letter to Corinth, the so-called reconciliation letter (which can be reconstructed from 2 Cor. 1:3-2:13 and 7:5-16), he tells his readers that he is not the master of their faith but a coworker for their joy (2 Cor. 1:24). What does this mean for the imperatives Paul formulated? The answer becomes especially clear in the Letter to Philemon.

Paul pleads on behalf of Onesimus, a slave who ran away from Philemon. In his flight he presumably stole money or did some other damage. Under Paul Onesimus became a Christian.

Now Paul asks Philemon to accept his slave as his brother. Paul would like to keep Onesimus with him, especially since the man was useless to Philemon in the past but has become useful to Paul (a pun: *onesimos* = "useful"). Paul does not say, of course, that Philemon should set Onesimus free, but he clearly hints that he expects Philemon to do that and to send Onesimus back to Paul.

So Paul has a very clear idea of what Philemon really should do. He even hints that Philemon actually owes him a favor. But only Philemon himself can make a decision.

Incidentally, concerning the social problem, we naturally cannot expect Paul also to design a plan to change society and resolve the slavery issue. That lay outside Paul's field of vision (and possibilities). But this does not exclude the possibility that acting in commitment to the *kyrios* will change society. Yet such change does not happen programmatically but indirectly, as an invitation.

In fact, the advice Paul gave Philemon was a double offense against contemporary society and its class interests. First, he sets himself against slaveowners. For if Philemon really frees the slave, then other slaves would become rebellious. But then Paul sets himself against the interests of slaves. For if Onesimus returns to his master voluntarily, he would be ruined for those who try to free the slaves by force (such as Spartacus).

Thus master and slave both spoil their relationship with their particular social class because through their commitment to a common Lord a new community is created.

Now let us take a look at Paul's peculiar argumentation. On the one hand, he says that he has the right to command Philemon to do what is now his duty (Philemon 8), especially since he owes Paul his being a Christian (v. 19). So here Paul is emphasizing his authority. Nevertheless, "on the basis of love" he wants only to appeal to Philemon (v. 9) and emphasizes explicitly that he did not want to make a decision without knowing Philemon's opinion, so that "your good deed might be voluntary and not something forced" (v. 14).

Even if Paul sees very clearly what the Christian Philemon should do now (and can even give good reasons for it), he does not write specific imperatives that Philemon has to follow; instead, he offers assistance in reaching a decision. After all, Philemon could have reasons to decide otherwise, and the letter makes clear that Paul would be willing to accept that, too.

If we want to get our bearings in the ethic of Paul, we can really speak here of a paradigm. Here are some indications:

In the church matters, paraeneses should not be given in a way that anticipates decisions. They should rather be aids that enable individuals to arrive at decisions on their own. In this process (as in Philemon) one must always show why (indicative!) people can make decisions.

At this point preachers could learn a great deal from Paul, but (and we have to put just as much emphasis on this) so could many critics of sermons (and church pronouncements).

If sermons (or church pronouncements) address an appropriate Christology to listeners (or readers) and in this way they learn what they *can* do, then we are dealing with the indicative. It is spoken "with authority." There is no discussion. Only two answers possible here: yes or no. Those who answer yes *can* do it.

Specifically what this deed will look like, however, cannot be stated with authority. Here we can only offer aids to decision-making, and they must remain recognizable as such. For the responsibility for the specific form of the deed always lies with the individual doer.

At this very point, however, the criticism often begins. Preachers and the church are reproached for not being willing to commit themselves; therefore they shrink from making a clear decision. This reproach is made for two (very different) reasons.

First, it may be made because listeners or readers have already decided. They have every right to do so. But now they demand that the preacher or the church arrive at the same decision as theirs. Yet if the preacher leaves the decision open because a specific decision is not at all possible, then the critics reproach the preacher or the church—not, however, for dodging a decision, for example, but in reality for not making obligatory *for everyone* what *they* hold to be obligatory and for that reason is obligatory for them.

The second reason for criticism lies in the critics' own insecurity. They know that they have to make a concrete decision, but they do not know how. If the preacher or church formulates a clear decision, then their insecurity is eliminated. It is indeed eliminated, but at what price?

The responsibility each individual has *toward his or her Lord* is rejected. When making a decision, everyone can now appeal to preacher and church. *They* are now responsible for what the doer actually does. But this is nothing less than a "change of gods."

If Paul had written to Philemon specifically what he must do, then Philemon—had he done it—would have been freed of responsibility both for his own deeds themselves and for the possible consequences (for slaveowners and for slaves). Philemon would not have acted as determined by his Lord but would have simply followed Paul's orders. Paul would then have become Philemon's "god"—even if Paul's orders had been well substantiated.

How about the "weight" of imperatives now? They have weight all right, but only in regard to the indicative that carries the imperatives and is announced together with them. They have no weight whatsoever in regard to the specific contents of the imperatives. For the responsibility for the specific deed always remains with the doers, and they are directly responsible to their Lord.

Anyone who talks about arbitrariness of action, or even of caprice, does not understand what is involved here. For we do not mean that people are free to decide any way they want, this way or that. We are not talking about the decision of a free (= autonomous) person but about the decision of a person whose freedom consists in being the slave of his or her Lord. We are talking about the decision of a person shaped by the *kyrios*.

Those who really expose themselves to the God of Jesus still have to take the risk of a concrete decision. And they will observe that it has nothing at all to do with arbitrariness or caprice.

And if someone else decides differently in a specific case? Then an uninvolved third person might say that Christians make arbitrary decisions, sometimes this way, sometimes that. But those who surrender themselves to the God of Jesus not only know that their own concrete decision is a risk; they also know that someone else's decision is likewise a risk. Hence they will understand when someone else decides differently.

It is obvious that such differences are often not easily tolerated. Sometimes they are not, as shown by the example of the quarrel between Peter and Paul in Antioch (see pp. 218-19 above). But where they are endured, the fellowship is not necessarily destroyed.

## 5. Summary: Everyday Worship

Summarizing the often observed tensions in the statements of Paul, we can say (with expressions that seem to go back to Karl Barth) that Christian ethics is an impossible possibility and at the same time a possible impossibility. We must not resolve this tension. From time to time, however, it may be neccessary to emphasize different aspects.

Looking at some ecclesiastical and individual efforts in the area of ethics, we may get the impression that generally the word *impossible* is not taken into account at all or gets less than its fair share of attention. Ethics is then formulated as human possibilities, and the contents are fixed by imperatives. Those whose deeds are limited to the contents are considered Christians (and sometimes one even speaks of anonymous Christians). And the opposite is also true: those who think of themselves as Christians or who want to be Christians, endeavor to accomplish the contents of the imperatives. Yet the question still remains: Are we dealing here with nominal or with genuine Christians?

When making this distinction, we must immediately warn against a misunderstanding. We are not trying to evaluate or judge the actual deed. Those who act as Christians are usually within the Christian tradition. In what Christians—authentic or nominal—have done in the past, they see exemplary action that for the most part even places demands on what is expected from doers, who then emulate this action. When they are successful, their deeds deserve recognition. Those who deny recognition because the deeds were not done "out of faith" (how do they know?) elevate themselves to the position of judge, performing a function that, as they should know, is not theirs to perform.

Yet we can speak of authentically Christian action only when it is performed by authentic Christians. It all depends on the doer, and therefore any discussion of "Christian ethics" misses the point if the doer is not taken into consideration. This, however, is exactly what is not only often but almost always overlooked today.

Paul never loses sight of the doer, not even when the subject is "ethics." In his last letter he formulates almost programmatically at the beginning of the monitory section: "I appeal to you therefore, brothers and sisters, by the mercies of God [which in the foregoing have been emphatically promised], to present your bodies [your whole selves] as a living sacrifice, holy and acceptable to God, which is your spiritual worship. Do not [therefore] be conformed to this [old] world, but be transformed by the renewing of your minds, so that you may discern what is the will of God—[namely] what is good and acceptable and perfect" (Rom. 12:1-2).

To summarize briefly, we can say that genuine Christian ethics is the worship of God in everyday life. And only when the specific deed is the worship of *God* can we speak of genuine Christian ethics.

Naturally, the demand here is not for a personal achievement by the doers who present themselves as a sacrifice. The question is, What power guides the doers: the old world or the divine mercies they have received? If the doers have received the mercies of God, they are no longer masters of their bodies. That this is God's will is perceived by Paul in Christ (and his self-giving). The discussion in Romans 1-11 is supposed to cause the readers to say that what Paul wrote has struck them hard and they have surrendered themselves to it. If this happens, then what they do in their bodies is no longer their own doing but God's doing, even if it is done through them.

Christian ethics as the worship of God is authentically Christian ethics only when the action of the doers takes place as the action of God. But since it is really an act of God, this action is an impossibility for human beings. They can neither plan their actions in advance nor programmatically determine the contents in advance. Those who attempt it do not take seriously the impossibility of the action. Nevertheless, the impossible becomes possible for renewed individuals, but it is the possibility of something that remains impossible for them.

The worship of God, to be sure, always takes place in the middle of a secular world; regarded from the outside, therefore, the action always remains a secular one. Yet the doers, who have offered their bodies and had their thinking renewed, do not know automatically what specific action must now take place. They should (and can) verify what the will of God is. For that they need a critical mind in the concrete situation. If they use it (in renewed thinking), they may succeed in doing what is good and acceptable—but also what is perfect?

Here we see the same boundary as that expressed in the *pre*-Matthean antithesis, "Be perfect, therefore, as your heavenly Father is perfect" (Matt. 5:48). Since here, however, it is not a question of coming as close as possible to perfection (which perhaps may be achievable with effort in a nominally Christian ethic—and those who succeed at it deserve our respect) but of the genuinely Christian ethics that is *God's* perfection, the worship of God in everyday life remains an impossible possibility.

But precisely because for the children of God it is the possibility of the impossible, nominal Christians may expect to become genuine Christians again and again and rejoice gratefully that they are coworkers of God (cf. 1 Thess. 3:2 and p. 196 above).

The criterion of a Christian ethics that is authentically Christian still remains: Is the worship *of God* taking place in the concrete secular deed?

## II. Developments and False Developments

Actually we should speak here of successful developments and failed developments in which the "approach" was continued. Yet for the time being we can only point to the tension suggested in our heading. After the foregoing discussions, we can ask whether successful developments are at all possible.

If we distinguish between Christology and ethics, we can trace the development of the christological statements, as has often been done, and at the same time ask the critical question, Has the beginning been followed or lost? If the latter is true, the Christology is said to be heretical. Hence it is logical to proceed in the same way with ethics. We would turn (individually) to the problems newly emerging at a later time and in other environments and ask what solutions we have discovered and considered. But how would we plan to judge ethical developments critically? In such a separation of ethics from Christology, do we not refrain all too easily from the christological substantiation of ethical decisions? But then ethics is no longer an aspect of Christology. We will soon show that exactly this happened very early on.

If Christian ethics is to be characterized as eschatological existence, then this means, first of all, that we can grasp it only point by point. Indeed, Christian ethics succeeds only in the *kairos*. The *kairos* itself knows no development, because points do not become a line. For that reason we must not try do construct a line from the points. It is unavoidable, nonetheless, that those who have repeatedly existed eschatologically have experienced this existence in an ongoing history and continue in an ongoing history, in "developments." This problem appeared even in the first generation. But in the second and third, it became even more pointed. How can we resolve this tension? Can it be resolved at all?

What is involved here can perhaps be made clear most simply with the example of the shaping—and the subsequent reshaping—of the concept of the imminent expectation of the Parousia.

Apocalyptic concepts were already present. This age is drawing to a close. At the end of the aeon God (or the Son of man on his behalf) will sit in judgment. Those who want to survive must prepare themselves in this life. When judgment day was expected imminently, which happened again and again, there was additional motivation to intensify one's efforts.

In their encounter with Jesus, people learned that he redefined this apocalyptic expectation. They could expect the coming of God at any moment. Yet God was now defined no longer as Judge but as Father. (Paul modifies the idea when he talks of the coming of the *kyrios*.) As a result, the imminent expectation takes on a new and quite different shape. Of course, the apocalyptic framework still persists as a philosophically predetermined concept, and consequently "the day" still remains a future expected at some point on the time line. Paul could expect it as a very near future—at least at the time when he was writing 1 Thess. 4:15, 17. But the view is steered away from this *concept* because something quite different becomes of sole importance. On the line of their passing (and ongoing!) life, people now *always* live in imminent expectation, for the possibility of eschatological existence *always* awaits them. If that happens in their lives, it immediately again becomes a future to be expected imminently.

Because of *this* imminent expectation the question of the apocalyptically imagined day is no longer important, nor is the date (1 Thess. 5:1). It can be regarded as near, or it can take its time. Those who today are "children of the day" (1 Thess. 5:5) do not need to ask about a day that is coming later. Living in *this* imminent expectation, they are not confronted with the problem of the Parousia's delay, which necessarily appears after a short time within the framework of the apocalyptic concept. (How Paul smooths over this problem becomes apparent if we compare 1 Thess. 4:15, 17 and 1 Cor. 15:51—in the respective contexts.)

This shaping of the apocalyptic *concept* of imminent expectation into the *focusing* of a life in imminent expectation could not always be maintained. Since the focusing made use of the terminology of the concept, it could easily be misunderstood as being apocalyptic. This led to the loss of authentically Christian imminent expectation. It was reshaped into the apocalyptic concept. Consequently, in the course of time the problem of the Parousia's delay had to come up, though it could not have arisen if Christian imminent expectation had been maintained. We can see this especially clearly in 2 Thessalonians and in 2 Peter. From the *always* expected *arrival* of the *kyrios* in people's lives now arose as doctrine the christological assertion of the *second coming* of Christ.

Since life and doctrine now separate, there are consequences for ethics. It must be newly conceived and given a different substantiation. Even in New Testament times such a development was protested, as is most evident in the Gospel of John. And this also had consequences for the new conception of ethics.

In our context the tension between *kairos* and *chronos*, between point and line, can be formulated as an opening question: Does ethics remain an aspect of Christology even in the second and third generation, or do the two go their separate ways? Precisely this question will be asked of a sampling of New Testament authors. We may assume that they all intended to maintain the approaches and to redesign them for their time and situation. The exegetical question then reads: How did they do that? Then we must ask in each case the systematic question: Did they succeed?

# A. The Ethic of Matthew

In discussions on Christian ethics the Sermon on the Mount has always played a special role, and it still does today. Yet there is disagreement as to how to understand it and how to appeal to its authority, as there was in earlier times. Thus we must try to present a well reasoned suggestion for understanding the Sermon on the Mount.

We must begin with the fact that the Sermon on the Mount is a part of the Gospel of Matthew. Though that should be obvious, it is still necessary to say it, because in discussions on the Sermon on the Mount it is nearly always ignored, and this prevents a proper understanding. Even in the formulation we must be precise. The matter we are concerned with is not the ethic of the Sermon on the Mount, nor is it the ethic of Matthew's Gospel. We are concerned with the ethic of the person who wrote this *book* (cf. 1:1), that is, the ethic of Matthew. Scholars agree that Matthew worked as redactor. This fact alone creates problems for the exegesis.

## 1. The Redactor Matthew

We assume the two-source theory, according to which Matthew drew on the Gospel of Mark and the so-called sayings source (Q), as well as a good deal of his own special material. By comparison (especially with Luke) we can verify that the redactor did not merely copy his sources word for word. Rather, he changed them somewhat and made certain emphases that his sources did not contain. Quite obviously he also created something new and gave his whole work an order that, while essentially following the thread of Mark's Gospel, also makes noticeable modifications. Thus exegetes have to differentiate between tradition and redaction. And this is exactly where some of them fail.

We may assume, of course, that a redactor will not adopt anything from his sources that contradicts his own conception. That does not mean, however, that Matthew exegeted his sources historically and then inserted them into his work, while preserving their original meaning. Matthew was not familiar with historical exegesis. We, however, must distinguish between the historical exegesis of the Matthean sources and the historical exegesis of the work as a whole. Even if the wording is the same or nearly the same, the results of the two exegeses need not be the same.

We can clarify the problem further by considering the so-called antitheses (5:21-48). Even though there is (and will probably continue to be) disagreement about which antitheses and which wording Matthew found before him, we may certainly assume that the third antithesis (5:31-32), in which divorce is prohibited, came from Matthew's pen (cf. 5:32 with 19:9). It is apparent that the third antithesis is not really an antithesis. In the other antitheses the thesis itself remains but is made more radical. Yet in Matthew's third "antithesis" the thesis is disputed. One commandment replaces another, but it *still remains* a commandment, just as the prior commandment was a commandment. When Matthew himself now creates an "antithesis," however, he lets us know how he understood the other antitheses: not as antitheses but as new theses, as newly formulated commandments.

We encounter exactly the same problem in the beatitudes (5:3-11). The first beatitudes (5:3-9) must be understood *as Matthew understood them* on the basis of the later beatitudes (5:10-11), which he created.

Since the goal of the exegesis of Matthew's Gospel is to establish its author's assertions, the best starting point will be the passages where we can recognize Matthew's style with sufficient certainty. From there we should then also exegete the sections the redactor left entirely unaltered or only slightly altered. In no case should the assertions of the authors of the sources, as established through historical exegesis, be used as an argument against the assertions of Matthew, as formulated in his work.

Even in a brief perusal of the book as a whole, some peculiarities immediately stand out. Into the framework Matthew adopts from Mark, he inserts five speeches largely assembled by himself: the Sermon on the Mount (chap. 5-7), the sending out of the twelve (10), the speech on parables (13), community rules (18), and the speech against the Pharisees and on the Parousia and the last judgment (23-25). We know that these are intentional speeches composed by the author because of the stereotyped expressions at the end of each speech: "When Jesus finished these sayings . . ." (7:28; 11:1; 13:53; 19:1; 26:1).

Another peculiarity of the book is the frequent occurrence of proof texts in the form of quotations, which are typical of Matthew (1:22-23; 2:5-6, 15, 17-18, 23; 3:3; 4:14-16; 8:17; 12:17-21; 13:35; 21:4-5; 26:56; 27:9-10). Matthew finally brings his work to a close with a grand mountain scene in Galilee.

It is apparent that the best place to start the exegesis is with these peculiarities.

## 2. An Exegesis of Matthew's Work in Overview.

We will begin with the final scene (28:16-20), because Matthew himself offers a summary of his work here.

> Now the eleven disciples went to Galilee, to the mountain to which Jesus had directed them. When they saw him, they worshiped him; but some doubted. And Jesus came and said to them, "All authority in heaven and on earth has been given to me. Go therefore and make disciples of all nations, baptizing them in the name of the Father and of the Son and of the Holy Spirit, and teaching them to obey everything that I have commanded you. And remember, I am with you always, to the end of the age."

One thing becomes immediately clear: this text speaks in a universal manner in terms of both time and space. Matthew is looking at the period from the resurrection of Jesus until the end of time. Exactly when this end and judgment (25:31-46) will come remains completely open. The date not only plays no role but also presents no problem. We only have to specify: no longer. For the motif of the Parousia's delay (cf. 24:48; 25:5) shows that former times must have been dominated by an apocalyptically understood imminent expectation of the end. But Matthew does not discuss this problem apologetically (as does, for example, 2 Peter 3:1-10); he simply goes beyond it in his presentation. When the eleven(!) disciples have their first (and last) encounter with the resurrected One, he sketches the program for the future of the church (cf. 16:18). The commission that the disciples received at that time was thus temporally unlimited from the beginning.

The spatial dimension can be regarded in a similar way. The commandment not to go to the Gentiles and Samaritans but to the lost sheep of the house of Israel (10:5-6), which was in effect during Jesus' lifetime (according to Matthew), is replaced by the commission to make disciples of all nations.

And this is what happens: now and in every future time disciples will baptize and teach. They are to baptize in the name of the Father and of the Son and of the Holy Spirit. And they are to teach obedience of everything Jesus commanded.

On this basis we can understand the other two peculiarities of the Gospel of Matthew. Everything that Jesus commanded in his lifetime—and whose observance is now to be taught—is found mainly in the speeches compiled by Matthew. But why Jesus in particular was in a position to give such instructions is expressed by Matthew with the help of quotations. In his work Jesus proved himself to be the one who fulfilled the Old Testament "promises." For this reason one could almost read from a multiplicity of events in Jesus' life that he was the expected Messiah of Israel. Thus, Matthew wants to prove in a verifiable way that Jesus was the expected Messiah.

The family tree with which Matthew begins his book also serves this purpose. Jesus, son of Abraham and son of David, was born at the end of the double "world-weeks" (three times fourteen generations; 1:17), that is, at a precisely predestined time.

Then Matthew connects the life of this Messiah Jesus to Moses. On the one hand, this is shown in the childhood stories, which exhibit a Moses typology (e.g., the motif of the pursued child). On the other hand, it is certainly no accident that Jesus delivered his first—and for Matthew probably most important—oratory on a mountain, just as Moses received the commandments on a mountain, and on a mountain in Galilee the resurrected One confirms the instructions he had given during his lifetime. Does that mean that Matthew saw the Messiah Jesus as the new Moses? This would naturally have had consequences for his understanding of the law.

The exegesis of the last verse of Matthew's book, of course, requires special caution. The statement of the resurrected One that he will be with his people until the end of time must not be understood too quickly in the way one could understand it if it were a statement from Paul. First, we must clarify *how* and *as who* the resurrected One will be with his people. Then we will begin to see the context of this thought: the resurrected One will be with his people as the one who in his lifetime gave the commandments that now must be observed; they must be obeyed all the more because in the meantime all authority in heaven and on earth has been given to the resurrected One. Yet if Matthew was born a Jew, which can hardly be doubted, we must recall the contemporary Jewish thought according to which Yahweh himself is in heaven, of course, and hence (still) absent, though present in his law. Accordingly, Matthew thinks of the resurrected One as in heaven. Yet he is with his people because his instructions, which he ordered them to follow, are with them. To put it more sharply: everywhere and always the church has Matthew's book. The church is to live by it and can live by it until the resurrected One returns in judgment. So Matthew's Gospel gives the church its holy scripture, just as the Jews have their holy scripture.

Now we have to fill this exegetical overview with content. Our main objective will be to clarify the connection between ethics and Christology.

### 3. Matthew's Image of Jesus: The Teacher of the New Righteousness

Within the Sermon on the Mount (5:17-19) Matthew presents discussions of the law that he himself shaped, as a synoptic comparison shows. The "Matthean" Jesus formulates here polemically: "Think not that I have come to abolish the law or the prophets; I have come not to abolish but to fulfill."

This polemic shows that there must have been people who did not share Matthew's view. In Jesus they saw the one who had abolished the law. We can hardly know exactly who these people were. They could have been Jews who accused Christians of not observing the law. Possibly such an accusation could have been well-founded, for there may have been Christians who had misunderstood Paul. When Paul had emphasized that human beings themselves could not clear the way to God by observing the law, they perhaps concluded: We do not need the law anymore at all. The result could then have been libertinism (cf. 7:21).

Thus Matthew emphasizes that in the church the law has not been abolished, and this is true for all of the law down to the tiniest detail. Rather, it must be "fulfilled," and in this context that means that it must be done, just as Jesus did it. For the church, however, it is also true that only those who do the law and teach others to do likewise (cf. 28:20a) will be called "great" in the kingdom of heaven.

In 5:20 we find the reason (as also formulated by Matthew): "For I tell you, unless your righteousness exceeds that of the scribes and Pharisees, you will never enter the kingdom of heaven."

Exegetes have often argued about this verse. The reason in part is the fact that the crucial verb can be understood in different ways, as will be discussed later on. The main reason, however, is that one often tries too hastily to harmonize Matthew's statements with those of others (mainly Paul) in order then to use the results in dogmatics. But the exegete must listen only to Matthew and must use the results reached that way, even if they seem strange to him.

Matthew sets up an opposition: on one side, the church, and on the other, the scribes and Pharisees. Both have the same goal in view: they would like to enter the kingdom of heaven. The prerequisite for that is "righteousness." Here the word does not express (as in Paul) the judgment of God over humanity, but the deeds that people must achieve on earth so that at the judgment God can pronounce the verdict: you are accepted by me. Even the structure of this verse prevents a premature application of Pauline ideas.

Now, Matthew denies that the righteousness of the scribes and Pharisees is sufficient to reach their intended goal. For that reason church members are challenged to a better righteousness, a righteousness that is far more than the righteousness of the scribes and the Pharisees. Only then will they reach their goal.

What is the "more" of the better righteousness? Two possibilities are discussed: the "more" may have either a quantitative or a qualitative meaning.

> Unfortunately, the term is not unequivocal. The Greek word *perisseuein* means to exist in abundance, to be present in excess. It is used, to be sure, mostly in its quantitative meaning, but it also occurs with a qualitative meaning.

If we understand the "more" quantitatively, it means that the scribes and Pharisees do too little; Christians must do more. In this case the result would be that as Matthew understands the matter, there is no fundamental difference between the ethics of the scribes and Pharisees and the ethics of Christians. For if the scribes and Pharisees did more than they do, that is, if they did as much as (Matthew's) Jesus demands of Christians, then they too would enter the kingdom of heaven. It is at least understandable that many exegetes hesitate to accept this interpretation.

If we understand the "more" qualitatively, however, we are then talking about a different kind of doing. Christian ethics would then be a different kind of ethics, for example, an ethics in which it is not simply a matter of fulfilling more imperatives but rather a question of imperatives that are founded on a christologically based indicative. Then there are *different doers* who perform the deeds.

Since the wording of 5:20 allows both interpretations, we must draw on other statements of Matthew for help in the exegesis of this verse. The simplest place to find the answer may be where Matthew establishes a "less" that is opposed to his "more."

Looking first in the immediate context, we see a reference to "the least of the commandments," which are not to be relaxed (5:18-19). Hence, not only is any "generosity" forbidden in regard to the commandments but also any differentiation between important and less important commandments. Instead, *all* the commandments must be kept, and the people are to be taught to keep *all* the commandments. Thus the "less" consists in not keeping all the commandments. Proceeding from 5:17-19 to 5:20, we conclude that the "more" has to be understood quantitatively.

> Formulated in a Pauline way this means that Christians will be acknowledged by God on judgment day only if they do more "works" than the scribes and Pharisees. Thus it is a question of one's own righteousness and thus the very thing against which Paul had fought so passionately (Phil. 3:9; Rom. 10:3)

If we want to avoid this exegesis, we must demonstrate that for Matthew it is not simply and only a question of sufficient *deeds*, but that he substantiates the imperatives with an indicative that enables the doer to follow the imperatives. I doubt, however, that such a demonstration is possible, especially since there are a number of other passages that are clearly edited by Matthew and confirm the above exegesis.

Matthew starts the last compiled speech with a sharp attack on the *practice* of the scribes and Pharisees (23:1-33). It must be strictly distinguished from their *teaching*. In fact, the scribes and the Pharisees sit on "Moses' seat" (23:2). For Matthew that is a thoroughly positive statement. Hence he advises his readers: "Therefore, do whatever they teach you and follow it" (23:3a). Thus the authority of the scribes and Pharisees is also to be acknowledged by the Christians. Against this background Matthew formulates the "less": "For they do not practice what they teach" (23:3b). Because their teaching and their practice do not agree, they are repeatedly called "hypocrites" (23:13, 15, 23, 25, 27, 29).

Today's widespread characterization of the Pharisees as hypocrites goes back to Matthew. It hardly agrees with historical reality. Quite the opposite! The Pharisees made a great effort—and with visible success—to observe the commandments of the law with painstaking exactitude. One example is Paul (Phil. 3:6), who moreover can vouch for his fellow Pharisees that in their efforts to fulfill the law they show a notable zeal for God, even if they have the wrong idea (Rom. 10:2). It is not their (perhaps exemplary) deeds but their theology that is criticized. Their God demands works from them, and accordingly they think that they can influence their God through their own performance (cf. Luke 18:10-14a). Matthew had obviously not seen this theological critique. He transforms the theological problem back into an exclusively ethical problem.

If Christians *do,* what scribes and Pharisees (regrettably only) *say,* they are certainly on the right path in Matthew's opinion. Everything depends on quantitatively sufficient action. Naturally, one can "have" a Christology (and Matthew "has" one, too), but it does not help people to act, not even if in itself it is "correct." For those who only say, "Lord, Lord," to Jesus cannot depend on that on judgment day (7:22). Only doing the will of the Father in heaven (which is taught entirely correctly by the scribes and Pharisees) will be decisive there. The outcome will be decided by whether what Jesus (the "Lord") commanded to do (e.g., in the Sermon on the Mount) has not only been heard but also done (7:24-27).

The fact that Matthew indeed makes God's decision on judgment day really dependent on human deeds is also shown by his interpretation (6:14-15) of the Lord's Prayer (6:9-13). The original text of the prayer, which Matthew takes from the sayings source, cannot be reconstructed with certainty, but the original sequence in the fourth petition can: forgiveness by God, forgiveness by the people. If God forgives people, they become free to forgive in turn. In Matthew's interpretation, however, the indicative is missing. God's forgiveness is made conditional upon people forgiving their debtors first. If they do not do that, God will not forgive them either. Hence people must earn God's forgiveness.

Along the same line is Matthew's reworking of Mark 1:15. Mark had begun with the indicative: "The kingdom of God has come near." It leads to the imperative: Repent! In repentance one receives the kingdom of God. Matthew reworks his model. Now Jesus'' first sermon begins with the imperative: Repent! The doing of the imperative is made urgent by announcing that the kingdom of God has come near (4:17). Matthew turns Mark's indicative into an amplification of the imperative.

> From time to time exegetes try to interpret 4:17 differently in order somehow to "save" the indicative for Matthew (in spite of the modified wording vis-à-vis Mark 1:15).
>
> One could then argue, for example, that because Matthew is no longer counting on the imminent inbreaking of the kingdom of heaven, he cannot use this indication of time to make action urgent. Yet here the redactor is dependent on tradition.
>
> Above all, however, Jesus' first sermon in Matthew now matches word for word the Baptist's sermon in the wilderness (3:2). If 4:17 contains an indicative, that must also be true of 3:2. To make such an assumption, however, is all but impossible. Rather, John motivated the call to repentence, and at the same time made it urgent, by pointing to imminent judgment. Now Matthew has Jesus repeat this very same sermon of the Baptist. Apparently Matthew failed to notice, however, that his model, Mark 1:15, contains an indicative and therefore differs fundamentally from the Baptist's sermon.

Can we have an ethic without an indicative? The result could perhaps be a nominally Christian ethic, but hardly a genuinely Christian one. Anyone who (for whatever reasons) presupposes such an ethic in Matthew (and naturally wants it also to be the result of his exegesis) will have to find strong arguments after what we have just discussed. Where do we find the indicative in Matthew?

Here we must not point to the traditions adopted by the redactor. Of course, an exegesis of the pre-Matthean parable of the unforgiving servant (18:23-35) shows that the imperative is based on the indicative. Matthew was able to understand the parable as an example and therefore to arrange it within his ethical conception.

Even the reference to the central significance the love commandment in Matthew does not help. It is true that he adds the commandment of love (19:19) to the list of commandments adopted from Mark 10:17. Evidently, he wants to put special emphasis on it. At the same time, however, he shows why he does it: the love commandment is the critical authority for practicing the law. Twice he quotes Hosea 6:6: "For I desire mercy and not sacrifice" (9:13; 12:7). In doing so, Matthew stays within the bounds of the contemporary Jewish discussion of the law, as it was carried on especially by the scribes, which then led into casuistry. If the literal obedience of any commandment resulted in a violation of the commandment of love, then (and *only* then) the commandment in question became invalid. For Matthew the commandment of love is, of course, the most important, but as such it is still one of many commandments God requires to be kept. Similarly, *for Matthew* the commandment to love one's enemy is a commandment to be kept (5:44). It exceeds the commandment of love (cf. 5:43) but at the same time remains an obligation required of Christians.

We must not, however, let Matthew's use of the word "love" lead us to the conclusion that here we have an authentically Christian motif. We can see no sign of the idea that love and love of the enemy can only be expected from those who have been changed by God's love and by God's love of the enemy.

The missing indicative in Matthew is mainly a result of the nature of his Christology, which has shrunk to a mere doctrine. We can become familiar with it by reading the Gospel of Matthew. Then we can know it. Matthew even tries to prove its accuracy, especially by using scriptural quotations and the family tree. But this "known" Christology is not designed to "reach" and change the readers. Therefore ethics is not an aspect of this Christology but merely a consequence. It is a desirable consequence and even a necessary one, since readers have to see that if they have a correct knowledge of the Christology, an action is also required. That, however, is a second step. Christology and ethics are separate entities.

Readers know, to be sure, that the one who in his lifetime proved himself (verifiably) to be the Messiah of Israel has now risen. But they have direct contact (in Paul's sense) not with the resurrected One himself, who now controls their lives, but with a book. It refers them to the past. They learn that the Messiah of Israel has proved himself to be a "second Moses," a teacher of a better righteousness who is authorized by God. This better righteousness is what readers are now supposed to do—if only because the bringer of the new law will return as judge at the end of the age and will judge according to the law.

Salvation is expected in the future; it is not already present. Through the new law, however, readers now have the opportunity to do what is necessary to achieve salvation. They do not know if their efforts so far will be sufficient to attain the goal. No one can know. That is why people should not even want to know (either for themselves or for anyone else). Matthew makes that clear with the parable of the weeds among the wheat (13:24-30). In the church there are good and not so good Christians living side by side. The latter Matthew calls "you of little faith."

> He cannot call them "unbelievers" since they have been baptized and have thereby become disciples (28:19). All members of the church are "believers," but if their deeds are insufficient, they are "of little faith."

Those of little faith are now supposed to try to overcome their deficiency in faith. Whether they succeed will be known only on judgment day, when the weeds and the wheat, the sheep and the goats (25:31-46) will be separated. Until then everything remains open. If the readers realize, however, that their salvation will not be decided until later, they will be urged to greater watchfulness (25:1-13) and thus to even greater efforts in doing the better righteousness.

## 4. The Sermon on the Mount

Difficulties in discussing the Sermon on the Mount can be traced largely to the undisciplined use of language. In former times this point was not seen and perhaps could not be seen, but today we can see it. When the topic is the Sermon on the Mount, very often what one understands by the phrase is not the sermon itself but something like a "sum" of Christian ethics or the central document toward which Christian ethics must be oriented. We are hardly ever conscious of the fact that this is possible only through a serious modification of the original meaning of the Sermon on the Mount.

There can be no doubt, however, that the Sermon on the Mount is an unambiguously definable entity. It is the first of the speeches Matthew shaped for his book. It follows that we must not identify the "Preacher on the Mount" with Jesus (as E. Lohse did; *Theologische Ethik des Neuen Testaments,* 44-51) but must make linguistically precise distinctions. The "Preacher on the Mount" is rather Jesus as Matthew understood him and portrayed him with the help of his redactional work. Thus the Sermon on the Mount must be interpreted within the framework of the Matthean ethic.

When, by contrast, we *reconstruct* the traditions that were available for Matthew for the shaping of his book (and not simply copy them from Matt. 5-7), we can interpret them for themselves. Then, however, we cannot speak of the Sermon on the Mount. *For there was no Sermon on the Mount before Matthew.* Hence anyone who uses the term *Sermon on the Mount* must really mean the Sermon on the Mount and must not use the term in a completely different sense.

Rather, the characterization of the Sermon on the Mount by Hans Windisch is apt: it contains the admission requirments for entering the kingdom of heaven (cf. esp. 5:20). Thus Christians are expected to perform works because it is the only way for them eventually to reach their goal.

Most of the requirements mentioned in the Sermon on the Mount are very demanding. For this reason the question whether they are fulfillable at all is asked again and again. Yet before we answer too quickly, we must first clarify the following questions. Are we thinking of the possibility of fulfilling the requirements within the framework of a present-day Christian ethic? Or is it a question of whether Matthew considered the requirements fulfillable?

Anyone who discusses this question as a current ethical problem quickly encounters difficulties and looks for ways out. For example, we can speak of an "interim ethic" (Albert Schweitzer) that is not valid for all times or for all people but only for the short time immediately before the end of this world. Or we can also switch to a "two-stage ethic": the strict requirements are not applicable to everyone but are addressed only to a small circle of people who are especially gifted or have taken on special obligations (e.g., clergy or monks). Finally, we can say that the requirements merely identify ethical goals, which are at least to be striven for, even if they are seldomly reached.

With these attempted solutions, however, we are already on the wrong path, because we have too hastily understood the ethic of Matthew as a Christian ethic for the present and have therefore misunderstood it.

The question can and must be: Did Matthew believe that his readers (and he) were capable of living according to the rules of the Sermon on the Mount? Since the author of the book does not reveal whether he even considered this question, a direct answer is not possible. At best we can hazard an educated guess.

Matthew addresses people who throughout their lives are on the move. Their goal, meanwhile, is eventually to be admitted to the kingdom of heaven. They can reach their objective only if they meet the admission requirements. Since we may assume that Matthew thinks this goal is reachable, he must have also thought it possible to meet the requirements.

Whether and how his readers (and he) succeeded is a quite different question; it is one that we simply cannot answer. If we want to make a guess, we can presume that Matthew and his readers fell short of the requirements. Then they may have expected, as was common in contemporary Judaism, that in the judgment unfulfilled demands could be weighed against fulfilled demands. But we must not conclude on this basis that Matthew thought the requirements were impossible to fulfill. The idea that the unfulfilled requirements are supposed to make us realize that we are totally dependent on the grace of God is beyond Matthew. According to him we can do works toward our salvation.

Finally, there is another question to be considered, which applied to Matthew, of course, but which still has to be asked, because it plays a role in the current discussion of the Sermon on the Mount. What is Matthew trying to achieve with the formulation of these demands?

The answer is obvious: he is concerned with the future salvation of humankind. For the sake of this future salvation people are to do the new righteousness now. The admission requirements for heaven will be fulfilled in the present, and if many people fulfill them, that will change the present as well as people's living and working together in the present. But for Matthew the accent does not lie on this "social component." Rather, for him it is on people being concerned about their *future* salvation. If the world they live in thereby becomes a better world, that is naturally a welcome side-effect—but only a side-effect. It does not get Matthew's immediate attention.

Therefore, the question whether one could have governed the Prussian state with the Sermon on the Mount (a question that Bismarck answered in the negative, but which, in a modified form, is occasionally answered in the affirmative today) is the wrong question to ask, because it presupposes that one could use the Sermon on the Mount directly to achieve a Christian ethic. Even if we interpret the Sermon on the Mount historically, the question proves to be inappropriate.

## 5. Checking the Exegesis

The foregoing exegesis (like any other) is subject to *testing*. Here we must keep in mind that this testing is and remains an entirely historical matter. The question is: Did we correctly understand what *Matthew* wanted to say to his readers?

Such an examination will surely confirm the possibility of a more comprehensive understanding than the one I have presented here in a somewhat shortened form. As an exegete I must also accept the fact that I have misunderstood Matthew. That would then have to be shown using the extant text—more precisely: using only it and only those passages in which Matthew's hand can be seen. The reason for differing judgments, nonetheless, lies in the tension between tradition and redaction.

The question that underlies the quarrels of the exegetes is simply: Who understands *Matthew* correctly? What is involved here is neither the question, What can the exegesis bring to a present-day Christian ethic? nor the question, Can what Matthew wrote to his readers be called Christian? Because, however, the Christian aspect in particular must not play a role in the exegesis, the exegete must be at pains not to introduce his (possible) prior understanding into his exegesis as prior judgment. To do so would be to ruin it.

Now, we must distinguish clearly between a testing of the exegesis and the theological checking of the results of the exegesis. This checking is accomplished by applying a "touchstone" (Luther) to the results of the exegesis. How I hope to find this "touchstone" (the "canon *before* the canon") and its contents was presented and substantiated earlier (pp. 18-22, 51-52).

The exegetical outcome now leads to a verdict. Matthew's ethic, of course, emerged from the Christian tradition, but we cannot call it genuinely Christian. It represents rather a relapse into the Pharisaic ethic. Likewise, the other verdict is that the ethic of the Sermon on the Mount is not a truly Christian ethic, either.

This verdict merely labels the Matthean ethic. It says nothing about its value. We cannot deny that the Pharisaic ethic is a demanding one; that in itself gives it considerable value. Those who model their lives according to this ethic set a high standard for their actions. They submit to demands that far exceed the usual. They exert themselves, and through their efforts they can achieve demonstrable success. Matthew even increases the demands of this Pharisaic ethic. His readers are to do not only what the Pharisees teach; they are to do more. For example, they are to love not only their neighbors but also their enemies. Everyone who succeeds at this earns high recognition. Therefore no one has the right to look down on people who live by this ethic. The Matthean ethic is a good ethic and—not least of all through the Sermon on the Mount—a downright exemplary ethic.

Hence it would be wrong to call the authentically Christian ethic a better ethic than that of the Pharisees or that of Matthew. It is not a better but a quite different kind of ethic. The difference between the two is rooted in different theologies. This again must be understood quite precisely.

Those who talk *of* their God as one who sets requirements and makes his relationship with people dependent on fulfilling these requirements have every reason to hold to the Matthean ethic and to make the Sermon on the Mount the standard for their actions. Following it promises achievement of the objective. The Matthean ethic is one aspect of *this* theology.

But those who talk *of* their God as one who has already come to them with his love—and of course without any precondition— must defend against the Matthean ethic, because it will lead them into temptation. Those who are oriented toward this ethic are involved in blasphemy against *their* God: they do not believe in his love because they do not want to receive it as a gift; they want to earn it themselves. But if they try to do that, they have already lost their God and *must* hold to the ethic of Matthew.

If, however, they believe in God's love—if they have let themselves to be transformed into people who love—they do not face this "must" anymore. Now they *can* act—out of gratitude. Yet if they then look at their deeds, they will be able to see that they correspond to what Matthew in the Sermon on the Mount (unfortunately) formulated as commandments that Jesus ordered his followers to do.

Is this a criticism of Matthew? We could call it that, but we should nevertheless be careful. When criticism becomes condemnation, it becomes unjust. For then it obstructs our view of the crucial question, which we can only ask in the first person singular now: Is the God of Matthew not far too often also my God? Do I not fall under his power again and again when I, who could be a genuine Christian, become a nominal Christian?

Here we can also give the main reason why this happens: *Christology becomes doctrine.* In this way it remains at a distance and is no longer received. Then ethics has to become an independent entity and is no longer an aspect of Christology.

If Christians cannot deal with ethics, they will not become authentic Christians just by making a greater effort or by reformulating the requirements as precisely as possible into concrete instructions. Rather, they can become genuine Christians only if they understand that they have not received the Christology. Then they will formulate it in such a way that it can be received and will wait for it to be received.

# B. The Function of Christology in Ethical Systems

Since exegesis is a auxiliary theological science, its results must not be adopted directly into a Christian ethic for the present time. Through exegesis we learn only what the author wanted to tell his readers in his time. We may assume that all the authors of writings that later found their way into the New Testament (which the authors themselves could not know) believed that they were developing an authentically Christian ethic for their time. Whether they were successful, however, cannot be decided through exegesis but only after a subsequent theological checking of the outcome of the exegesis.

Now it is obvious that among exegetes there are divergent opinions about the author's intentions in a great many New Testament scriptures. We can regret that fact, but at the same time we must see that even a consensus of exegetes would not directly produce anything for developing a genuinely Christian ethic for today. By all appearances, this is often overlooked. Exegetes are not content to view their work solely as an auxiliary science. So they easily fall into short-sighted argumentation by refuting the results of other exegetes—more often than not with good reasons. Yet at the same time they claim (or at least give the impression) that their arguments are relevant for present-day ethical decisions. At this very point, however, they exceed not only their competence as exegetes but also their possibilities. This is especially fateful when they do not interpret entire scriptures but employ the "quarry method." Then present-day ethical decisions are supposedly substantiated with the help of the exegesis of short sections (e.g., the household rules) or even single verses.

To reach the goal pursued in the present work, it would make little sense to portray now the ethics of all the authors of New Testament scriptures. We could only do that exegetically, and since the results of the exegeses would remain in dispute, the judgments made checking the exegeses would also differ from each other. Therefore we will try a different path. We will start with the always indispensable checking of the results of the exegeses. We have already seen some of the important viewpoints while portraying the ethic of Matthew. We will now take these up and discuss them, using further scriptures from the New Testament.

One of these viewpoints is marked by the catch phrase "heresy and ethics." When the authors of the New Testament writings fight heresies or heretics, the issue almost always involves differences in Christology. Since ethics is an aspect of Christology, we face a double problem. First, do the authors who, in their own opinion, are fighting a wrong Christology see that this Christology goes hand in hand with a wrong ethic? Or do they totally fail to see the connection and fight only the wrong Christology or only the wrong ethic? Incidentally, we have to consider the possibility that the opponents do not make the connection either. The second problem is this: does correcting the Christology at the same time correct the ethics? In other words, is ethics seen as an aspect of the Christology, or do the authors correct both the Christology and the ethics, or perhaps only one of the two?

The authors of the New Testament scriptures faced very different problems and hence produced quite different solutions.

## 1. The Solution of the Author of 2 Thessalonians

With the overwhelming majority of exegetes, I assume that the Second Letter to the Thessalonians did not come from Paul's pen. The parallels to 1 Thessalonians in construction and formulation show that the author not only knew the first letter but while writing must have had it on his writing table and used it. (For details see my commentary on 2 Thessalonians.) The author independently drafted only two sections, 1:5-10 and 2:1-12. Thus this is where the exegete finds the main concern of the author's statement.

We find the "heresy" the author is fighting in 2:2. There are people who claim (either by spirit or by word or by letter) that the day of the Lord is already here.

There is disagreement as to what the author actually means in this sentence that is formulated in a rather nebulous context.

First, we may assume that he is polemicizing against statements in 1 Thessalonians to which the "opponents" are apparently referring. The imminence of the Parousia, which is announced in 1 Thessalonians, is expressedly denied.

Yet we must clarify this immediately. In 1 Thess. 4:14-17 Paul had (still) supported the *idea* that the Parousia was imminent. At the same time, however, he tried to steer away from this apocalyptic idea by inviting readers to an eschatological existence in the present (1 Thess. 5:1-11). Those who today already live in accordance with the coming day make obsolete the apocalyptic question of a date.

In later times the coexistence of *idea* and *attitude influenced by the idea* could easily lead to misunderstandings. If interest is focused on the idea, the date becomes a problem. If, however, it is focused on the attitude, the idea can easily be lost—and not replaced. We cannot know with certainty which was the case for the opponents of the author of 2 Thessalonians.

The opponents may have been apocalyptic enthusiasts who thought that the Parousia was now really quite imminent. As an ethical consequence, they neglected the tasks of everyday life. To worry about these so close to the end would have made no sense. But then their motto could not have been that the day of the Lord is already here. One would have to translate 2:2, disregarding the Greek wording, as follows: "The day of the Lord is immediately at hand."

In my opinion, it is more probable that they were Gnostic enthusiasts who, based on their dualistic anthropology, believed that in their "spirit" (i.e., in their self) they were already perfected. Then the ethical consequence would be that what they did with their "body" was unimportant, for it could not affect a salvation that had been attained once and for all. The author formulates this Gnostic thought apocalyptically because his conceptual world is that of apocalypticism. He then formulates the presence of the salvation claimed by the "opponents" so as to have them assert that the day of the Lord is already here. (We have here the same idea as in 2 Tim. 2:18, where the Gnostic view of being already perfected in the self is formulated apocalyptically: the resurrection has already taken place.)

The two exegeses have one thing in common: the author of 2 Thessalonians opposes the concept that what humans do in the present time is *theologically* insignificant.

The author views the thesis of the opponents that the day of the Lord is already here as an excuse to justify "living in idleness" (3:6, 11). Accordingly, in this letter he calls upon his readers to work in all seriousness on the shaping of their everyday lives.

Even if we do not succeed in clearly determining the opponents' Christology, which led to neglecting and even disregarding ethics, it is still clear that the author uses Christology to confront ethical abuse. Yet he does not formulate this Christology so that his readers receive it as Christology but drafts it as a doctrine (1:5-10), which he binds to an apocalyptic timetable (2:1-12).

In the author's view it is out of the question that salvation is already present (through Christology) even if simply for the reason that before the day of the Lord certain intervening events must happen, and they have not yet occurred (2:3b; 4:6-10). The writer is quite vague (probably even intentionally) about exactly what these events are. They are of no interest for him either. What is crucial for him is to move the day of the Lord into the future. In this way he succeeds in extending the present and gaining a limited amount of time for now, which must be filled and properly shaped.

That, however, can happen only with the greatest seriousness, for at the revelation of Jesus (1:7)—that is, at the Parousia that is expected after the intervening events have taken place—the "Lord Jesus" will come down as judge from heaven with the angels of his might and inflict a horrible judgment on the disobedient. The only ones to escape will be those who believed "our testimony" (i.e., the testimony of "Paul"; 1:9-10).

The attitude the author wants to instill in his readers on the basis of *this* concept (and the only one he can instill) is therefore not the anticipation of salvation, which *enables* them to shape their everyday lives. Rather, the conviction of the correctness of this concept makes the reader afraid. Will he survive judgment? Only through obedience can he escape fear and attain salvation in the future.

The readers are to obey the "gospel of our Lord Jesus" (1:8). This phrase, which occurs nowhere else in the New Testament, is almost certainly a creation of the author.

> The context shows that the author's understanding of the term *gospel* in this phrase (and of other terms as well) differs from that of Paul. The gospel for Paul is an active power, just as the *kyrios* is for him a power acting from heaven. It sets upon people, takes them over, shapes them, and governs them. When Paul talks about obedience to the gospel (cf. Rom. 10:16) or obedience to the faith (Rom. 1:5), this obedience means surrendering oneself. The writer of 2 Thessalonians, however, uses *obey* in the sense of "follow." Jesus is not the Lord because he himself is now active. Until his revelation he remains in heaven (1:7b). Nevertheless, Jesus can be called *kyrios* because he has given his gospel, which humankind is now supposed to know.

> The "gospel of our Lord Jesus" has merged with the testimony of "Paul" (1:10), and therefore the two are identical. It is to be followed as long as this old aeon lasts and hence until after the intervening events (2:3b; 4:6-10). Thus for the author the term *gospel* has become a formulaic summary of "truth" (cf. 2:10, 12, 13), and this truth itself is doctrine that can be handed down (cf. 2:15; 3:6). Such a gospel (as well as the testimony of "Paul" in 1:10) demands "faith" in the sense of approving recognition, of "holding to be true." This recognition leads to "achievement" for all who come to "love the truth" (cf. 2:10). The crucial point is that the gospel demands that it be done.

This very understanding of the term *gospel* is operative even in our time and has all but replaced the Markan and Pauline understanding (at least in the widespread linguistic usage of the church). That is the case especially when people use the term as a formula without reflecting on the content and then on that basis try to substantiate an ethic. Then they do not say, "The gospel enables us to . . ." but "The gospel demands that . . ."

According to the author readers are supposed to look at the deeds of Paul to see what the gospel (or "the truth") demands of them. The author describes in detail how Paul behaved in Thessalonica: he was not idle and did not eat any one's bread without paying for it. Rather, he himself worked in order not to burden anyone (3:7-10). Thus Paul is an example.

The author took over the material for this statement from 1 Thess. 2:9. But the context in which he uses it is significant. He takes the main theme from 1 Thess. 1:6-7. There the terms *example* and *imitator* are used in reference to each other. Paul, however, uses them to make a christological statement: The *kyrios* (as "example") shaped Paul. As a shaped person he is an "imitator" of the *kyrios*. Then the "imitator" (i.e., the person shaped by the *kyrios*) shaped the Thessalonians, who themselves as "imitators" of Paul (i.e., those shaped by Paul and through him by the *kyrios*) subsequently shaped others (cf. pp. 191-98 above). This idea of a "received" Christology is foreign to the author of 2 Thessalonians. He turns it into the idea of an imitation of Paul's behavior and takes its content from 1 Thess. 2:9.

Naturally, the writer cannot take the *kyrios* as his starting point, for he (still) remains in heaven. For this reason alone he is beyond consideration as an example to imitate. But Paul can certainly be brought in for this purpose. His behavior is pictured for the readers, so that they may know what they have to do. This appeal for imitation is emphasized by the author's assumption that while Paul was in Thessalonica, he left the church the command: "Anyone unwilling to work should not eat" (3:10). If the readers are obedient to Paul's "testimony" (1:10), that is, to the tradition they received from him (3:6), they will prove themselves worthy (1:11) "when the Lord Jesus is revealed from heaven" (1:7) and will receive salvation.

Thus the author offers no indicatives but only imperatives. Nowhere in the letter can we find the idea that the *kyrios* is now acting or wants to act and that *insofar* we can speak of a present salvation. The author does not see that his opponents' assertion might contain a proper concern that could be taken up and modified. The presence of salvation asserted by the opponents is rejected so completely that salvation can be expected only in the future.

Therefore the author is not interested in eschatological existence but in existence for the *eschaton*. He does not use the apocalyptic conceptual world in order to make christological statements based on it. Rather, his argumentation is immediately apocalyptic. Jesus' coming again is drafted as a doctrine that informs about the future. As a result, what the author recommends as Christian ethics is not genuinely Christian but a relapse into Pharisaic ethics.

## 2. The Solution of the Author of the Pastoral Letters

We will assume that the two letters to Timothy and the Letter to Titus have a common author. It could not have been Paul, since the letters look back upon a church long in existence. We must assume the first third of the second century A.D. as the approximate time of composition, especially because of the developed form of the church office.

The ethic of the pastoral letters was very popular for a long time (and often still is even today). It corresponds to the "ideal of a Christian bourgeoisie" (M. Dibelius), which owed its existence not least of all to the pastorals.

The goal is "a quiet and peaceable life in all godliness and dignity" (1 Tim. 2:2). To reach this goal, the author urges his readers to make supplications for those in high places (1 Tim. 2:1-2). The shape of this quiet and peaceable life can be characterized as a middle road between extreme life-styles. For example, no one is to be a drunkard (1. Tim. 3:3; Titus

1:7). Yet abstinence is not demanded, for a little wine is to be taken along with water (for health's sake; 1 Tim. 5:23). Thus moderation is advised. The author warns against riches, which bring with them great temptations (1 Tim. 6:9-10). That does not mean, however, that poverty is presented as an ideal; rather, the ideal is modest sufficiency. Those who have food and clothing should be content (1 Tim. 6:8). They are to do good with their riches (1 Tim. 6:17-18) but with reasonable reflection. Not every poor person is to be helped. The author explains with the example of caring for the widows that there must be a real need, not one that is the person's own fault (1 Tim. 5:5-6, 11). Thus one has to test whether the recipient is worthy of the gifts.

What is demanded of officials (bishops, deacons, and elders) fits into this image of the "bourgeoisie." They must not be drunkards, violent, quarrelsome, or lovers of money. Rather, they must be above reproach, temperate, sensible, respectable, hospitable, and apt teachers. In particular, they must be good managers of their own households (cf. 1 Tim. 3:2-5). Yet these are really not just "official" virtues but virtues that apply to everyone. Thus ecclesiastical office proves to be a bourgeois vocation.

Of course, on the fringe of this desired quiet and peaceable life, suffering can appear. The author knows that Christians can encounter suffering, as he shows especially with the example of Paul (2 Timothy). But in such cases this is not a consequence of the life officials and Christians lead (how could it be?) but a consequence of the doctrine they advocate.

Now, it would be unfair to discount this ethic prematurely because of its "well-tempered bourgeois character." After all, we have here justifiable demands, about whose details, of course, there can be varying opinions (depending on the taste of the time). Yet for that time and that environment, we can absolutely call this ethic exemplary, for it corresponds fairly precisely to what was thought to be ideal in those days.

Then the question arises: Should Christians therefore be model citizens? There is no reason to argue against this idea.

Why should they not be? It is quite a different matter, though, to ask whether this ethic can be a standard for what is genuinely Christian and whether it can therefore be adopted today (even if modified) as an authentically Christian ethic.

If we want to look at the problem of what is genuinely Christian, we must first look at how this ethic emerged. The author faces critics who represent a different doctrine from his and who have developed an ethic in connection with this doctrine. But in the discussion that now becomes necessary he encounters difficulties he cannot resolve, because he does not relate dogmatics and ethics.

We may assume that the heretics themselves called their teaching "knowledge" (*gnosis;* 1 Tim. 6:20). Exactly what that teaching was is hard to determine.

> The opponents are "of the circumcision" (Titus 1:10). They want to be teachers of the law (1 Tim. 1:7). Yet we should not overestimate the Jewish influence (cf. the prohibition of marriage; 1 Tim. 4:3) even if the myths they support are labeled Jewish (Titus 1:14). We read about "myths and endless genealogies" (1 Tim. 1:4), about "profane myths and old wives' tales" (1 Tim. 4:7). Yet the content of these statements remains rather vague. It becomes clearer perhaps when the heretics claim "to know God," although they (allegedly) deny him by their actions (Titus 1:16). That they are then described (literally) as "puffed up" (1 Tim. 6:4; 2 Tim. 3:4) points to the probability of enthusiasm.

The only concrete piece of information is found in the heretics' claim that the resurrection has already taken place (2 Tim. 2:18). On that basis, the writer can only be talking about Gnostics, who are characterized by an anthropological dualism.

> The Gnostics could say that the resurrection has already taken place (as it was also said that the day of the Lord has already come; 2 Thess. 2:2; cf. p. 252 above). The idea is that the soul living in the body has already experienced salvation—and indeed irrevocably. As a consequence, the body can

either do whatever it wants (libertinism) or is no longer allowed to do anything (asceticism).

We must doubt whether the author really understands the heretics' teaching, for he does not discuss it. Not only does he himself refrain from any discussion, but he also explicitly forbids any discussion among his readers. It would only breed quarrels (2 Tim. 2:23) and is therefore unprofitable and worthless (Titus 3:9).

The author does not succeed, however, in presenting the content of his own doctrine. Of course, he occasionally uses formulations taken from Paul and speaks of righteousness not because of works (Titus 3:5) and of "Christ Jesus . . . who gave himself a ransom for all" (1 Tim. 2:5-6). For the author, however, these expressions always remain formulas. For the most part he refrains altogether from quoting such statements and speaks of doctrine as "what has been entrusted" (1 Tim. 6:20; 2 Tim. 1:12, 14), or he uses the terms "sound teaching" and "sound doctrine" (1 Tim. 1:10; 2 Tim. 1:13; 4:3; Titus 1:9; 2:1). Presumably, he wants to express the idea that in contrast to the questionable views of the heretics, his doctrine is reasonable.

Thus the author simply places the two doctrines side by side, and then, without reference to them, he deals with ethics. Here his embarrassment becomes especially clear. Since he did not understand the doctrine of the heretics, he does not see that their ethic grows directly out of their doctrine. He actually draws two not only different but even opposite images of the heretics' deeds and behavior.

On the one hand, the writer lists in a catalog of vices all the things on which they are to be reproached. They are lovers of themselves, lovers of money, boasters, arrogant, abusive, disobedient to their parents, ungrateful, unholy, inhuman, implacable, slanderers, profligates, brutes, haters of good, and so forth (2 Tim. 3:2-4). This lack of restraint is said to be connected with false doctrine, because its spread causes envy, dissension, slander, and wranglings (1 Tim. 6:4).

On the other hand, the opponents are open to quite different reproaches. They follow the purity regulations (Titus 1:14-16) and forbid marriage and the enjoyment of certain foods (1 Tim. 4:3). Presumably, they also reject the drinking of wine (cf. 1 Tim. 5:23). Thus the heretics are in no wise unrestrained people but ethical rigorists. The author calls this rigorism "physical training" that is "of some value" (1 Tim. 4:8).

It is hard to say how the author brought the two sides together for himself, for only *one* image of the heretics can be correct, after all. On the basis of their Gnosticism with its dualistic anthropology, we would have to say that the heretics must in fact have been rigorists. Since the author, however, does not perceive this, he refutes each "misbehavior" individually.

Against the abstinence from certain foods, the author emphasizes that God created them. What is created by God is not to be rejected (1 Tim. 4:3-4). He counters the opponents' prohibition of marriage with the creation story. The woman (not Adam) has of course given in to temptation, but she can be saved through childbearing if she continues "in faith and love and holiness, with modesty" (1 Tim. 2:15). But how can this be harmonized with the writer's statement that one cannot reach salvation by works (Titus 3:5)?

The image of the heretics' lack of restraint was drawn by the author himself. We might come to his aid with the fact that in his time the usual style of polemics against heretics included representing them as morally defective. Yet he gladly adopted this motif, for it helped him make his intended point: Christians must not fall victim to such a lack of restraint but should lead a quiet and peaceable life in all godliness and dignity.

Thus the ethic of the author of the pastorals is neither theologically nor christologically nor eschatologically substantiated. On the contrary, it is designed in reaction to a different ethic, which the author imputes to the heretics. Of course, it is their *doctrine* that is sinister to him. That is why he wants to fight it. But he does not succeed, and he advises his readers not to occupy themselves with questions of doctrine. They are not to discuss it with others either, because they can assume that their doctrine is "sound" apostolic doctrine. All that matters for them is ethics. They are to lead a respectable bourgeois life, a life that is reasonable, open to scrutiny, transparent, and that travels the middle road between dangerous extremes. That is exactly the life that is thought to be exemplary and desirable in a civilized environment. In the author's opinion, those who lead such a life can assume that they are leading a Christian life. In any case, they have the "correct" faith.

The question must be asked: Did the author not anticipate a wide-spread view in today's church? Yet we must also ask: Did the author not anticipate the view of those who mourn the loss of ethics in today's church and now want to make up the deficit by treating ethics independently?

## 3. The Solution of the Author of James

Though the Letter of James has the literary form of a letter, it is not a letter but a loose collection of paraeneses from various sources. There are echoes of wisdom literature, as well as the monitory traditions of Greek civilization and Hellenism. In addition there are often references to material in the synoptic Gospels.

The author apparently collected various materials of various kinds and fitted them together without a recognizable structure. For that reason it is relatively easy to reconstruct sources through literary criticism and then to interpret them. Yet through these exegeses we still do not arrive at the author's views.

Thus, for example, we may (in spite of 5:7-11) exclude the possibility that *this writer* entertained an imminent expectation of the Parousia, for the *kyrios* who is to come is clearly God (cf. 5:11). Nor will we be able to determine precisely what *this writer* understood by "the perfect law, the law of liberty" (1:25) or "the royal law" (2:8). The same is true of the other material he adopted, especially since at no point is it possible to detect whether and where the author himself made changes in his sources.

Yet it is certain that the author would like to use all these traditions as statements of Christian ethics. He expresses that formally by mentioning the name of Jesus Christ in the preface (1:1) and in an address that refers back to the preface (2:1). (Otherwise, surprisingly enough, the name of Jesus Christ does not occur in the whole document.) Yet is this alone enough to Christianize ancient monitory traditions?

A merely statistical observation will reveal why the author falls back on this particular material: the 108 verses of the letter contain 54 imperatives, and it is precisely these imperatives that the author is interested in. They hold the borrowed traditions together and reveal the author's intention: with great emphasis he wants to exhort his readers to action.

Why he considers that necessary is explained in 2:14-26, which may have come entirely from his own pen. It concerns the question of faith and works, a problem that, as far as we know, was first formulated in this way by Paul. Thus the author is writing in the post-Pauline period and seems to be polemizing against Paul.

The question whether faith can save without works (2:14) seems strange in view of Paul's statements. But the idea that "a person is justified by works and not by faith alone" (2:24) seems to be formulated expressly against Rom. 3:28. We should note that the word *alone,* which in Paul is missing but of course implicit, is expressly stated by the author, but only in order to be disputed.

Now we must be more precise about the nature of the polemic. It is not aimed at Paul himself but at the understanding of Paul's *wording* in later times. At this point we can leave open the question whether the author saw this difference. Probably, he did not.

For Paul faith is always a "reliance upon," which is lived concretely in the body. Therefore in his writings faith always *implies* "obedience." Deeds are then "fruit" but not "works" to be accomplished by people. Only with this understanding was Paul able to formulate Romans 3:28.

If, however, one changes the content of what Paul understands as faith and still uses the same word in spite of the new content, what happens? The Pauline expression is quoted word for word, but what Paul meant by it is totally destroyed.

This is exactly what must have happened in the post-Pauline period, and it is where the author begins. *Faith* has now come to mean the acceptance of doctrines and facts. The author illustrates this with the example of demons, who have such "faith" if they believe that God is one, that is, if they are monotheists (2:19). But if (using the *wording* of the Pauline expression) one asserts that God justifies people not by works but solely because of this "faith," then with the disqualification of works, human deeds drop out of sight altogether. The result may be libertinism or at least indifference toward human behavior. At the same time justification gets a different place. The situation is no longer, as in Paul, that "justified people" are now able to act and do act; instead, justification by God is moved into the future. And the prerequisite for justification is no longer (as for the Pharisees) proof of deeds done; rather, justification requires only the "faith." Those who have "the right faith" can be sure of their future.

For the author, however, the right faith alone is not enough for justification. At one point there is even a brief hint of the Pauline understanding of faith: the (present!) shuddering of the demons shows that their "faith" is without salvation (2:19b). Nevertheless, the writer's attention is still focused on future justification. And without doing works, his readers will not attain it.

The author's polemic against the Pauline wording and its new contents—which are presumably known to the readers, since they evidently refer to it—could (at least theoretically) have been conducted in a way that would clarify the word "faith" and correct its content. Yet this attempt would presuppose that the author was aware of the linguistic difference.

At the same time, of course, we must admit that in practice such an attempt is almost always doomed to failure. Words whose contents have been ruined are unusable. In many cases this can still be demonstrated in today's "ecclesiastical language usage." Such words must be replaced by others.

The author now takes the following path: with an eye on future justification, he ascertains a deficit in ethics and begins to work on it. He takes up his readers' understanding of "faith" (which he himself probably shares) and demonstrates the absurdity of the hope that one can expect salvation from such "faith." Such "faith" will not achieve justification by God— certainly not "alone," but only together with works, and works are actually more important (2:24). This means, however, that the element of "obedience," which the Pauline understanding of faith always implies, has wandered away from faith (and stays away!). The author adds it to faith as an independent entity, as work, and even puts it first.

Naturally, we can look one by one at the paraeneses that the author adds to his writing. Then we will engage in noteworthy deliberations on ethics and probably be able to ascertain a remarkable ethical level. Therefore there is no reason to disqualify the ethics of the paraeneses or the ethics of the author of James.

Yet the writer of James does not offer a genuinely Christian ethic. Because Christology is completely missing, the adopted imperatives lack an indicative. The outcome of this ethic is not eschatological existence.

## 4. The Solution of the Author of 1 Peter

In its present form the First Letter of Peter is a letter (more precisely, an encyclical) that the "elder myself and a witness of the sufferings of Christ" (5:1; note the first person singular!), who calls himself "Peter" in the preface (1:1), sends to churches in Asia Minor. They are under pressure from two sides. The first pressure is of a social nature. The author writes to readers who, because of their nonconformist life-style, have fallen into conflict with their heathen environment (4:4) and therefore must endure many reproaches and insinuations (3:14, 17) and perhaps even more (1:6). The other pressure is of a political nature. Persecution of Christians on a big scale has begun (4:12; 5:8-9). In this context the readers have to reckon with the possibility of being brought to court (4:15) and enduring suffering.

There are reasons to assume that the letter was not all written at one time but developed literarily in two or three steps.

According to this hypothesis, the oldest section (1:3-4:11) is a kind of catechism. Christians—perhaps even applicants for baptism—are taught what Christian faith and life are all about. At the same time they are informed about possible negative consequences for them personally. Then in 4:12-5:11 the previously written catechism is brought up to date in the current situation, in which the persecution of Christians is actually (4:13) afflicting the whole empire (5:8-9). Finally, either at the same time or later, the whole work is placed into an epistolary framework with 1:1-2 and 5:12-14.

For the presentation of the author's ethic, of course, this hypothesis has little significance, since both the parts and the whole are almost certainly from the same writer. Yet the hypothesis makes it possible to treat the ethical problem in a more differentiated way.

Thus the author wants to help Christians who have become socially isolated and hence are under pressure. In addition they are threatened with persecution by the state, which the author himself already seems to have experienced, since he calls himself a witness of the sufferings of Christ (5:1). The way in which he tries to help them is noteworthy.

Literarily, he uses the same method as the author of James. He compiles various traditions of various kinds. A recognizable organization is lacking, and therefore a division is hardly possible (apart from a closing in 4:11 and a new beginning in 4:12). The writer draws not only on a wealth of monitory traditions (including especially household rules; 2:13-3:7) but also on hymns and confessional formulas (1:20; 2:21-25; 3:18).

Thus one could say that he connects life and doctrine even while selecting his materials. Yet he does not place the two·side by side but joins them together in many ways. It is significant that (and how) he always relates both to the addressees.

The author does not make statements that are crucial for his ethics by telling his readers what they must do, but by talking to them about *who they are,* how they became who they are, how that can be translated into concrete behavior and action, and what the resulting consequences are for them personally. Thus it immediately becomes clear that the author's ethic is not oriented mainly toward deeds but looks first at the doer.

The doers, however, are those who are in "exile" (1:17) and live in this world as "aliens and exiles" (2:11).

> This characterization of Christians is typical of the author. Elsewhere in the New Testament the wording used here occurs in a positive sense only in Heb. 11:13 (as opposed to Eph. 2:19). The importance that the writer places on using the reader's foreign status in a positive way is conveyed in the preface: "To the exiles of the dispersion . . ." (1:1).

Of course, the readers, like their neighbors, live in this world. The author emphasizes that this is what they are supposed to do, and then he gives them examples of how to do that. Yet it is crucial that they are not at home in this world, and that means that they are not governed by it. They have become foreigners.

> Here we can point out that the author expresses the same content that the summary in Mark 1:14-15 does, but he uses a different terminology. Those who in the old aeon are living the inbreaking dominion of God are no longer at home in this world.

That this is exactly what happened to the readers (and is supposed to happen again and again) can be expressed by the author in various ways. He begins with what is largely already known to his readers but must be said to them again and again. Then he talks in general, using traditional expressions, which occur in large numbers in this writing. Here the author only touches on things lightly, as it were, in order to give his readers the overall picture once again. When discussing acute problems, however, he argues more thoroughly. Then he develops inherited christological statements independently and in relation to the problems. In this way Christology becomes an immediate help in overcoming existing difficulties. Yet sometimes general talk also changes into specific talk.

For example, the author can say to his readers, "You were ransomed from the futile ways inherited from your ancestors ... with the precious blood of Christ" (1:18-19). But he can also express this ransoming with the term *new birth*. Through the resurrection of Jesus Christ the readers receive "a new birth into a living hope" (1:3). Or: "You have been born anew ... of imperishable seed, through the living and enduring word of God" (1:23), and for that reason are "like newborn infants" (2:2). "For Christ also suffered for sins once for all ... in order to bring you to God" (3:18). Many such terse statements occur throughout the letter. The author is always concerned with the reception of Christology. His readers are supposed to perceive *who* they are (and have become), so that they may live from that. They are supposed to receive the indicative, so that the received indicative can be lived.

> The association of the indicative with the imperative, as well as that of the imperative with the indicative, reminds us of Paul. Hence the author has often been called a student of Paul. Of course, we can hardly say whether he really was. The adopted material shows that he drew from a broad stream of Christian tradition. How he deals with diverse traditions from different sources is significant. He neither simply repeats them nor combines them additively. He takes on a middle course, which he sees in the ethic of Paul. And then he succeeds in shaping his ethic from that middle way, while incorporating the adopted traditions. In this sense, he really is a "student" of Paul, because for him Paul's theology is, to coin a phrase, "the canon within the canon."
>
> In carrying out his intentions, he proceeds quite independently. We see that especially in two of the more

common characteristics. He likes to put the imperative first (especially when it occurs in an adopted tradition) and then begin the indicative with a substantiating *for*. Also, the "imperative" often occurs in the grammatical form of a participle, which is difficult to imitate when translating from Greek into our language (and that is why the participles are translated as imperatives). Because the author uses the participle, the (intended) imperative appears to be less than an order that has to be followed, for those who are challenged to do something are already addressed as people who are doing it (2:1, 18; 3:1, 7; etc.).

Exactly the same association of the indicative with the imperative is seen when we survey the author's larger contexts. An example of this is the household rules (2:13-3:7). The writer adopts imperatives from material that is familiar in the surrounding world. But this is precisely where he does not want to offer his readers imperatives.

That is what, for example, the author of the pastoral letters does (cf. 1 Tim. 2:8-12; Titus 2:1-5), thereby presenting bourgeois ethics directly as Christian ethics. The household rules in Col. 3:18-20 and Ephesians 5:22-25, however, are different. They are "Christianized," of course, but always in stereotyped phrases. The author of the 1 Peter goes much further.

In many and various ways the writer brings the indicative into the adopted ethic of the household rules. That happens even in the introduction (2:11-12). The sources contained rules for citizens. The author does not present them to the citizens, though, but expressly to "aliens and exiles," that is, to those who he assumes have received the indicative. Now, as it happens, they are (for whatever reasons) maligned as evildoers by the citizens (the "Gentiles"). The "aliens and exiles" are now to prove such a reproach wrong by living according to the household rules. As "aliens and exiles" they actually *can* do that.

Thus the author is guided by an apologetic interest. That is why he resorts to the household rules. On the basis of this interest, he also structures his work in a systematic way.

The question has been raised, whether the request for loyal behavior toward political authorities was a component of the household rules at all. Should the author's household rules begin at 2:18? Yet this immediately raises further questions. Why the unusual order of slaves, women, men? And if slaves are addressed in a Christian community, do the owners of the slaves not have to be addressed too? Or were there no slaveowners among the Christians?

Such questions fail to recognize that the writer's "household rules" are not bourgeois household rules. Rather, the author creates something new (whatever one wants to call it) by organizing different traditions—including household rules—according to subject matter and introducing them with 2:11-12.

When the author begins with the command to be subject to the human institutions (2:13-17), he first addresses the "bourgeois" theme. The address to the slaves, which surprisingly now follows, (2:18-25) is not aimed actually—and certainly not exclusively—at the slaves. Rather, they are addressed because the author wants to show, by using them as examples, what it means as "aliens and exiles" to be pressured as outsiders in the middle of citizens. Thus with these two sections the author develops the thematic tension of 2:11-12. Then he focuses on the intracommunity aspect. Because his concern is to help the weak who are under pressure, he first addresses the women (3:1-6) and then only briefly the men (3:7). From 3:8 on he again addresses all the readers.

Within this framework we can see how the author presents his argumentation. His demand that the readers subject themselves to human institutions (2:13-17) is substantiated above all by their ability to do so. They are not simply citizens, from whom obedience is demanded, but as "servants [Greek: slaves] of God" they are "free people" (2:16). That is why "for the Lord's sake" they can be subject to the emperor, the governors, and their officials, especially since they, even as the bearers of governmental power, are (only) "human creations" (as the beginning of 2:13 is correctly translated).

We can see the uniqueness of the author's statement even clearer if we compare it with Rom. 13:1-7. Here also Paul uses an adopted piece of tradition, which, however, he does not change in order to "Christianize" it. According to this tradition, which presumably originated in Hellenistic Judaism (though not in Paul's opinion!), every authority is instituted by God. Thus it has divine dignity, and its officials are servants of God. It follows that everyone who obeys the authorities is doing God's will.

This, however, is exactly what the author of 1 Peter does not want to say. According to him it is God's will that the readers refute the unjustified accusations leveled against them by doing what is right. Yet if they do right, they are doing exactly what those who hold governmental office are commanded to do. By submitting as free people to the existing order, they "silence the ignorance of the foolish" (2:15).

This thought is continued immediately in the address to the slaves (2:18-25). The initial theme is again subordination and corresponds to the traditional requirement in the household rules. But now the author introduces a distinction between good and bad masters, thereby touching on the theme of unjust suffering. Subordination is required even with unjust masters. In this way the writer can talk about the unjust suffering experienced not only by slaves but also by Christians. His words to slaves are carried over to all readers. They live (the author assumes innocently) in an oppressive situation that is hardly bearable, but that should not surprise them (cf. 4:12). This idea is substantiated christologically. For if the Christology that the author gives the readers is really received by them, then they can expect nothing different as aliens in this world.

Quite probably, the author had a hymn at his disposal for his christological statements in 2:21-25 but must have adapted it. Formulaic material (e.g., "Christ also suffered for you"; 2:21) is embellished with motifs from the passion story and is thus made visual. This visualization is then applied to the situation of the slaves and the Christians: "When he was abused, he did not return abuse; when he suffered, he did not threaten . . ." (2:23).

Those who suffer unjustly are promised that they are living the life of Christ. The fact that images used in the Christology are enriched with images from concrete situations makes it clear that here we are dealing with a Christology that is supposed to be received.

When the author then addresses wives (3:1-6) and their husbands (3:7), his statements always remain within the bounds of what was usual in the household rules. But also within the church he points out a feature (of those who are weaker) that he thinks is important for the influence that Christians can have on the outside world: through their subordination and behavior wives can influence their husbands and can win them over to the church (3:1-2).

Yet the author does not substantiate his ethic only christologically (cf. also 3:18-22, which is introduced with a substantiating *for*). On the basis of his Christology he can also substantiate his ethic eschatologically. "Through the resurrection of Jesus Christ from the dead" those who have a "new birth" have a "living hope." For them an "inheritance that is imperishable, undefiled and unfading" is "kept in heaven" (1:3-4). Since the future joy is certain but not yet present, the "aliens and exiles" have to "suffer various trials," to test the "genuineness of their faith" (1:6-7). What that means for ethics is discussed in a summary in 4:7-11.

> When the author says here, "The end of all things is near" (4:7), we must not understand it in the sense of an apocalyptic imminent expectation. He has no date in mind but rather employs a traditional phrase in order to express the idea that the life of Christians is determined from the standpoint of the end.

Those who live their lives from the standpoint of the end, in the sure hope of gaining the inheritance, live soberly (and not in enthusiastic rapture, as the opponents do, according to 2 Thess. 2:2). This soberness includes not being overextended ethically. Only the gift each one has received is to be lived for one's neighbor. In this way the readers prove to be "good stewards of the manifold grace of God." The indicative always precedes the imperative. God is present when Christians speak, and for that reason it is "the very words of God" that are uttered. Service takes place "with the strength that God supplies." The whole existence of Christians as Christians is thus a glorification of God. What they are forming is the lived worship of God (cf. Rom. 12:1).

If, however, as the extreme case of pressure, a "fiery ordeal" comes upon Christians (4:12) in the form of a persecution by the state, in the author's opinion the threshold of pain has not been crossed. Even now he remains true to his approach. Hence persecution can neither astonish the readers nor be something unforeseen and strange for them. On the contrary, there is reason to rejoice because the readers now share the sufferings of Christ even more intensely and thus the coming glory (4:13). The author has only one concern: it must really be a question of suffering "for the name of Christ" (4:14).

Beside Christology the author then brings an ecclesiological aspect into his argument: the readers are not alone in their suffering. It has come to "your brothers and sisters in all the world" (5:9). And the author can point to himself with a double designation. As an elder among other elders, he is both a witness to the sufferings of Christ and (as such) a partaker of the glory to be revealed (5:1).

For the first time in Christian literature the term *martys* ("witness") occurs here with a suggestion of the sense of "martyr." At the same time the motif of the primacy of Peter in Rome occurs for the first time; the letter claims to be written by "Peter" from Babylon (i.e., Rome; 5:13). The two seem to be connected and to lead the author's statement another step forward.

Since pseudonymous letters almost always originated in the place to which they were addressed, it is most likely that the author was an elder in a church somewhere in Asia Minor. The persecution began in Rome, and Christians in the East knew that Paul had become a martyr in Rome. That is why Peter is named within the framework of the letter (1:1-2; 5:12-14) as the author of this writing from "Babylon." *As a martyr* Peter has primacy. This martyr, together with the actual author, who is a fellow elder and a witness of the sufferings of Christ (5:1), comes to the aid of the churches oppressed by the persecution that began in Rome.

Naturally, when in our day political activity is demanded of Christians beyond the bounds of their own church, we cannot appeal directly to the First Letter of Peter. After all, readers in those days had no opportunity at all to engage in external political activity.

Nevertheless, we should not fail to hear the voice of our author in such discussions. Indeed, he showed his readers that an existence of Christians that is christologically and eschatologically founded is already in itself a political act. It takes place in the world, and the world is amazed that Christians live the way they do. They themselves endure being aliens and exiles. They do not seek persecution at all, but they are not surprised when it comes, and they certainly do not complain about it (4:12). For they are sure that they are following in the steps of their Lord (2:21).

## 5. The Solution of the Author of Colossians

In all probability, the Letter to the Colossians did not come from Paul's pen. Of course, the letter is quite reminiscent of Pauline thought, and the argumentation in particular can be called Pauline. In addition, however, there is an abundance of un-Pauline characteristics in language and style, and there are, above all, ideas that are completely unknown to Paul or at least never occur in his other letters. Thus it is almost universally assumed that Colossians was written by a student of Paul.

The main characteristic of the ethic of the author of Colossians is the always close relationship between indicatives and imperatives. Formally, the structure of the letter reveals the following. Out of the "teachings" (chap. 1-2) comes the "paraenesis" (chap. 3-4). That even happens explicitly, as emphasized especially by the reference in 3:1 ("you have been raised with Christ") back to 2:12 ("you were also raised with him"). Furthermore, the association of indicative and imperative often occurs within both parts of the letter. In the first part christological statements are directly transformed into paraenesis (1:21-23; 2:16-23). And when in the second part the author falls back on traditional forms for the paraenesis (catalog of vices and virtues, 3:5-13; household rules, 3:18-4:1), he substantiates the imperatives again and again with indicatives (3:9-10, 12-13, 15; etc.). To this extend there is agreement with Paul.

For an overall understanding of Colossians, however, something else is more important: the author discusses heretics, whose Christology has direct consequences for ethics. And now he turns against both in his polemic: against Christology and ethics. It is noteworthy here that (and how) he preserves the connection between the two.

It is not very easy to describe the heretics' position precisely. The main reason is that the author never describes it in itself but always brings it directly into his polemic. The writer could assume that his readers were familiar with the heresy; after all, they were endangered by it. But we must depend on reconstruction. The attempts at reconstruction, however, show that we are dealing with a syncretistic formation in which the motifs of various religious and philosophical origins occur side by side: Jewish and Gnostic ones, but also overtones of mystery cults. Often we find only allusions. Therefore it is difficult to perceive how these themes were connected to each other and how important they were for the overall picture. That reminds us to be careful in our exegesis.

We get a relatively clear picture of the ethic of the heretics against whose "human way of thinking" (2:18) the author is polemizing. There are "legal demands" that have to be fulfilled (cf. 2:14). The author talks of "human commands and teachings" (2:22). Certain times (festivals, new moons, and sabbaths) have to be observed, as well as certain food regulations apparently of an ascetic character (2:16). Taboos (also regarding sexual intercourse?) are to be maintained (2:21). It is a matter of chastising the body (2:23). Thus we have here a dualistic anthropology: the body is despised, and salvation is expected only for the self.

Now, the author says, to be sure, that everything goes back to human tradition (2:8). At the same time, though, one has to make sure that the ethic is substantiated "theologically." The heretics understood themselves as Christians and indeed as Christians of a higher kind. They looked upon their doctrine as "philosophy" (2:8). The word is not to be understood here in its classical Greek sense but in the Hellenistic sense of a doctrine of myths, which drew from ancient tradition and imparted knowledge about redemption—though redemption only for the self. The self strives for "the things that are above" (3:1). Its goal is the divine world, the *pleroma* ("fullness"; 2:9). But the *pleroma* can be reached from the material world only if the intermediate powers do not interfere. Yet these intermediate powers demand worship in return (2:18). By doing so they prove themselves to be the "gods" of human beings.

Such worship of the intermediate powers takes place through the fulfilling of "legal demands." Those who let themselves be determined by these powers show their self-abasement (2:18, 23) toward these cosmic "rulers and authorities" (2:10, 15) represented as persons, toward the *stoicheia tou kosmou* ("elemental spirits of the universe"; 2:8, 20), and toward the angels (2:18). Thus, because of these intermediate powers, fulfillment of the ethical requirements is necessary to salvation. Without the fulfillment of the "legal demands" there is no salvation for the self.

The cult must have also played a role for the heretics. This is suggested by the verb *embateuein* (2:18; literally, to enter, to scrutinize exactly upon entering). The word occurs in the language of the mystery cults as a technical term for the rite of entrance. Those who dedicate themselves to such (in the author's view, self-chosen) worship (2:23) experience upon consecration visions of the cosmic intermediate powers.

No matter how and where these heretics imagined Christ in this cosmic hierarchy (presumably at the top, next to the *pleroma*), for them simply being a Christian was not enough for salvation. To be sure, forgiveness of sins had been accomplished through the cross but not redemption of the self. This could be attained only if Christians themselves made their contribution in ethics and the cult by orienting themselves toward the "philosophy."

The author now argues against this philosophy theologically (in the precise sense of this word), and he substantiates his theology christologically. For him it is a question of who the *God* of Christians is: the elemental spirits of the universe or Christ (2:8). If it is not the elemental spirits of the universe, then their legal demands cannot enslave Christians. Therefore, the fulfillment of these demands cannot be required as a prerequisite for the attainment of salvation.

> To put it as Paul might: what human beings want to achieve by means of their own deeds (through "works of the law") has already been achieved—through Christ. In order to show this, however, the author uses concepts that are different from Paul's. He adopts the "world view" of the opponents, presumably because he shares it himself (see below), and now he argues from the inside, as it were, against the opponents' doctrine.

For the author the cross has a central significance, yet he interprets the cross more comprehensively than his opponents do. Not only did the cross bring the forgiveness of sins, but also Christ has erased the whole record, a document directed against people, by nailing it to the cross (2:14). And its creators, the rulers and authorities, were disarmed at the cross. They were exposed publicly by Christ and made to look ridiculous by Christ's triumph over them (2:15). Thus the cosmic intermediate powers and their legal demands have been cleared out of the way. They are not gods anymore and thus can no longer block the way to heaven. The heretics and the author are equally interested in the way to heaven. But now, he says, this path has been cleared by Jesus on the cross. In this way the desired goal, the *pleroma*, is reached directly. No longer do we need the cosmic intermediate powers and their legal demands, because we can take our bearings directly from Christ and thus directly from the goal. For in Christ dwells the whole divine *pleroma* (2:9).

Since Christ is the "head of every ruler and authority" (2:10) and Christians are oriented towards Christ, they can share in his victory over the cosmic intermediate powers. To show how this applies to his readers, the author reminds them of their baptism and inteprets it. For in their baptism they have already died to the elemental spirits of the universe and been raised with Christ (2:12). Hence they are people who have already reached their goal.

Here the author adopts the image of dying with and being raised with the deity, which was already familiar at the time. Paul also uses it (Rom. 6:3-6), even if in a modified form and for direct ethical substantiation. In this way he avoids the assertion that Christians are already raised with Christ. For Paul the resurrection of Christians remains in the future. In the present Christians have a new way of life that is defined by the resurrected Christ. Paul especially values this so-called eschatological reservation because of his experiences with enthusiasts in Corinth. The assertion of an already accomplished resurrection of Christians can lead to a perfectionism that brings with it the loss of ethics.

Is the author of Colossians more "careless" at this point? He says exactly what Paul carefully avoids saying. We must keep in mind, though, that unlike Paul he does not argue using the category of time but the category of space.

The author does not want to understand the claim that Christians have been raised with Christ in baptism in the sense of a perfectionism that makes ethics superfluous. For that reason he first formulates only the indicative within the framework of his cosmological world view. For even as those raised with Christ, Christians remain "below," on this earth. At this point the indicative then leads into imperatives. But since the indicative is not expressed in the same way as in Paul, that also gives the imperative a different shape. It is not a question of anticipating the future—and hence not a question of eschatological existence. Rather, for Christians it is a matter of seeking the "things that are above," for Christ is there, seated at the right hand of God (3:1). That is what Christians should set their minds on and not—because they are still below—on things that are on earth (3:2). Thus, for those who are raised with Christ, salvation is actual a reality but still a hidden one (3:3). It is not simply at one's disposal but must be lived until that time "when Christ who is your life is revealed" (3:4). So those raised with Christ are also on their way. How this being on the way can be shaped is developed from 3:5 on by the author, who repeatedly substantiates the imperatives with indicatives.

It is interesting that the idea of the Parousia occurs here (and only here in this letter), and it means a future event that Christians are approaching (not one that is approaching them and already governs them). The author, thinking entirely in spatial categories and arguing within these categories, has to work with a "cosmological reservation": even the Christians raised with Christ are still "below." This word *still* forces us at least to take a look at the category of time. Because time on the earth is the "place" for ethics.

Without doubt, the polemic against heresy is the central focus in Colossians. The author has written this polemical document for the sake of this particular discussion. We must now keep in mind, however, that it is not the author's intention to set his own (correct) "doctrine" over against the "doctrine" of the heretics. He is not concerned with the isolated problem of orthodoxy. Rather, the difference shows up in the life that the heretics live and demand of others, that is, in ethics. For this life is what first becomes visible: Christians are to observe special times (festivals, new moons, sabbaths); they are to subject themselves to asceticism and observe the precepts of taboos. The author polemizes against this ethic as a supposedly Christian one. But he does not do so with arguments from the ethic itself in order to contradict it within itself. Instead he argues theologically by revealing the "gods" of this ethic and then stripping them of their power with his Christology. Then on the basis of his Christology, the author finds his ethic.

We must also keep this point in mind in regard to the Christology that the author develops in chapter 1. Since it comes at the beginning, it has the effect of laying a foundation, which in the author's view is what it is supposed to be, and he keeps it free from any polemic. The crucial question, however, is how these christological statements came about. And there we cannot overlook the fact that the Christology was created from the ideas and the conceptual world that occur in the interaction with the heretics.

There is a consensus that the author followed a model, presumably a christological hymn, in 1:15-20. We cannot be certain where he altered the model. It may even be that we have here an older tradition that goes back to a pre-Christian hymn. It probably comes from the realm of cosmic mythology, which dealt with overcoming from below the dividing line between heaven and earth. The hymn was then christologized to express the belief that Christ was the one who had overcome this separation. Then, of course, the author added further emphases of his own.

As a result we have a wealth of christological statements, which (except for Ephesians, which is dependent on Colossians) do not occur again in the same way: Christ is the "image" (= hypostasis) of God, the firstborn of all creation, in whom all things were created in heaven and on earth. In Christ all things hold together; the fullness (*pleroma*) of God dwells within him; and so forth.

Now, we must not isolate this Christology from the polemic and turn it into a doctrine. The author developed it (even while following models) on the basis of the specific situation with which he was confronted. Thus, to use a modern terminology, we have here a "Christology from below," whose help is to be used in overcoming ethical differences. The "material" for this Christology comes from "below." Given the world views of the author and his opponents, the use of this particular material is immediately understandable. But if we now reverse the direction, if we turn the "Christology from below" into a "Christology from above," we necessarily fall into the realm of christological speculation.

For there is not only the danger of isolating ethics from Christology. There is also the danger of isolating Christology from ethics.

The author of the Colossians shows in model fashion that Christian ethics is always an aspect of Christology. If this connection is not preserved, both will be ruined.

## 6. The Solution of the Author of Hebrews

The Letter to the Hebrews is not a letter but a scholarly essay largely shaped in the form of a speech. The unknown author himself calls his treatise a "word of exhortation" (13:22). The fictitious ending of the letter (13:23-24) was added to the essay either by the writer or by someone else. There are, of course, occasional direct addresses and also specific allusions (5:11-12; 6:10; 10:32-34; 13:7), yet the author does not address a particular community that he wants to help in its concrete situation. Rather, he wants to make "typical" statements that are important for many communities in (about) the third Christian generation (2:3). In that regard we can say that the author addresses the "church of his time" with his word of exhortation.

The author believes his readers (or listeners) are in danger, though not because of heresy but because of fatigue. Now, it is significant that this fatigue in his church concerns both doctrine and life. The author relates the two to each other.

We must make this very point right from the beginning because there has been a recurring dispute as to whether the writer's main interest was his Christology or ethics. As a result, the emphasis is usually placed according to where one's own interest lies. For the author, however, it is not at all a question of an alternative. For him ethics is really an aspect of Christology. Accordingly, he uses Christology to eliminate the ethical shortcomings of the church in his time.

On the one hand, the author detects in his readers a deficit in doctrine. They have stopped at an inadequate stage of knowledge and become dull in understanding (5:11-14). Although they actually could already be teachers, considering how long they have been Christians, they must again be taught the basic elements of doctrine. Since they are still unskilled in the "word of righteousness," they need milk instead of solid food. Yet if they were "mature" (i.e., adults in doctrine), that would become visible in their life-style: they would be practiced in the use of their faculties and could better distinguish good from evil.

Thus the writer challenges his readers to leave the basic teaching behind and not deal repeatedly with the fundamentals. Among such "fundamentals" the author includes repentance from dead works, faith toward God, and instruction about baptism and the laying on of hands, the resurrection of the dead and eternal judgment.

> What the author lists here seems in some degree "modern." It is generally the picture of Christian doctrine as normally understood today: a usually vague idea of faith in God, an (often also unclear) idea that Christians must do "good works," baptism and the laying on of hands as customary rites, and expectation of the resurrection of the dead and judgment.

Then, however, the readers also show signs of fatigue in their actual behavior. In earlier times Christians endured sufferings for the sake of their faith (10:32-34). But that was long ago, for in the meantime they have almost become timid about suffering (12:4). They lack endurance (10:36). They are growing weary (12:3). Hence they are in danger of falling away (6:6). Readers must be warned not to sin willfully (10:26-31; 12:16-17). Already some have even been "neglecting to meet together" (10:25).

On the other hand, corresponding to the deficit in understanding is the readers' indifference in life-style. The eschatologically living community has transformed itself into a church and established itself in the world. This church deserves the author's warning, which receives a special emphasis when he brings into play the motif of the impossibility of a second repentance (6:4-6; 10:26-27; cf. 12:16-17).

> Exactly what the author means by this is exegetically disputed. In the history of church and of dogma the problem has often played

a significant role and also been the object of theological criticism (by Luther, among others). This criticism is indeed appropriate when these particular passages are misused in a biblicist fashion. If we interpret historically, there should be no doubt. The author was not trying to say that *for his readers* there is no possibility of repentance in spite of their failure. If he had meant that, he either would not have needed to write at all or would have written quite differently. Rather, he had to warn against their calmly carrying on as before because, after all, they had the "institution of confession" and therefore could count on the forgiveness of sins. The possibility of a (second) repentance that was *planned* in this way is by all means disputed by the author.

Precisely in connection with these assertions it becomes clear at what point the author begins to encounter signs of fatigue in his readers. Those who tire in the shape their faith takes in real life show that they are really unskilled in the "word of righteousness." It has not yet been received in their lives, and they think that they do not have to receive it because they can count on the forgiveness of sins. In this way, however, "on their own they are crucifying the Son of God and are holding him up to contempt" (6:6). This means that they are thereby abolishing the basis for their existence as Christians: the sacrifice of Christ. Yet there is no further "sacrifice" through which they might now be able to attain forgiveness of sins. It happened *once* and hence at the same time *once for all* (7:27; 9:12).

Thus the readers do not need admonitions at first in order to stay on the right path or to get back on it; rather, they need a more comprehensive understanding of the sacrifice of Christ. Only when they have gained this understanding can they overcome the signs of fatigue in the shaping of their lives. That is why the author of Hebrews expounds his Christology. This exposition is done in service to soteriology, and in this way his Christology is supposed to become an immediate aid to living.

A comparison with corresponding expositions before and by Paul will aid our understanding. With the formula, "Christ died for us," the death of Jesus is announced as a salvific death. Paul continues this approach when he specifies "*died* for us" in the (likewise adopted) statement, "Christ *gave* himself for us": Christ did not *live* to "please himself" (Rom. 15:3). In accordance with his Christology, Paul paints the "life of Jesus" as self-giving love (Gal. 2:20), as obedience (Rom. 5:19), and so forth. He explains this most vividly when he adopts the hymn of Christ and interpretively expands it in Phil. 2:6-11. The exposition of the Christology is written with a soteriological interest: Paul wants to guide his readers to a more comprehensive understanding of the offered salvation and thus provides the opportunity to understand and shape life more comprehensively on the basis of this salvation. Christians can and should become people who are shaped by the *typos* Christ (1 Thess. 1:6-7; 1 Cor. 11:1) and are living as such. They live "christologically." Paul himself carries the "death of Jesus" in his body in order to make the "life of Jesus" apparent to others (2 Cor. 4:10-12). (Cf. also the quite parallel exposition of Christology in 1 Peter 2:21-24: it is supposed to encourage "christological life.")

Using a modern expression, we could say that the author of Hebrews has written a "narrative Christology." Incorporating ideas that originated in the cult (sacrifice, high priest), the atoning *death* of Christ is portrayed as the *self*-sacrifice of the true high priest. This does not mean, however, that the author is setting up something like christological speculations that today could be expounded as "doctrine," developed further, and brought into one system with other Christologies. He proceeds, rather, in the other direction. Because he wants to lead the church of his time out of its fatigue, he makes more vivid the soteriological meaning of "died for us." For this purpose he adopts old ideas, whose understanding he can assume on the part of his readers.

The One who gave himself as a sacrifice is, on the one hand, separated from humankind: he was without sin. At the same time, however, he is closely bound to them: he has sympathy for their weaknesses and was tested as they are (4:15). In every respect he was like his brothers and sisters (2:17). Because he suffered and was tested himself, he can help others who are tested, especially the readers. Christology is always related to soteriology.

Because of his obedience, the Son attained heavenly perfection (5:8-9) and "is seated at the right hand of the throne of the Majesty in the heavens" (8:1; cf. 4:14; 7:26; 9:24; 12:2).

Thus the author of Hebrews adopts the image of the myth: the Redeemer (the "Son") comes from heaven for the redemption of humankind and then returns again to heaven. His earthly life is vividly portrayed: redemption takes place in the self-sacrifice of the high priest. This alone is the basis of salvation. Accordingly, any mention of the resurrection of Jesus is missing in Hebrews (as also in the hymn of Phil. 2:6-11). It does not fit into this schema as a "salvation event."

To this "Son" who is exalted into heaven, Christians on earth are now on their way as the "wandering people of God" (E. Käsemann). Corresponding to the christological statements that are more comprehensive than the "basic elements" (5:12) is a more comprehensive understanding of the Christian life-style, to which, as an aspect of the Christology, the author again invites and admonishes his readers.

As an illustration he refers to the past and in particular to the past of the church that has grown tired. The readers are asked to recall those earlier days (10:32-36). At that time they lived their faith, for after they were enlightened they endured hard struggle with sufferings and were exposed to abuse. They were partners with those so treated and also endured the plundering of their possessions, because they knew that they had a better "possession." They must not abandon this confidence. (Cf. Paul's quite similar argumentation in 1 Thessalonians.)

The author can also refer to the past, however, by connecting with the traditions of the Old Testament. The validity of sacrifice in the old covenant is not questioned; the sacrifice of Christ is the "better" one (9:23). The law has only a "shadow" of the things to come, but it does have the shadow. It offers a wealth of examples for the paraenesis.

From time to time, the central conception of the author of Hebrews has been called (mainly because of 1:1-2) one of "salvation history." But that (like the expression itself) is very misleading. The author only seems to trace the way of God as a path through Old Testament history to the coming of the "Son." The "cloud of witnesses" (12:1), which he details especially in chapter 11, did not receive what was promised because God "provided something better" (11:39-40). So if the author is portraying something like a "historical line," then he is not especially interested in it. He looks back to the past from "something better" and shows that even then these witnesses had to prove themselves in situations that were similar to those of his readers.

The old covenant is really replaced by the new covenant. Now the church can and should run with perseverance the race that is set before them. The church will succeed, however, only if it looks to Jesus, the pioneer and perfecter of the faith (12:1-2). In this the members of the church are supposed to help each other (3:13; 10:25), to inspire one another (10:24), and take care of what is lame (12:13). For in this world they remain strangers and foreigners (11:13) who have no lasting city but together are looking for the city that is to come (13:14).

Thus with his Christology the writer offers tired Christians crucial help for living. He composed it because he recognized that the reason for their fatigue was that the "basic elements" of doctrine no longer had soteriological power. He tries to remove this deficit in soteriological power by explicating the traditional Christology and thereby portraying it as a *helpful Christology*. It can reach his readers because in working it out, he uses ideas that were familiar to him and his readers.

If, in a church that has grown tired, we orient ourselves toward the basic concept of the author of Hebrews, we must ask the following question: How would a dogmatist today have to design a Christology that would help tired Christians *directly* to overcome their fatigue?

# C. Ethics in the Johannine Circle

The Gospel of John and the three Johannine epistles show broad agreement in language, style, and conceptual world, and it is this agreement that distinguishes them from the other New Testament scriptures. When we ask about the ethics of the authors, however, we must not let this impression deceive us. Naturally, we might expect them essentially to agree in their ethics, but exactly the opposite is the case. For it can be shown that the ethic of "John" is fundamentally different from that of his school.

Judgments about the literary findings form the point of departure for perceiving this difference.

There is a nearly unanimous consensus that the author of the Gospel was not also the author of the letters. There is disagreement, however, as to whether in the letters we are dealing with one or several authors (which is much more probable in my opinion). We can assume, nevertheless, that the letters originate from a relatively small circle.

Concerning the Gospel there is a nearly unanimous consensus that chapter 21 was subsequently added to chapters 1-20 by a different author. The most obvious suggestion is to give the responsibility for this subsequent chapter to someone in the circle in which the letters originated.

With a probability that borders on certainty, however, chapters 1-20 are not in their original form, either. It is easy to isolate a number of sentences that are not in harmony with the remaining context, which offers a "present eschatology" (see below). Apparently this was later thought to be one-sided and thus contradictory to the doctrine of the "church" at that time. Hence there was an "ecclesiastical redaction" (R. Bultmann) that added sentences with a "future eschatology," which were supposed to provide balance and mitigate the one-sidedness.

Thus we have to differentiate between the original Gospel on the one hand and the ecclesiastical redaction of this Gospel, the added chapter, and the three letters on the other.

The original Gospel was probably written by the disciple "whom Jesus loved" (cf. 13:23; 19:26; 20:2). We do not know his name, and we must also hasten to add that it is uncertain whether the author ever gave himself that designation. This identification of the author of the original Gospel with the disciple whom Jesus loved was carried out by the ecclesiastical redaction (19:34b, 35) and the author of the subsequent chapter (cf. 21:24 and 21:7, 20), and it happened after the death of the author of the original Gospel (cf. 21:23). We call this unknown disciple "John."

Students of this disciple (cf. the *we* in 21:24) then annotated and edited the work of their teacher, adding chapter 21. The annotation and expansion were necessary because the "Johannine School" had to defend itself against attacks (including those from the "church"). It looked back on the work of its teacher, felt obligated to him, and wanted to preserve his legacy, but in a later time and in a new situation. Such was also the aim of the three letters.

These literary findings already suggest that we should not be too quick to assert the unity of the ethic of John and that of his school.

## 1. The Ethic of John

If we look for ethics in the (original) Gospel, we are at first astonished to find that specific instructions and admonitions are completely absent. Actually, only one single ethical term occurs: love (used sometimes—and with the same meaning—as a noun and as a verb). How this love is actually to be carried out, however, is not stated, except in the washing of the disciples' feet (13:1-7).

In addition, love is never (in contrast to the synoptic tradition) for the little ones, the oppressed, or those in need. What is more, it is never for outsiders. The "new commandment" that Jesus gives his disciples and leaves behind for them (farewell speeches!) is that they love *one another* (13:34-35; 15:12, 13, 17). The object of the disciples' love is exclusively the disciples. That leads to the question, Does John restrict love of neighbor to mutual love within the circle of disciples? And if this is the case, does that not turn the fellowship of the disciples into a conventicle?

Explanations of this peculiarity have been sought in order to make understandable this restriction of love by John. This then raises the possibility of criticizing the content of the Evangelist's statements about love and at the same time substantiating the necessity of such criticism.

Thus, for example, scholars have pointed to the special situation of the farewell speeches, which is supposed to have occasioned this restriction. One theory is that John and the circle around him were so besieged from the outside that this led to a certain introversion. Another hypothesis is that in the circle around John love toward outsiders did not work, and John now wants to indicate that it cannot work if love is not practiced first within the circle. Therefore, he gives a one-sided emphasis to love toward one another.

Yet all these explanations are attempts to deal with a problem before sufficiently testing whether this particular problem really exists. Even considering all the differences between the explanations, they have a common denominator: the view that John must be excused because of his ethic. But then the crucial point is missed, and it is missed because of a desire to get a hold on the ethic too quickly—more precisely, to derive from the ethic of John a Christian ethic for today. To understand the ethic of John, however, we must not draw any hasty conclusions.

If we want to understand reciprocal love, we should first note that the word *love* for John is not an exclusively ethical term. Rather, it is also used theologically and christologically in a way that is especially characteristic of John, in order to specify a mutual relationship. The Father loves the Son, and the Son loves the Father. The Son loves his disciples, and the disciples love the Son. The Father loves the disciples, and the disciples love the Father (cf., e.g., 14:15, 21, 23, 31; 15:9-10, 12-13; 16:27; 17:23-24, 26).

Here we have—even if in different terminology—the same thing that occurs in Paul as the paradox of indicative and imperative. Those whom the Father and the Son love are themselves thereby enabled to love. Only they can love, and therefore they are exhorted to love with the very love that they themselves have experienced. They can fall out of this love. Therefore they are challenged to remain in this love, which corresponds to the love of the Father for the Son and of the Son for the Father (15:9-10). Only when they themselves love, do they receive the love of the Father and the Son. When they love, however, they love not only those whom they love; they also at the same time love those from whom they have received this love, the Father and the Son.

Thus John always uses the word *love* in a way that expresses reciprocity, and that is the paradox: love creates community, but it creates community only where community already exists. And vice versa: only where community exists, can love create community. This reciprocity is a basic element of what John means by the word *love*.

Yet if the indicative always takes the form of reciprocity, then the imperative must also take this form. Because love for John is always love for one another, it cannot include those who live outside this relationship.

Thus it has nothing to do with *restricting* love to the small circle of the disciples, and the reproach that the Johannine community led a conventicle existence does not, *as a reproach*, hit the real problem. For the problem is in the language. The use of the same word by John and by the other authors of New Testament scriptures must not lead us to a hasty conclusion that they always mean the same thing.

Our language has no equivalent for what John understands by *love*. Thus we must rely on circumlocutions. In doing so, we should keep the following difficulty in mind. The lack of a corresponding word in our language could be an indication that its meaning is completely foreign to us. That impedes and may even impose limits on our understanding.

There can be no doubt that the mutual love of the disciples is more than a mere attitude, conviction, or feeling. Rather, love of one another has to be given some kind of form—visible form. For if the disciples observe the commandment of Jesus to love one another, *everyone* will know that they are his disciples (13:35). Thus loving one another takes place in a circle that is closed but not closed-*off*. For it happens publicly. Yet this can mean only one thing: it takes place visibly.

Thus for ethics the question arises, What takes place so visibly when the disciples love one another that everyone can recognize it? What happens in the public eye?

Here, too, we must try not to answer prematurely. For example, we could point to the keeping of the commandments, which is often the topic, though in various contexts. It cannot be a question of following the law of Moses (1:17). Yet single commandments with specific contents are never mentioned. The only assertion is that whoever loves Jesus keeps his commandments (14:15, 21; 15:10). Instead of the keeping of the commandments, the subject may be the keeping of Jesus' words (15:20); likewise, the commandments can be reduced to *one* commandment: to love one another (15:12). Thus we go around in circles if we take all the statements into consideration, and we cannot escape the impression that John meticulously avoids becoming specific in any way.

Then we must also keep in mind that this commandment is not just one that the *disciples* are to obey: Jesus himself received it from the Father and kept it. Here the content of the commandment is called "eternal life" (12:49-50), and John has Jesus say that he gives those who belong to him eternal life (10:28). But if the disciples follow this commandment, does that mean that they "form" eternal life by their loving one another? Then, of course, we can understand why the commandment is called a "new" commandment (13:34), but at the same time we must ask whether it can be given a visible form at all.

John's view seems to be that this is indeed possible. For he says that Jesus did "works" not only that all could see, but also that all have seen (15:24). These works, however, are not simply and only works of Jesus but also at the same time works of the Father, and they have a special function. For if Jesus' words were not enough, then at least these works should have instilled faith in Jesus (14:10-11). And if the disciples believe in Jesus, they will not only do the same works that Jesus did; they will do even greater works than his (14:12).

Since the disciples, by loving one another in the public eye, give form to exactly what Jesus lived, the questions, what is formed and how is it lived, can be answered only on the basis of Christology. For without Jesus the disciples can do nothing (15:5). They are to do as Jesus has done to them (13:15). Jesus, on the other hand, can do nothing on his own, he does only what he sees the Father doing (5:19). Thus we have a circular movement.

Hence the quest for John's ethic proves to be a quest for his Christology. Insofar we can say that ethics and Christology are identical for John.

Now, we cannot describe the the full breadth of John's Christology here, especially since disputed issues would have to be discussed. Until now, no consensus has been reached concerning which ideas from the history of religions were adopted by John and how they were modified by him. Therefore we will confine ourselves to those characteristics of Christology that are important in our context.

The starting point for John's concept and argumentation is a cosmological dualism: God and world, above and below, light and darkness, truth and falsehood stand opposed to each other. John breaks out of this concept of a strict dualism only to the extent that he views the world as creation (1:3, 10).

In (Gnostic) dualism the world is fallen matter in which a few sparks of light have survived—specifically, *in* human beings (anthropological dualism). These sparks of light can be redeemed in two different ways. Either a redeemer from heaven can redeem the spark of light in the material body, or redemption can be attained through Gnosis (knowledge).

Even if John understands the world as the creation of God, he holds to his view that without God the world is lost. Therefore the separation between God and humankind, which is deadly for the world, must be overcome. Yet that can happen only if initiated by God. How it happens is expressed by John with the motif of "sending" (or "mission"). Here we are talking about an all-embracing event. The sending not only determines the Christology (which can then be presented and considered as such); at the same time it is also an ethical category.

The starting point is God (1:1). God loves *his* world (1:11) and proves his love by sending his Son into the world with the aim "that everyone who believes in him may not perish but may have eternal life" (3:16). As one sent by the Father and one who loves the Father, the Son does works together with the Father and chooses those who belong to him in the world (15:16). As those who are chosen by the Son and love the Son and thus at the same time are chosen by the Father and love the Father, the disciples are now also sent into the world. This is expressedly formulated as an analogy: "*As* the Father has sent me, *so* I send you" (20:21; cf. 17:18). Thus for the Son as well as for the disciples, the mission consists in giving form to love for one another. Yet only when they practice this, can they know that their mission is from the Father (7:17).

If up to this point we can almost speak of something like a closed system, the real problem appears where John considers and reflects on the fact that one is sent and is supposed to be sent into the world, but God and the world are separated. That is why loving one another is an impossible possibility in this world. This becomes especially clear if we consider that the commandment that Jesus received from the Father has as its content eternal life as loving one another. But can loving one another be made visible as eternal life in this world? The outcome would have to be a *theologia gloriae.*

This is also emphasized by the "present eschatology" that is a characteristic of John. In the "church" of his time eschatology had again become a "doctrine of the last things." Parousia, resurrection of the dead, and judgment were expected in the future (cf. pp. 228-30 above). John has Jesus announce what is expected as already present for the faithful, and he realizes that he is in contradiction with the widespread belief of his time.

For example, when Martha is faced with the death of her brother, she has the traditional hope of the resurrection of the dead on the last day (11:24). Jesus corrects this idea: he himself is the (expected) resurrection. Those who believe in *him* will live (even if their physical lives remained threatened by death), and whoever lives and believes in him will never die. According to this word of Jesus, everything now depends on Martha. She is asked, "Do you believe this?" (11:25-26). Everyone who hears Jesus' word and believes the one who sent him *has* eternal life and does not come under judgment but *has* passed from death to life (5:24; cf. 3:18-19). Those who believe in Jesus love him, keep his word, and are also loved by the Father. Then, however, Father and Son will come to them and dwell with them (14:23) *even now* (and not just in a later Parousia).

If eternal life is lived *now,* the "present eschatology" of John is only logical. But does that mean, then, that there is nothing more to be expected in the future? That could have dangerous ethical consequences. Yet John does not expressly reflect on the future. He meets the dangers of a "present eschatology" in a different way.

With the help of a "cosmological reservation," John confronts the possible misunderstanding that the life currently being lived, the loving of one another, can be directly read as eternal life. That cannot be, because the world is still the world. Of course, through the sending into the world there is much to see. Yet one must be able really and truly to *see* in order to see that eternal life happens. This paradox between seeing and really *seeing* is expressed in many ways in John's Christology.

It is expressed, for example, when John uses sources or incorporates individual bits of tradition into his works and interprets them. His models contained a number of striking miracle stories. One would think that these visibly extraordinary events would lead to faith (as was obviously assumed in the tradition; cf. Acts 2:22). But John opposes just such directness. Jesus, to be sure, finds faith in Jerusalem because of his doing signs. Yet he does not entrust himself to those who come to faith that way (2:23-25). The royal official who begged for the healing of his son first has to hear: "Unless you see signs and wonders you will not believe" (4:48). Nicodemus tries to derive a legitimation of Jesus from the visible signs that Jesus has done: he must be a teacher sent from God (3:2). But Jesus corrects this (contemporary) view by referring to birth "from above" (3:3) and "of the Spirit" (3:5-6).

Thus, for John such deeds of Jesus are perfectly visible. But those who cannot really *see* misunderstand them as divine miracles that directly evoke faith. They are visible only as signs, in the sense of indications. Whoever sees them becomes aware of the one who does them. Then those who see are asked whether they listen to him. The Baptist was also such a "sign" (1:8).

Corresponding paradoxes are also decisive for the prologue. With the Son, God really comes into the world, but he only "dwells" here (1:14a) and comes just as a son. Yet those who can really *see* now see God's glory in the world (1:14b). When the light shines in the darkness, it is really there, and the darkness does not overcome it (1:5). But the world just cannot really *see*, and that is why it does not recognize the light as light. Those "who were born . . . of God" (1:13), however, can truly *see*. Therefore in the world they recognize the light as light and have received the power to become "children of God" (1:12). In John's spirit we can interpret: they have eternal life and love one another.

This christological paradox between seeing and really *seeing* enables us to understand immediately what is the dominant characteristic of the Johannine ethic: there are no imperatives with specific content. This is true of no other New Testament scripture. For John, however, it is impossible for the disciples to be told what specific form their mission should take in the world. For if they receive specific instructions and follow them, there is an immediate danger that eternal life will take shape in the visible doing. What the disciples do can be seen and must be seeable. But that does not mean that one can really *see* it. Since the important thing is *seeing* really and truly, what is to be truly *seen* cannot be given a visible form.

Thus, because the disciples' deeds take place in the world, they must remain ambiguous. Therefore the road the disciples travel in the world is not a glorious road—either in the eyes of the world or in their own eyes. They themselves are afraid in the world (16:33). Yet Jesus' road was not a visibly glorious road, either. The world misunderstood Jesus and persecuted him, and his road on this earth ended at the cross. If John, nevertheless, calls it a glorious road (12:28) and sees the cross as an exaltation (3:14; 8:28; 12:32), this was not visible; rather, John says it as someone who can truly *see*. For those who can really *see*, the crucified One is the exalted One.

If this paradox is ignored, a misunderstanding can easily result: what we must truly *see* changes into something that we can see with our eyes (and thus establish scientifically). Then we say that the Son was there in divine glory. And if he was not there in divine glory, then he was not really in the world at all. This misunderstanding, which led to a docetic Christology (the Son only *seemed* to become human), is old and was already fought by the Johannine school (cf. pp. 302-4 below). John stresses, however, that the one who really became flesh, who really became human, died visibly on the cross. Only from there can he then also establish ethics for the disciples: ethics must really be done in the world.

Then, however, we must also note the difference between John and Paul. For John the cross is not a salvific event. The salvific event is, rather, the descent of God into the world, the

sending of the Son. But since salvation does not exist visibly
in the world, he argues with the *cosmological* reservation: in
the world we cannot see—but must always truly *see*—that it is
a question of salvation. If the world lets this salvation end on
the cross, that is no counterargument. Those who can really
*see*, see that the crucified One is the exalted One.

Paul, by contrast, argues with an *eschatological* reservation
when, against an enthusiastic perfectionism, he stresses that
the resurrected One is the crucified One. For those who in
the ongoing old aeon are oriented toward the resurrected
One do not, therefore, lead lives of glory but always carry in
their bodies the death of Jesus (2 Cor. 4:10).

Paul uses temporal concepts (*already/not yet*), whereas
John uses spatial concepts (*above/below*). With his (only so-
called) present eschatology, however, John crosses out the
spatial concepts familiar to him from church tradition.
Hence eternal life for him is not the anticipation of a future
life at the consummation; rather, eternal life is life determined
"from above"; it is true life or life in the truth. But the world
cannot really *see* it.

Because the world truly *sees* nothing, it must do something
about Jesus because of his claim, and it finally puts him on the
cross. Likewise, with its hate it persecutes the disciples (15:18-
19; 17:14). Yet that must not cause them to flee from the world.
Jesus asks the Father to protect them from the evil one (17:15),
but he does not take them out of the world. He sends them even
farther into the world, just as he himself was sent into the world
by the Father (17:18). The disciples' place is the world, and into
the world they are sent.

Because the disciples are, of course, in the world but not of
the world, they can truly *see* (indicative). They can *see* that Jesus
has given them the glory he received from the Father. Hence
Jesus can ask that he and the disciples may be one, as he and the
Father are one (17:22). What the disciples do on their mission
is exactly the same thing that Jesus did on his mission and that
the Father did when he sent his Son into the world.

But how are they to make that real when they are sent into
the world? Are they not asked to give visible form to something,

knowing beforehand that the world, of course, can see it and even must be able to see it, yet cannot really *see* it at all? With such an indicative, what does the imperative look like? The actions of the disciples are still always specific actions.

Only in one passage is the imperative, to love one another, filled with a specific content: the disciples are to wash one another's feet (13:14). We must not weaken this to a mere gesture or omit "one another." It is, rather, a real, reciprocal action whose spirit is perverted if we turn it into a liturgical rite. The washing of feet is the lowly service of a slave. When all the disciples do it for one another, each one forgoes being what he is in the world and according to the standards of the world.

Now, John expressly says that this is an example that Jesus gave the disciples by doing it himself (13:15). As an example the content of the imperative has an exemplary significance, since loving one another naturally goes beyond the mutual washing of feet. How this example is to be translated into other concrete action is still not said. Nor can it be said. Even so, every time reciprocal love takes place, we must ask whether the specific action corresponds to the example. Since it is the example that Jesus gave his disciples, Christology still remains the only standard for the action.

The action is of course supposed to take place before the eyes of the world, since it is, after all, the visible form of the disciples' mission into the world. But what is the "success" of this action? The world can physically see it, but does it really *see* it? Making the world truly *see* is not within the power of the disciples. The world can understand it as the exemplary behavior of humans toward one another and perhaps even pay tribute to it. According to John, however, something else is more likely: the world is offended by it, turns hateful, and persecutes the disciples. The world simply sees in the disciples' actions only what appears before its eyes.

Yet if the world—because it is the world, after all—cannot truly *see* at all, how does the sending of the Son stand a chance of being received by the world in the way the Father intended? Obviously, not at all, since this circle (only those who can really *see*, really *see*) seems to be impenetrable. Yet this should not surprise the disciples—much less bring them to the point of giving up on loving one another *before the eyes of the world*. The imperative remains, since it comes with the indicative.

Perhaps John is suggesting, if ever so cautiously, at least one possible way in which this circle might be broken. At the Jewish festival of Booths he has Jesus say (in 7:17): "Anyone who resolves to do the will of God will know whether the teaching is from God or whether I am speaking on my own" (that is, as a man, as the world). Likewise, we could say: those who see the disciples' love of one another and live this love of one another as they see the disciples live it, can experience, *while living* this love of one another, that they are not living their own love but rather are living the love that God has brought into the world through the Son. They *can* experience this *while* loving one another, and then they can truly *see*. That, however, is always a miracle and therefore impossible for the disciples to plan. No one can come to Jesus unless drawn by the Father (6:44a). Only those who are "born from above," who are born of the Spirit, "can see the kingdom of God" (3:3, 5). The Spirit, however, blows where it chooses (3:8).

We close this section with the following thoughts. How did John manage to take ethics almost completely back into Christology without giving up ethics? There is no certain answer to this question, because the origin and provenance of Johannine theology are obscure. Accordingly, views about it are still controversial today. Yet we can offer some general thoughts and then use them as a starting point: In the course of the ongoing "history of the church," somewhere around the end of the first century A.D., John made his own mark, and it is quite obvious that he did so by reaching with a correcting hand into the tradition from which he came and in which he lived.

It is, of course, problematic even to talk about a history of "the" church in that time. After its beginnings, the church developed in quite different directions, as shown by the New Testament scriptures, which originated as snapshots, so to speak, at different times, in different locations, and in different traditions. There seems to be no direct line that leads to John. We do find, however, some common characteristics that developed in the period before A.D. 100, and which we can, with all due caution, recognize as the Johannine background. A certain institutionalization took place. In these sociologically describable entities (churches, church provinces), which were then more clearly distinguishable than earlier, Christians reflected on their own self-understanding.

The past with Jesus (the earthly One and the resurrected One), which earlier determined people directly in their present time, now became a past that was really past, and they became conscious of it. The Christian imminent expectation (see p. 73 above) again became (as in apocalypticism) the expectation of a future with the Parousia of the *kyrios*. In between was the present, which received its own significance between past and future. The present itself was experienced less and less as time in which God was trying to, and repeatedly did, break in with his salvation. Rather, Christians reflected on how to form the present as well as possible.

For help with that, they turned to Christology. With time, however, Christology became more and more the doctrine of a salvation that had happened in the past. Thus it expressed the people's conviction but was no longer really received by them. So Christology and ethics separated. For ethics people could also turn to statements in the Old Testament or to the bourgeois ethics of the surrounding world. Salvation had departed from the present. The institution claimed to be different from other, "worldly" institutions because of its origin and tradition. Its dogmatic theology *and* its ethic constituted what was understood as Christian.

Even if development did not proceed everywhere with equal uniformity and speed, the general trend is reasonably clear. Also, the development that followed this trend was virtually unavoidable and therefore was hardly considered a problem by those who experienced it. After all, "eschatological existence" within a community in ongoing time cannot simply be prolonged indefinitely. Since that is impossible, there is a danger that eschatological existence may be lost altogether. And a Christology that has become doctrine is not sufficient protection.

John obviously saw that and thus became the first "reformer" of the new church. Where and from which traditions he got the criteria for his reformation, must remain open. At any rate he was not satisfied with what had developed. He took the "doctrine of the last things" that he had found and turned it into what we call "present eschatology" today; in this way he attempted to emphasize salvation in the present. Then his use of the categories of space, rather than those of time, helped him in his presentation to avoid the possible misunderstanding that present salvation is at the disposal of human beings. The world remains the world. (In essence, this makes the same assertion as when formulated in the categories of time: the kingdom of God breaks into the [still] ongoing old aeon.) God's mission happens from above and comes into the world: in the Son. Here John (in contrast to Matthew and Luke) does not describe the past with Jesus simply as a past that is past, but in a way that makes it directly transparent for the present. As John knows and does not question, Peter had earlier played an important role in the church and for the church. But that is the past and no longer has any direct bearing on the present. What matters today is the disciple that Jesus loved. John probably understood himself as this (or a similar) disciple. He is the disciple who lives totally on the basis of mutual love. Jesus loves him, and he loves Jesus. For that reason he now has himself sent into this mutual love. Around him a circle of disciples then forms and lives this love for one another before the eyes of the world.

## 2. The Ethics of the Johannine School

With his "reformation," John had tried to solve critically the problem of the connection with tradition. But after his death (cf. 21:22-23) his circle of disciples soon faced the very same problem. For John's reformation had become history.

This becomes especially clear where the "new commandment" (John 13:34) is called the old commandment, which has accompanied the circle from the beginning (i.e., from the time of John), but which nevertheless is to remain the new commandment (but now: of John) (1 John 2:7-8; 2 John 5).

This past now becomes the content of a new tradition. The
disciples still feel obligated to their teacher. They appeal to his
authority and expressly identify him as the disciple whom Jesus
loved (John 21:24). But now the question is: Do they deal with
this tradition as critically a John did?

Even if we cannot always draw a clear line of separation, in
the dealings of the disciples with tradition we have to
differentiate (at least basically) between the *concern* that
John had and the *form* that the concern took in John's time
and was fixed by him in his (original) Gospel.

We can perhaps formulate the concern—even if in later
terminology—in the following way: *The church must always be
reformed.* The institution that arose through tradition cannot
guarantee that the sending of commissioned disciples into
the world will really happen as a sending "from above."
Related to this is the fact that there can be no specific
instructions that tell precisely what form love of one another
must take. Of course, Christology is supposed to be
maintained as abiding in the love of Jesus (John 15:9). But
since the disciples live in the world, they must decide ever
again and ever anew how to live visibly before the eyes of the
world what the world cannot really *see*. To express it in
categories of time, in the "Christian imminent expectation"
the expected Lord is expected at any moment—and again
and again—as the one who is to come. But can that really be
maintained with the ongoing passage of time?

The charismatic leader is dead. The tendency is simply to
continue the work that he left behind rather than his
concern. But this results in a shift in emphasis: instead of
carrying on John's reformation, his followers look back to
the reformation he implemented and orient themselves
toward it.

Instead of dealing critically with tradition (and now also with
the new tradition), the Johannine school adopts the new
tradition, which now becomes its standard. Yet in later times
even that is not entirely simple. At some points a critique of
tradition is necessary. The literary expression of this critique is

found in the so-called ecclesiastical redaction of the Gospel of John.

In order to understand the concern of "the church," we must assume that it observed the circle around John and then also his school. What it saw and heard there, however, did not agree with its own theology. The doctrine of the last things, which was thought to be indispensable, was missing, as were the sacraments. This critique was heard in the Johannine school, which became insecure and attempted a "balance."

The future eschatology that was missed by the church was slipped into the Gospel of John. If John had Jesus say that anyone who believes has eternal life and does not come under judgment but has passed from death to life (John 5:24-25), the Johannine school adds that all who are in their graves will hear the voice of the Son of man "and *will* come out"—those who have done good, to the resurrection to life, and those who have done evil, to the resurrection to condemnation (5:28-29). Also looking into the future is the redactional statement that keeps repeating almost like a refrain: "I *will* raise them up on the last day" (6:40, 54; cf. 6:39).

John's idea that the bread that came down from heaven is Jesus and that whoever eats of this bread will live (6:51a) is continued in a solidly sacramental way by a lengthy added section (6:51b-58). The bread that came down from heaven is called Jesus' "flesh" and even "the flesh of the Son of Man." This is followed (totally without preparation in John's original text) by reference to the blood of the Son of man. Then, using a different Greek verb that literally means "chew" or "crunch," the text stresses that those who "eat" Jesus' flesh and drink his blood have eternal life—and *will* be raised up on the last day. The food of the Lord's Supper is a means to immortality.

Finally, baptism is also introduced through redaction (3:5). The birth "from above" and "of the Spirit" is integrated into the church doctrine of baptism by inserting the phrase *of water*: birth from above and bestowal of the Spirit happen through baptism (by water).

If we ask about the significance of this church redaction, it is only partly true to say that the Johannine school parries the critique by creating a "balance" between the doctrine of the church and the exaggerations of John. Superficially, this is of course true. But it is more important to see that the Johannine school had already understood John's statements ecclesiastically—and that means, dogmatically—no longer in the way John intended them.

> When John says that those who believe have passed from death to life, he means that *in the world* they have life "from above," true life. But John does not say that they are therefore already resurrected. Hence the future is certainly not anticipated here in such a way that it must be expounded anew in the revision. When people look for bread, and John says that the bread of life that they are seeking (subject!) is Jesus (predicate noun!), the eating of the bread is not meant to be actual. In the Johannine school this becomes solid eating. When John speaks of birth from above or of the Spirit, he is talking about an uncontrollable, ever repeating happening. The Johannine school understands it as a one-time action of the church.

Since the Johannine school gets involved in the church's theological critique of John's statements, it gets involved in the church's statement of the problem. It reveals thereby that it also understands John's statements in the sense of a theology. Based on this new presupposition, the Johannine school is now prepared to admit the one-sidedness of the Johannine statements. Through this misunderstanding it in fact creates a balance.

The interest of the Johannine school in dogmatics as an isolated topic also becomes clear at another point. With church doctrine it seeks an accommodation, but with the Christology of heretics it argues much more abruptly.

> The heretics' position can be seen quite clearly, if indirectly, in the polemic against them. They are docetic Gnostics who deny the real incarnation of Jesus Christ (1 John 4:2-3; cf.

2:22; 2 John 7). Since the cross would then also be without meaning for them, they obviously reject the Lord's Supper (1 John 5:6).

It is unlikely that the representatives of the heresy were also libertines (in spite of 1 John 2:15-17; 5:4). Either these accusations are part of the traditional polemic against heretics, or there is a misunderstanding, since the heretics believe that they are without sin (1 John 1:8) because they possess the Spirit (4:1). They are called false prophets (4:1) and even antichrists (2:18).

It is worth noting, however, that these heretics not only consider themselves Christians but *also* appeal to John. The author of 1 John says about them: "They went out from us, but they did not belong to us; for if they had belonged to us, they would have remained with us" (2:19). Hence there was a split in the Johannine school, and it happened because of a difference of opinion about the "right" Christology.

How this disagreement developed is relatively easy to explain. In John's Christology, the Father came into the world in the Son. Hence the glory of the Father is *really* in the world. Yet the world cannot see *this reality* because it cannot really *see*. Thus it is characteristic of this Christology that *people* receive the Christology only if they can really *see*. If they cannot really *see*, they always see only the world.

If we resolve the paradox of seeing and really *seeing*, the two ways of seeing are no longer distinguishable, but then neither are people. Now *all* will be presumed capable of seeing. But *what* do they see? Now that becomes the problem. The alternative between seeing and *seeing*, which originally rested with people, now shifts and becomes an alternative in judging the reality of what is seen. In other words, Christology is objectified and thus becomes a doctrine. This is a debated point, because from the standpoint of John's paradox, different emphases can be placed.

When we argue from below and strictly observe the separation between above and below, we get the following result. Since the coming of the Father in the Son did not happen visibly, since it could not possibly happen visibly because of the separation, the Son *cannot really* have come into the world. Jesus was only the apparent body of the Christ. Thus it is a Christology that can be described as a doctrine, but it is docetic.

If we argue from above, however, and in doing so forget John's cosmological reservation, then the Father is not only really in the Son but also has come into the world in a *really visible* way. What is now proclaimed is not only "what we have heard" but at the same time, and with emphasis, "what we have seen with our eyes . . . and touched with our hands" (1 John 1:1). This *Jesus* Christ came by water and blood (1 John 5:6). Thus baptism is a new birth that has really happened (cf. John 3:5); above all, Jesus' flesh can be eaten and his blood can be drunk at the Lord's Supper (John 6:54).

Both Christologies grew from the same roots, the Christology of the Johannine school (whose scriptures later entered the New Testament canon) and the Christology of its opponents (who, we must not forget, were also a Johannine school). Both schools in quite similar ways either misunderstood or no longer understood the statements of John. They played down *the people,* who either really *see* or do not see in the world, and now became interested only in the *object of the seeing.* Christology became a knowable doctrine. The question is no longer whether Christology is received or not, but rather: Who has the "right" Christology?

*If* we talk about heretics in this context, we should not name only the Docetists as such, and we certainly should not do it for the reason that they are fought in the canonical scriptures. Anyone who removes the cosmological reservation from the conception of John and speaks of a visible and therefore available reality is no less a heretic.

What about the ethic of Johannine school (which has become "canonical")? Does it, like Christology, become a topic by itself? Or are there relationships? If so, what do they look like? The problems to be dealt with here in part interact with each other and also often concern the opponents, even if indirectly.

The author of 1 John is above all interested in having his readers hold to the right creed. The criterion for its rightness is acknowledgment of the real incarnation of Jesus Christ. The older confession, "Jesus is the Christ" (4:2) is polemically sharpened against the heretics: anyone who does not confess *Jesus* (and that means, anyone who includes only the heavenly Christ and not the human Jesus in the confession) does not come from God but has fallen to the spirit of the antichrist (4:2-3). The antichrist is, to be sure, a figure that is expected in the end time, according to the doctrine of the church, but here he is viewed as already at work now (cf. 2:18). Yet his present activity does not consist in determining the actions of the human beings but rather in tempting them with a false Christology. There is hope only for those who represent the right Christology (3:2-3), which also includes acknowledgment of the salvific significance of the cross. Yet here the author falls back on traditional formulations without explaining them (1:7; 2:1-2; 4:10). Such dogmatic statements are then, of course, followed again and again by paraeneses (cf. 2:3-6 after 2:1-2; 2:28-3:24 after 2:18-27; 4:7-5:4a after 4:1-6). Nevertheless, the advocated life-style is neither more fully explained nor substantiated theologically.

The crucial characteristic of this life-style is love for one's brothers and sisters. Quite obviously, the author has adopted John's love for one another but understands it in a completely different way. For the "brothers and sisters" are for him a precisely defined group. [The author of 1 John and the present author use only *brothers,* but we follow the NRSV in adding *sisters.* —Trans.]

The brothers and sisters include only those who are members of the orthodox community. They are the only ones who believe that *Jesus* is the Christ and therefore the only ones who have been born of God (5:1). That is why it is not (Christian) faith in general but "our" faith that will conquer the world (5:4). Only the "orthodox" faith believes that *Jesus* is the Son of God (5:5). Hence there is only one criterion for the rightness of faith: belonging to the community of the author. Any who leave this community show thereby that they have fallen away from the right faith and thus are no longer brothers and sisters (2:19).

They can even be called simply godless. For everyone who does not abide in the teaching of Christ (which can be found only in the author's community) does not even have God anymore. But whoever abides in it has both the Father *and* the Son (2 John 9).

The author of 1 John, however, fights not only the Christology but also the claim of the opponents. When they refer to an anointing, he emphasizes that *his community* has received this anointing (2:20). Very probably, he is alluding to the baptism that has already happened and cannot be lost, as well as to the instruction in correct Christology that came with baptism (2:27). Thus the community has a double "possession." But what does it do with it?

Here the author gets into linguistic difficulties when he uses the same word, *sin,* in completely different ways. On the one hand, he asserts that "those who are born of God do not sin, but the one who was born of God protects them, and the evil one does not touch them" (5:18). Since in the author's view this being born of God applies to his community, it constantly lives without sin. On the other hand, the author characterizes a professed sinlessness as heresy (1:8, 10) and talks about the forgiveness of sins that for Christians is not only possible but repeatedly necessary (1:9; cf. 5:16). These statements seem contradictory, but this is due to his careless use of the language. Presumably, he did not notice it himself at all (as even today the same words are used unconsciously with different meanings). When we look for definitions, the apparent contradiction is resolved.

First, it is certain that when the author *polemizes* against a professed sinlessness, he is trying to counter a claim of his opponents.

Docetists can actually claim to be without sin. But by that they do not mean that their body commits no sin in its concrete deeds. Their body does not interest them at all. For the cosmological dualism between below and above (to which they hold, as their Christology demonstrates) corresponds to an anthropological dualism, which is analogous to kernel and hull. Only the kernel (the soul) is redeemed by the heavenly Christ (not by *Jesus* Christ). Hence the *kernel* is without sin and lives in the hull, in an "apparent body." For the Docetists *this* sinlessness is a possession that cannot be lost.

Now, the author wants to contest the claim of the opponents. When they claim sinlessness, he calls that a delusion. In doing so, however, he does not notice (or does not want to notice) that his argument misses the point of his opponents' claim. When he holds sinlessness to be a delusion, he means that life *in the body* is not possible without sin. But the Docetists did not make that claim at all.

Nevertheless, the author does adopt one idea from the opponents' assertion. He would like to reclaim for his community a possession that cannot be lost. For this unlosable possession he himself now uses the word *sinlessness,* which he borrowed (though only as a word) from the opponents. For his community he now claims that there is no sin for those who are really born of God. They are, after all, children of God and remain children of God, and that is proved by the fact that they love their brothers and sisters (3:8-10). Thus sinlessness for the author is identical with belonging to the community. As long as someone remains in the orthodox community, he or she can be said to be without sin. But those who separate from the community prove already by their departure that they were not born of God. By separating they commit "mortal sin" (5:16).

Yet how this term is to be understood is the subject of exegetical debate, which is connected with the occasionally voiced assumption that 5:14-21 was added to 1 John by later redaction. If that assumption is correct, we can consider what the meaning of "mortal sin" might have been *in the author's source.* Yet we cannot apply this meaning directly to 1 John.

In our present 1 John the statement is clear: whoever separates from the orthodox community and falls into heresy commits mortal sin. For the Johannine school it is true that *extra ecclesiam nulla salus* (there is no salvation outside the church).

This has immediate problematic consequences for ethics. In its center is the requirement of brotherly love. The self-understanding of the community leads to a strict exclusivity in this area. Those who live outside the community do not come under the love commandment. Those who have fallen away are expressly excluded. They are no longer brothers and sisters. Hospitality may no longer be extended to them (2 John 10). Even a greeting is to be denied them, for whoever greets them shares their evil deeds (2 John 11). In the strictest statement, it is even forbidden to pray for those who have committed mortal sin (1 John 5:16).

One should not try to tone down these individual statements with a so-called critical exegesis. Apart from the fact that criticism does not belong in an exegesis (cf. p. 12 above), the historical exegesis of individual statements must be done within the framework of the whole writing. Then we can see that the brotherly love of the Johannine school is bought with a lovelessness that is unparalleled in the New Testament scriptures. This cannot be ignored in the exegesis of pericopes, even if the terms that are used in them seem to give a different impression.

Now, the author of 1 John naturally also knows that there are violations of the law within the "sinless community," and for these he also uses the word *sin*. Those who deny *this* sin deceive themselves (1:8) and make a liar of Jesus Christ (1:10), whose blood, in fact, cleanses from all sin (1:7). Here the author is moving completely within the context of the "church" of his time. Unfortunately, we must deal with such sins. Yet we know that these sins are not mortal, even if they involve "unrighteousness" (*adikia*—1:9; 5:17; the NRSV reads "wrongdoing" in 5:17). For if these sins are confessed, we may count on forgiveness and cleansing from all unrighteousness (1:9). This institution of the instrument of penance is embedded in the institution of the Johannine school. For the readers are asked to practice intercession for *these* sinners, because upon their petition God will give life to those who have not committed a mortal sin (5:16). But *only* to them. Of course, there is still the obligation to walk as Jesus walked (2:6). But if that is not, or not always, accomplished, it does not by itself mean exclusion from the community and thus the loss of one's salvation. This is true, however, only if those who have committed sin that is not mortal do not commit mortal sin. Therefore they must remain "brothers and sisters"; that is, they must remain in the community with the "right" Christology.

Thus the Johannine school ruined nearly everything that John wanted to accomplish with his reformation. Christology and ethics again parted company. Christology became an intellectual possession, which then became a constitutive element of the community. Within the community there was an endeavor (and we may assume a serious endeavor) to live as good a life as possible. If that failed, there was always a way out. And instead of John's "indirect" mission (John 13:35), there were soon direct missions as well (cf. 3 John 7). The *reformation* of John had become an *institution*.

# Epilegomena

## *The Problem of Founding a Christian Ethic on the New Testament*

The self-understanding of the church includes the idea that it has a commission in the world. John expressed this idea in his language as follows: through the Son the Father sent the members of the church into the world as disciples of Jesus. John saw the special nature of this mission in the manner in which disciples had always talked and acted, which never happened in a visibly unambiguous way. The students of John, however, wanted to produce clarity and fled again into the very institution from which John had tried to liberate them.

In the history of the church after the New Testament, this development from the pre-Johannine church through John to the Johannine school repeated itself many times. Hence the founding of a Christian ethic on the New Testament can succeed only if we see that all of the twenty-seven books of the New Testament are testimonies of the history of the church. That is, the history of the church does not begin at the point where the church is first expressly mentioned in the sense of a sociologically definable entity, but rather where individual people encountered Jesus and were invited and enabled to exist eschatologically. Expressed in a Johannine way, the church is where people are led through mission into loving one another. Thus the church is not something that is visible here or there; the church *happens*.

Is this special nature of the church still seen today? Not when mission is institutionalized. As institutions, churches are part of the world. When they do not see that, they try to take God into the world. By claiming to make his actions visible and describable as *his* actions, they take over God's role. We often see the consequences of this even today: the churches become the "schoolmasters" of the world. With specific imperatives, they declare what God demands of the world and of humankind. At this point, however, the churches should back off.

If they do not (and as institutions they would not do so willingly), they should state clearly that they are speaking as the "world." To publish "words of the church" as pronouncements or instructions on how to act is a "worldly" business. Naturally, the result may be something meaningful and worthy of consideration. But making such assertions is not a part of the mission of the church. Precisely for its mission's sake, the church must be interested in maintaining its self-understanding as the church.

The sending of the church into the world has only one single purpose: to communicate the indicative to humankind again and again. Anyone who thinks that this is too little has not yet really understood the nature of the indicative. For the indicative is precisely what makes possible an action that can be called authentically "Christian." Yet since it cannot be *perceived* as authentically Christian, it may be possible to have a nominally Christian material ethic, but never an authentically Christian one.

The fact that the true church is always becoming the secular church is probably unavoidable in this world. Here every church has, almost as its distinguishing characteristic, its own theology and within that theology its own Christology.

For most church members *dogmatics* is almost an occult science, and thus they cannot be directly guided by it in their lives. Differences in doctrine are discussed almost exclusively by the respective experts. As a consequence, ethics is treated apart from dogmatics.

In regard to *ethics*, however, the members of the church in particular are involved—often in a very committed way. That always happens without regard to Christology, and even when the experts intervene in this discussion, ethics remains a separate subject. Of course, there are verbal indications and also regular assertions that life is related to doctrine. Yet the connection between dogmatics and ethics is hardly ever made explicit.

The extent to which we have come to terms with the distinction between dogmatics and ethics and no longer feel it as a problem is shown by a common practice. The members of different churches and even the heads of churches work toward a common Christian ethic. That happens in spite of varying theologies, whose differences are known and allowed to stand because they cannot, at least for the time being, be overcome. How then can we arrive at a common ethic?

The fact that ethics is always an aspect of Christology seems to be as little recognized today as it was in the tradition in which John found himself and into which the Johannine school fell again and again.

Is our situation today not the same as that of the Johannine school? As Christians we must constantly take a stand on this subject or that, as must everyone else. Yet people for whom the true Christian message is the deciding truth about their lives cannot extract from this message special arguments for opinions on, say, marriage, education, the social order, or politics. Here they must argue like everyone else for their opinions on this or that topic, and indeed with arguments that can be accepted equally well by both nominal Christians and genuine Christians.

Christianity does not grant an individual superior knowledge of politics or ethics. On the contrary: as soon as what is authentically Christian is put into a nominally Christian ethic, it is lost.

Can it still can be saved?

Mark 10:27!

# Index of Definitions and Proposals for Linguistic Precision

313

# Index of Subjects (selected)

314

# Index of Biblical References (selected)

# Index of Authors (with selected bibliography)

Bultmann, Rudolf, 2, 6, 33, 38, 46, 180, 188, 215, 285
———. *Theology of the New Testament*. New York: Scribners, 1951.
———. "Welchen Sinn hat es, von Gott zu reden?" (1924). In idem, *Glauben und Verstehen* 1. 2nd ed., 1954, pp. 26–37. (ET: *Faith and Understanding* 1. New York: Harper & Row, 1969.)
———. "Das Problem der Ethik bei Paulus" (1924). In idem, *Exegetica*. 1967, pp. 36–54.

Dibelius, Martin, 255
———. *Die Pastoralbriefe* (Handbuch zum NT). 1913.

Ebeling, Gerhard, 34
———. *Das Wesen des christlichen Glaubens*. 1959, pp. 50–51.

Harnack, Adolf von, 32 Cf. Agnes von Zahn-Harnack. Adolf von Harnack. 2nd ed., 1951, p. 46.

Jeremias, Joachim, 34
———. *Das Problem des historischen Jesus*. 1960.

Käsemann, Ernst, 34, 218, 283
———. "Das Problem des historischen Jesus" (1954). In idem, *Exegetische Versuche und Besinnungen* 1. 1960, pp. 187–214.
———. "Sackgassen im Streit um den historischen Jesus." In idem, *Exegetische Versuche und Besinnungen* 2. 1964, pp. 31–68.
———. *Commentary on Romans*. Grand Rapids: Wm. B. Eerdmans, 1980.
———. *The Wandering People of God*. Minneapolis: Augsburg, 1984.

Klausner, Joseph, 110, 112
———. *Jesus von Nazareth*. 3rd ed., 1952.

Lapide, Pinchas, 112
———. *Er predigte in ihren Synagogen*. 1980.